Ted Mack and America's First
Black-Owned Brewery

Ted Mack and America's First Black-Owned Brewery

The Rise and Fall of Peoples Beer

CLINT LANIER

McFarland & Company, Inc., Publishers
Jefferson, North Carolina

ISBN (print) 978-1-4766-9167-1
ISBN (ebook) 978-1-4766-4999-3

LIBRARY OF CONGRESS AND BRITISH LIBRARY
CATALOGUING DATA ARE AVAILABLE

Library of Congress Control Number 2023010635

© 2023 Clint Lanier. All rights reserved

No part of this book may be reproduced or transmitted in any form or by any means, electronic or mechanical, including photocopying or recording, or by any information storage and retrieval system, without permission in writing from the publisher.

Front cover image: November 5, 1971; Oshkosh, WI; Photograph of Theodore Mack at a press conference announcing the purchase of the Oshkosh Brewing Company by Peoples Brewing Company in Oshkosh. Oshkosh Brewing Company (© Oshkosh Daily Northwestern—USA TODAY NETWORK). Background © Rolling Stones/Shutterstock

Printed in the United States of America

McFarland & Company, Inc., Publishers
Box 611, Jefferson, North Carolina 28640
www.mcfarlandpub.com

To Regina,
thank you for all the love and support
over these many years.

Table of Contents

Preface   1

Introduction   3

1—From the Red Dirt of Alabama   7
2—A Beer Born of Resentment   21
3—Introducing Mr. Mack   32
4—United Black Enterprises and the Famous Beer from Milwaukee   44
5—Buying Peoples Beer   58
6—Race in Oshkosh   71
7—Overcoming   83
8—Growing Pains   92
9—Black Beer   104
10—The Hidden Truth About Big Beer   117
11—Government Contracts   124
12—Grasping at Straws   133
13—Last Ditch Efforts   141
14—Ted Mack's Legacy   150

Chapter Notes   163
Works Cited   181
Index   191

Preface

This book is the story of Theodore Mack and his journey to becoming the first black brewery president in America's history. There have been a number of articles[1] written about Mr. Mack and his short, but tumultuous tenure at the helm of the Peoples Brewing Company of Oshkosh, Wisconsin, but none really cover the story of the man himself, the mission he was on when he purchased the brewery, or the myriad of factors that caused his eventual failure.

This book is the first to provide a complete history of Mr. Mack before the brewery, and it relays the uplifting narrative of his passage from the sharecropper fields of Alabama, to the boardrooms of corporate America. It also examines the history of black beer in America, the corruption of the major brewers, and the failures of the federal government.

My research, conducted through the archives of the Peoples Brewing Company, newspaper accounts, and personal interviews, allowed me to paint the full portrait of Theodore Mack and Peoples Beer. The foundational information for this history was found in the Henry Crosby archives at the University of Wisconsin–Milwaukee. If facts are not referenced, assume they derive from there.

Introduction

The dream wasn't supposed to end like this, on a dull, frigid day in June in Oshkosh, Wisconsin. All the hard work, all the money, all the hope: all for naught. Lives had been threatened, lifesavings decimated, beliefs shaken. Those beliefs—a belief in the American dream, a belief that success followed hard work, a belief that equality would be won through industry—would most likely be reexamined and questioned in the decades that followed. Only the year before, in fact, Theodore A. (Ted) Mack, Sr., had told friends and stockholders, "Maybe no black man can make it in America. I'm beginning to think 'maybe not.'"[1]

Though we can't know exactly how he felt on June 18, 1974, a chilly Wisconsin summer day, as people perused and picked over the scattered remnants of his dream, it is hard to believe Mack could have felt anything but utter defeat. In fact, about the same time his life's work was being sold off, he told U.S. senators during his Congressional testimony about the shuttered brewery, "I try not to go to that part of Oshkosh because it hurts me too bad there to go down on that end and even see the place."[2] While he'd always been so good at putting on a positive, upbeat façade, even when the defeat was imminent, he'd lately been wearing the truth out in the open. It was evident in the letter he wrote to stockholders and the Board.[3] It was evident in the letter the Board had to write him—demanding he hold a meeting to provide an update on the situation with the brewery.[4] And it was evident in his tone and somber mood at that meeting at Jabber's Bar.[5]

Ultimately, Mack must have known it was over. Peoples Brewing Company, *his* company, had been seized by the U.S. government—the same government that had promised to help him turn it into a great success—and all he could do was sit on his hands and wonder where he went wrong while bargain hunters inspected the remains of the brewery to see what they might walk away with. The bottles were already gone. Pabst and Leinenkugel had bought them earlier and hauled them away—over 12,000 cases of new beer bottles to be washed, sorted, and then eventually filled with their own products.[6] Locals bought unused bottle caps and labels, office furniture, and delivery trucks. Everything else would eventually go too: fermenting tanks, bottle washers, labelers, cappers, and even the 5,000-pound copper brew kettle (removed by actually demolishing the walls of the brewhouse).[7] These would all go into service at some other brewery.

In short time, everything was sold, allegedly raising between $114,000 and $125,000.[8] It would have been helpful if that money was applied to the debt of over $400,000 that Mack and his partners owed the government, but unfortunately that wasn't the case. Instead, the money was going to the account of a private Milwaukee auction company, Klein Industrial Corporation, which bought the brewery and its contents from the Small Business Administration six weeks earlier for only $24,000[9]—yet another questionable decision made by the SBA that would later raise questions about the way it conducted business with Mack.

The lawsuit that Peoples Brewing Company had filed against the SBA and the Department of Defense—the last grasp at the only straw they had left—had already been dismissed,[10] so once the brewery's possessions were sold off, the whole episode would be over, at least publicly anyway. It was an episode that had started less than a decade before with the dream of buying an established business—a brewery no less. But in truth, it was more than a dream, much more. Mack said so himself, telling the Associated Press in an interview that "if the black man is going to survive in this country, he is going to have to get into the corporate structure. While the white man will give you welfare, you can really believe he is not going to give you industry."[11]

Peoples Brewing Company was to be his industry, his corporate structure. And it should have been a roaring success.

But then, while Mack seemed to be a master of PR, adept at controlling the message, he found there were many other things that were just too far out of his control. There was racism, of course, but this was nothing new to him. He'd been battling racism, racists, and bigots all his life. He knew how to rise above them and how to ultimately beat them. The problem was the type of racism. It wasn't the kind that hid its face behind a white mask and burned a cross on your front lawn. That was the type Ted was used to. But this was another type. This type smiled at you, gave you confidence into thinking you were safe, and all the while worked behind the scenes to destroy you. It was organized and actively worked for their downfall. This was the kind of racism they had faced in trying to run Peoples. And to some, it was this racism, wrapped up in a system that "kept him down,"[12] that was to blame for the demise of what should have been the great American success story.

But it was more than just racism. Mack's decision to purchase a small brewery in a small town in Wisconsin couldn't have come at a worse time. The brewing industry was coming under control of a handful of large brewers, and they didn't believe in the fairness of the market. Over time, little by little, they had systematically taken over smaller brewers that got in their way. If they couldn't be taken over, they forced them to close through corrupt business practices. The brewery that Mack chose to buy was a mere 75 miles from three of the largest breweries in America, and so it was subsequently squarely in their crosshairs.

Mack had also put a lot of faith into help that had never materialized. He first had assumed that the black community, his community—the one he'd worked so tirelessly to help for all those years—would rally around him and the brewery. He'd also assumed that, because of their status as the only minority-owned brewery in America, and because of the lofty rhetoric and platitudes about "helping the Black man" that never ceased to flow from Washington, Peoples would be a shoo-in to gain lucrative government contracts. But neither of these hopes panned out either.

And between his big plans and small budget, Mack also spent more than he had while trying to expand operations and sales. He took a number of risks and gambled much of Peoples' money in the hopes of some big gains. Those gambles could have paid off had it not been for the tempest of other elements that battered and bashed the small brewery before those gambles had time to start showing dividends. For Mack, it seemed the fates were against him.

But to be fair, some blamed Theodore Mack himself for the failure of Peoples. In their book, *The Breweries of Oshkosh: Their Rise and Fall*, authors Ron Akin and Lee Reilherzer intimated that it was Mack's ambition, perhaps more so than any other factor, that caused the brewery's ruin. They wrote, "[Ted] Mack had not come to Oshkosh with the goal of running a moderately profitable regional brewery. His aim was much higher."[13] Likewise, Vernon Wiedenhaft, who at 26 years old worked for Peoples Brewing Company as a bottling lineman when Mack arrived, told me that "[Ted Mack] tried to go all over with [Peoples] instead of keeping the beer local, as it had been for the previous 60 years."[14]

Frankly, it's hard to blame these and others for seeing Mack as the face of Peoples' downfall. After all, he was the very public face of Peoples, and the company—brewing beer in Oshkosh since 1911—closed within two years of his purchase of it. From the moment that purchase was finalized, Mack was in a different newspaper seemingly every week. He crisscrossed the state giving presentations and speeches as the "first black brewery president in America." He was celebrated by politicians and the African American press. He was given positions on political advisory committees. He became a public figure. So, when the Peoples Brewing Company shuttered after 62 years, Mack was conveniently portrayed as the primary cause.

But ultimately, with a whole gallery of factors to blame (including himself), Mack pointed his finger directly at the Small Business Administration as the cause of his failure. According to him, the SBA gave him and his partners the loan to buy Peoples with the promise of helping them succeed. That promise was comprised of two parts—assistance in getting federal contracts, and technical assistance in running the brewery. Peoples got neither. At a Congressional oversight hearing about SBA mismanagement in 1974, the same one in which he admitted the pain the whole episode had created, Mack told the panel, "we did not get anything (contracts or help) in that area. We signed the loan guarantees, and now the SBA wants us to pay them back about $400,000. They did not do their job but they want us to pay them back."[15]

But the truth about why Peoples Brewing Company closed in 1974 is much more complicated, and it is made up of all of these different causes, each a different story to tell. From systemic racism to opposing ideas of black power, from government abuses to capitalist corruption, from bravado and hubris to bad timing; the story of Peoples Beer—how it started and how it ended—is a tragic one that combines all the best and worst of American business and society in the Midwest in the 1970s. And to tell this tale, the best place to start is not in Milwaukee or Oshkosh, but much further south: in Alabama in 1930.

1

From the Red Dirt of Alabama

Theodore (Ted) A. Mack, Sr., was born on May 8, 1930, not too far from the small town of Prattville, Alabama, located in Autauga County (about 20 miles west of Montgomery). The country was idyllic in songs and poems, which recounted good times and green farms as far as the eye could see. In truth it was much less ideal than that. It was the Cotton Belt and fewer than 70 years removed from the Civil War. It was a place of muddy fields, intense poverty, Jim Crow and the Klan. Anyone born here was in for a difficult life. Some more than others. This was especially true for Ted Mack.

Mack's family had deep roots in the area, going back to the births of his grandparents on his mother's side. This may be true as well for his father's side, but there is no evidence of who his father was, and Mack never spoke or wrote of him (in fact, his mother, Earline, kept her maiden name and passed it on to Ted and most all of her other children). His grandparents were born in 1851 and 1859, and most assuredly spent their early childhood as slaves.[1] This would have been a dour history shared by most of the people in the area. In fact, for the most part, anyone that Ted would have met growing up (in the black community anyway) would have been either the offspring of former Cotton Belt slaves, or former slaves themselves (a sad life detail to share with others, to be sure).

Earline was born in 1896, joining an already large family of eight other siblings. Luckily, at four, she was too young to be listed as "Farm Laborer" in the 1900 census, though four of her older brothers and sisters held that occupation (her father was listed as "Farmer"). That fact changed upon the next census, though. In 1910, when she was 14, she, too, was recorded as "Laborer" along with the others.[2] In 1920, some things had changed much, while others remained the same. Her father was no longer in the household—he presumably died in the intermediate ten years—and at 24 years old, Earline had a daughter named "Elsie Bates." Under the column labeled "Occupation," Earline and her older brother, William, both listed "Farm Laborer."[3]

None of this was really unusual, though. In fact, looking up and down the column of sheet number 15 of precinct 3 for Autauga County Alabama's census roll for 1920, most of the 99 other entries say the same thing—"Farm Laborer." Of the over 1100 other pages of census rolls for the county in that year, the vast majority of listings' occupations likewise state the same, which evidences another sad fact of Ted Mack's early life—like most everyone that he would have known growing up, Ted Mack was born a sharecropper.

At the end of the Civil War, contrary to the wishes of the majority of Congress, many large Southern landowners (most, in fact) who supported the Confederacy were allowed to keep their property. While before the war Southern plantations were mighty agricultural machines that supplied the nation and the world with cotton and tobacco, after 1865 the land was idle, unsown, and unproductive. The problem the landowners had, of course, was a lack of a labor force due to the emancipation of their slaves. Another problem was little capital after most of the South's cash was consumed during the war. In other words, they no longer had people to work their land for free. To make matters worse, and the reason lawmakers in Washington, D.C., even cared, without their crops and the income raised from them (not to mention the associated income based on taxes and peripheral expenses), the Southern states themselves would be tossed into poverty. This would in turn make it immensely more difficult for the nation as a whole to recover from the travails of the previous decade. So, the solution that was arrived at was an exchange-based farming system known as sharecropping.

Sharecropping seemed, to the now ruined but very obstinate Southern elite, like a convenient solution to the problem. Instead of hiring their laborers outright with capital they didn't have, landowners could instead make an arrangement with local farmers (that is, emancipated slaves), allowing them to work a portion of the property—usually ten acres—in exchange for a share of the crop they produced. The landowners-turned-landlords supplied the land, and the newly freed slaves supplied whatever was needed to farm it.

For emancipated slaves, this was a far cry from the "40 acres and a mule" they thought they'd receive from the U.S. Government. Promised at first by Major General Sherman in 1864, freed men and women were quick to celebrate a world where they would be granted land on which to settle and farm after a lifetime in chains. Sherman even promised them the coasts of Georgia and South Carolina—this would be their very own region to settle as they wished. These dreams were dashed, however, when President Andrew Johnson turned the land back to the Southern owners, effectively crushing the hopes of emancipated slaves who had longed for their own soil to plant, till, and harvest. Now they were faced with working the farms owned by the very same people who had terrorized them for the past hundred years.[4]

Sharecropping, then, was yet another mechanism to exploit the country's most vulnerable—a population of tired, starved, and unskilled people still recoiling from a lifetime of forced servitude. What made it even worse was the insatiable greed of the white, Southern landowners.

While the sharecroppers did indeed receive a plot of ten acres on which to farm, they still had to procure the items needed to actually conduct the farming. The implements used to work the farm—the plows, shovels and hoes—might be owned by the farmers (and frequently were), but the seeds they actually planted had to be purchased, almost exclusively on credit from local merchants. This was the start of a vicious credit system that kept sharecroppers in their place and let local merchants and landlords exploit the most helpless population in the country.

Even worse were the living conditions these people suffered. On the same ten acres the sharecroppers worked was found the smallest, meanest, and most ramshackle of buildings—the sharecropper's shack. These were simple and crudely made, assembled with rough planks of thin wood nailed together so clumsily as to be barely standing. Sunlight streamed through the gaps between boards, and they lacked glass windows, insulation, electricity, or running water (toilets were outhouses in the yard, and water was drawn from open wells or nearby springs).[5] Scorching in the summer and freezing during the winter, these shacks crowded the landscape of the South through the 20th century. While a source of misery for their tenants, they were a goldmine for their owners, the farm's landlords. They rented them out to their sharecroppers who had no choice but to live in them as they had no other place to dwell.

To add to their tenants' suffering, landowners demanded they grow only the valuable cash crop (cotton in Ted's case) and nothing else. They were not allowed even a measly vegetable garden from which to feed their family, nor could they keep animals, like pigs, cows, or chickens, for food (though horses or mules for pulling ploughs were permitted). Nothing could take away from the crop-bearing acreage they rented and farmed. But because the sharecroppers needed food and other necessities, making them a convenient (and conveniently captive) population, landlords operated general stores or commissaries to sell them the most basic of provisions. To say these shops lacked variety is an understatement. Their stock amounted to little more than corn meal, fatback pork, and molasses. Malnutrition was rampant, as were maladies like hookworms and rickets, ailments all but forgotten in most other parts of the country.[6]

Another injustice was found in the financial situation sharecroppers were forced to live under. None of what was supplied to them was ever free. Nor, interestingly, did the landlords or merchants bother with collecting money from them as payment, at least not right away. Instead, everything, from seeds to shack and equipment to food, anything and everything sharecroppers bought, was supplied through a credit system called a crop lien. Throughout the year, landlords kept track of the items the farmers acquired from them. Every month they added rent for the shack, the groceries taken from the commissary, and anything else used or purchased. Merchants, meanwhile, had also been keeping track of what was owed for the seeds or other equipment rented or bought. This was added onto what the landlord was owed. Also added on were random charges like "supervision fees," which were supposed to compensate the landlords for the work of being landlords. And, of course, on top of all of this was added interest at extravagant rates.

The books were balanced at the end of the growing season when the farmers brought their crops in. Every year, assuming the crop didn't fail, the landlord took his share of the crop "owed" to him for supplying the land, and then an additional amount considered recompense for everything the farmer used in credit throughout the year, like rent, groceries, and supplies. Likewise, local merchants would do the same, charging the farmers for the seeds and anything else they might have been furnished (plus interest of course). And, as in any good grift, the landlords and merchants kept the books, while the sharecroppers often couldn't read. So, in the end, there was small chance of knowing how honest the tallies really were. Most of the time, they weren't, a fact commonly known by all.

In fact, there was a joke recited in those days about a sharecropper who presented all but two bales to the landlord at the end of the season. After conducting his tally on what the farmer had charged over the last year, the landlord told the farmer he owed exactly the number of bales presented. After hearing this the farmer brought out the two other bales he'd held back. The landlord wiped his brow and admonished the farmer, saying, "I wish you'd told me, now I have to add it back up again, so it come out right!"[7]

The joke was based on the cruel truth of sharecropper economics. By the time the credits were all added up and the value of the cotton bales taken into account, the farmer was usually left with very little, or—as was sometimes the case—still owed the landlord money (the balance of which was added to the next year's credit). If they did somehow manage to eke out a little profit, it wasn't much at all. It's estimated that the average income of a sharecropper family was less than 65 cents per day in the early 1940s,[8] which amounts to less than $12 in 2022.

Through this system it was next to impossible for sharecroppers to get ahead. Instead, they were almost always playing catch up with what they owed the landowners. So, what should have been a satisfying transaction at the end of a hard year of farming was instead a soul-crushing moment of despair. The future would have indeed seemed bleak as they faced yet another year of farming to fill the pockets of others all the while knowing there was no way out of the cycle.

Daily life, too, was a terrible routine that consisted of getting up when the sun rose and working in the fields until the sun went down. The cycle stopped when farmers were too old to work, too injured to work, or dead. There was usually no escape from this life. A mere six years after Ted's birth, Edwin Embree, a businessman who studied and then wrote about the situation in the Southern states, summed up the situation thusly:

> The cultural landscape of the cotton belt is a miserable panorama of unpainted shacks, rain-gullied fields, straggling fences, dirt, poverty, disease, drudgery, monotony. Submerged beneath the system which he supports, the cotton tenant's standard of living approaches the level of bare animal existence. The traditional standards of the slave required only subsistence. The cotton slave—white or colored—has inherited a role in which comfort, education, and self-development have no place. For the type of labor he performs, all that is actually required is a stomach indifferently filled, a shack to sleep in, some old jeans to cover his nakedness.[9]

In essence, after the Civil War, the emancipated slaves, and eventually their ancestors, swapped one kind of slavery for another. Sharecropping lasted until the late 1940s, when it was finally cheaper to replace this type of human labor with machinery and automation. When that happened, thousands of sharecroppers with little to no education were turned out, and most of them migrated to larger cities in the north, where they tried to find menial jobs or simply continued living in poverty. For young black children growing up in the Cotton Belt, there was really little to hope for or aspire to, and the opportunity for a better life would have seemed pitifully remote.

On April 16, 1930, William Thompson, the census taker for Precinct 3, Autaugaville, Alabama, penciled in an entry for Earline Mack (though misspelling it "Erline"). At that date, 22 days before Ted Mack was born, Earline was renting a house on a farm and listed "farmer" as her occupation. The household at the time had five members (including Earline), none of the four children were attending school, but instead, at the ages of 12, 9, and 4½, they were most likely helping their mother in the fields.[10]

By 1940 the household had grown to eight,[11] and at times there might be even more. For the first 17 years of his life, according to Mack himself, he lived in a two-room shack on a ten-acre cotton farm, cramped with sometimes up to 13 people—himself, his mother, three sisters, three brothers and five first-cousins.[12] How they managed to cram so many bodies into a small shanty is anyone's guess, but they somehow made it work.

Having large families was not at all unheard of. Tennant farmers and sharecroppers often had a multitude of children out of necessity because they were seen as resources to work the farm, just like their slave-ancestors were. So, while undoubtedly uncomfortable with the living conditions (to say the least), a large family like Mack's could certainly help increase the productivity of the acreage they were expected to cultivate. They might have even worked for other farmers in the area who needed help. In other words, children were assets of the farm, not just children. And it was for this reason so few sharecroppers (both black and white) were able to attend school with any regularity—they were needed at the farm.

But at least while they were young, and not quite strong enough for the more physical demands of farming, some children were able to get a basic education. Fortunately, Mack was one of these. According to the 1940 census, at nine years old he was attending the second grade (the appropriate level for a nine-year-old)[13] most likely at a regional (segregated) school taught out of the church where his family attended worship services every Sunday. There was no other option, as formal schools (that is, publicly supported schools) for young black children simply didn't exist anywhere nearby.

However, as Mack intimated much later in his life, Earline was very religious,[14] and so she would have raised her family according to the lessons of the Bible anyway. Learning scripture alongside the alphabet must have been fine with her, and at least the young Ted Mack would get some form of education (more than most others got). But though Mack and his classmates would have learned at least some of the fundamentals normally taught in a grade school (alongside Bible stories), their education would have been far less advanced than what was enjoyed by white children in the state-run elementary schools. Such disparity was common in those days according to Edward Redcay, an early advocate for black education in the South, who, in 1935, observed:

> [Black children's] school terms average 2 months less than the white school year; attendance is difficult and irregular; enrollment is congested in the first three grades; buildings are dilapidated and inaccessible; and teaching equipment is meagre or lacking. Even more serious is the instructional situation under which large numbers of unqualified teachers are still retained and paid salaries averaging less than half of the white school salaries. Dominating all else is the problem of financial support, involving a current annual expenditure of $87.22 per child for the Unites States as a whole but an annual expenditure of only $12.57 for the average Negro child.[15]

1. From the Red Dirt of Alabama

White children received a full academic year of instruction (eight months) from actual teachers who were trained as educators. Black children like Mack, by comparison, usually had a six-month school term to make sure they were still available during the planting and harvest seasons. For these kids, school was a luxury, taking a backseat to the farm. For white children, in contrast, an early education was compulsory and important to their future. Mack, his siblings, cousins, friends, and all the other black children living in the rural South were not nearly so lucky.

Racism, segregation, bigotry: these were daily experiences for Mack and other poor black residents of Alabama at this time. Often, growing up in the South, or even simply living there, could prove dangerous for African Americans guilty of nothing but having dark skin. Between 1877 and 1950, there were 299 black people lynched in Alabama, and of these, four were killed in Autauga,[16] perhaps not far from Ted's house. As in all lynching cases, people took it upon themselves to punish black people for perceived crimes. The punishment, of course, was death, which the crimes rarely if ever justified, and only on rare occasions was the person lynched even verifiably guilty. Rarely, too, were the victims given an actual trial, and to establish their guilt all that was needed was an eyewitness, a white eyewitness, and sometimes even less than that.

On May 1, 1904, a black man named Gaines Hall was brutally executed in Autauga County. The previous day, an African American had allegedly attempted to rape a white woman while buying "greens" from her at her home. After a brief struggle in which the woman began screaming for help, the man fled. That night, a crowd seized Hall at a nearby town and brought him to the scene of the crime where he was identified by the woman as her attacker. Satisfied that he was the perpetrator, the mob hung him from a tree, and then "riddled his body with shot."[17] He hung from the tree for days before finally being cut down by the sheriff and buried in an unmarked grave at the foot of the same tree he was killed on. In the subsequent weeks and months, the sheriff would refuse to look into the lynching[18] and the local judge would refuse to hold a special investigation.[19] The matter, celebrated by the local paper, would eventually be dropped and forgotten altogether.

Starting in sixth grade, Mack's education continued past church-turned-elementary-school to the Autauga County Training School. Substituting for the junior and senior high schools attended by the white youth, these training schools were often the first formal school many black children in the Cotton Belt ever went to (considering that if they went to elementary schools they were most often of the ad-hoc type that Mack attended). Created in the early 1900s, training schools were supposed to teach employable skills to black teenagers across the South.[20] In those early, post–Civil War years, the white majority refused to fund traditional academics for black teenage sharecroppers at formal high schools. They believed that students weren't mentally capable of getting anything out of traditional academics anyway and therefore weren't worth spending the money on. However, that white majority accepted the idea of those same teenagers learning technical knowledge that might make them employable (they understood that a poor, out of work population was worse than a poor working population). For this they would spend money.

The technical skills taught to Mack and his classmates focused on subjects that the white community thought would be "useful" for the black community. Teenage boys were taught how to plant and grow crops (the cash crops of the South), how to manage farms, and how to use farming equipment. The teenage girls, conversely, were taught to clean and organize the home, make and mend clothes, do laundry and other household tasks. In essence, both were being taught to work for wealthy white people as their farmers and housekeepers. As segregation ended, many of these training schools eventually transitioned into typical, traditionally academic high schools equal to the schools attended by white teens. But not all did. In fact, this type of "education" lasted even into the 1960s in some parts of the South. The Autauga County School Board, for example, fought to keep the Autauga County Training School, the same one that Mack went to, training kids to farm and serve in the home (and to keep them segregated) as late as 1968.[21]

In 1965 students in Greenville, Alabama, held protests and boycotts over the training school they were forced to attend. In one student's words,

The Autauga County Training School in Autaugaville, Alabama, where Theodore Mack attended instead of a traditional high school before his family moved to Montgomery, Alabama (Alabama Department of Archives and History).

"you just learn two trades up there: how to pick cotton and how to take care of white folks' babies." Outside of the South this education wasn't really good for much (not that it was very valuable in the South either). One former student of Greenville's training school applied to Colorado State University but was rejected and told he wasn't prepared for college. None of them were. Such was the training at the training schools.[22]

This was the type of "education" Mack had to look forward to when he started the sixth grade. Despite its shortcomings, though, Earline was insistent he take advantage of what was available, and so he made every effort to make the best of it, though it took some time and work for him to do so. Every day Mack trudged 14 miles to and from the training school, down muddy, red dirt roads in the desolate Alabama countryside. As he plodded along, every morning and afternoon, a bus carrying white kids passed by (often hanging out of the windows to taunt him or throw rocks) on their way to and from their formal schools.

Earline would see to it that her son eventually went to one of those schools too. When he was 17, and facing the last two years of education, they moved to nearby Montgomery. Mack was able to settle into Booker T. Washington High School. This was a huge break for him. Not only did his new school give him traditional academic preparation, it also provided an organized sports program that would become vital to Mack's future. Though he played almost all sports, as his future would demonstrate, he seemed to shine in football. Allowed to play only other black schools, his high school football team excelled. He once said that they were so good that "at halftime the first team wouldn't even dress for second half. We'd be in the stand with our girlfriends, watching the game."[23]

Despite his sharecropper background, despite the shortcomings of his early education, and despite his time spent pursuing sports, Ted Mack still ranked third in his class when he graduated in 1950. The fact that he graduated at all was astounding when only about 14 percent of black students completed high school that year.[24] Considering where he came from, his accomplishment is exponentially more impressive. Unfortunately, it wasn't impressive enough for the University of Alabama, the college he hoped to attend. "My application was denied," he later wrote, "not because of academic reasons but solely because I was black."[25] The same would happen to any black person hoping to go there. It would take another 15 years and armed soldiers to get the school to finally desegregate. At first, he accepted his fate, deciding to study at the Alabama State College for Negroes (now Alabama State University), but he never got the chance to attend. Instead, like many other poor, black Southerners, he was drafted into the U.S. Army and sent to Korea.

In the Army, Mack would find the same type of segregation and racism that hounded him on that small dirt patch in Alabama. Though President Truman integrated the military in 1948 by issuing executive order 9981, it would take years for that order to really be followed.[26] Officers still kept black and white soldiers segregated, especially on the front lines. This would change by the end of the war, but when Mack initially entered the Army, he would have most likely served in an all-black unit. But, as usual, he endured, rose above the injustices he suffered, and found a silver lining.

Since the U.S. military's founding, sports have been closely tied to service. As far back as the 18th century, soldiers, sailors and marines passed the time engaged in sport of all types, sometimes involving skills they needed or used in battles, like horse racing or fencing. Team sports, loosely organized on military bases, also became popular, especially in the 19th and 20th centuries. On any given day, barring other duties that needed to carry out, it was common to find baseball games being played at Army bases throughout the country. In 1882 the Naval Academy at Annapolis introduced football to the armed services when they founded a team. Eight years later a team was founded at the U.S. Military Academy at West Point.

As years passed more and more teams were added at bases around the U.S., complete with stadiums, uniforms, and bands. At first, they played local college teams until the early 20th century when college sports were formalized and schools only played each other in different conferences. Past that point, service teams began playing each other. At a time without television or internet, finding ways to pass time on a military base was important, and so sports programs, especially service football programs, became treasured.[27] Mack, thanks to his playing time and experience from high school, got a spot on a team and began playing service football for the Army.

With names like Randolph Field Ramblers, Camp Peary Pirates, and Camp Davis Fighting AAs, armed forces service football teams played at a high level and were enthusiastically followed by football fans as well as scouts from college and professional organizations. Mack found out while playing for one of these teams that his ability on the field could earn him a scholarship to a college "up north," a non-segregated college—a good college. Mack asked his high school coach to send out game films of him playing, and his accomplishments were impressive enough to score an interview with Ohio State University, the ambitious Big Ten conference school in Columbus. Equally impressed by his character and background, Ohio State awarded him a scholarship, and in March 1953, Ted Mack became the first black player from Alabama to play at a Big Ten school.[28]

Moving to Columbus brought Mack under the tutelage of Woody

1. From the Red Dirt of Alabama

Hayes, the famed Ohio State coach in his second year of what would become one of the most celebrated coaching runs in college football history. Woody had a reputation as a no-nonsense leader who valued hard-work and commitment to the game almost more than anything else. In his 28 seasons as the Buckeyes' coach, he led the school to 13 Big Ten Conference titles and five National Championships, the first of those was in 1954, two years after he took the job and one year after Ted arrived.[29] Coach Hayes was beloved, a legend, even after getting fired in 1978 for punching a Clemson player in the nose after he intercepted an Ohio State pass.

Mack played with the freshman football team that fall of 1953.[30] He earned his freshman sweater and numerals that November and joined a fraternity, settling into his life as a college student. His coach proved to be a powerful motivation in his life at this time, making sure he kept ahead in his courses, tutoring him when he needed it, and telling him that he was lucky to be there, that he had a chance to improve things not only for himself, but for other black people as well.[31] Hayes was a big believer in recruiting from the black community, and became one of the first to recruit black players to a major college team. Despite the image he earned later as a shouting, wailing tyrant of the sideline, he seemed to genuinely care for his players, at least that was Mack's impression.

One day, the coach mentioned to him that they were going to try to get him another job. "Good, I can always use a little more loot!" was Mack's response. Hayes snapped at him to get in his car, and then immediately drove them both to East Long Street, which was, according to Mack, the "roughest ghetto area in Columbus." Hayes parked the car and looked at him. "Take a look around here, son," his coach instructed him, "Which world do you want to live in? This one or the one the university can offer? Don't ever call money, 'loot.'"[32] Mack would remember that lesson for the rest of his life.

That season, 1953, the Buckeyes went 6–3, and alumni and fans were already clamoring for Hayes to be replaced. Instead, the university kept him on and in 1954 he led the team to the first of three National Championships they claimed with him as head coach. Mack should have been part of that team, he might have even played in that game, or perhaps the championship of 1957, but instead he changed his path, left Columbus, and moved to Milwaukee. He later said that the reason he left Ohio State was because he wasn't very good and got injured,[33] but there might have been another reason for leaving.

On June 3, 1954, while laying bricks for a smokestack, 100 feet off the ground, Mack's oldest brother, Thomas, fell through the scaffolds and plunged to his death. On the same scaffolds were two more of his brothers, Will and Richard, who must have witnessed the event.[34] According to Thomas Mack's obituary, much of the Mack family, including their mother, Earline, had moved to Middletown, Ohio (about 90 miles from Columbus and Theodore) so it must have been a hard loss for the family[35] (according to one report, his widow, upon hearing the news had to be treated by medics[36]). Ultimately, only Ted Mack knew why he gave up a scholarship that same June, moved to Milwaukee and enrolled at Marquette University, but whether because he wasn't very good and got injured, or he couldn't carry on so close to a family tragedy, fate would lead him away from Ohio State and to the city that would become the setting for so many seminal moments of his life.

In Marquette's 1957 yearbook, *The Hilltop*, Ted is pictured as a member of the varsity football team of 1956. That year, the yearbook notes, the team went a winless 0–11. The same story held true for the following year as well, when Ted was again part of the winless varsity team in 1957. In only three more years the university would indefinitely end its intercollegiate football program completely, citing the financial burden it put on the school (they claimed they lost $50,000 to it the preceding year). Clearly, for Mack, the draw at Marquette was academics, not athletics, and perhaps it also provided a chance to forget the tragedy of Ohio. In the yearbook for his senior year, 1958, he's noted as a member of the "Veteran's Brigade" and of the Sociology Club, and that year he graduated from Marquette University with a bachelor of science in sociology. He had finally achieved what he set out to achieve so many years before—his education. Now it came time to decide what to do with it.

The path that took him to this point in his life was marked at every

1956 Marquette University Varsity Football Team, Theodore Mack is in the second row from the bottom, seventh from the left, number 76 (Department of Special Collections and University Archives, Marquette University Libraries).

1. From the Red Dirt of Alabama

Far right in the top row, Theodore Mack in 1958, proud senior and soon to be graduate of Marquette University. Mack was a member of the Veteran's Brigade and the Sociology Club at the school (Department of Special Collections and University Archives, Marquette University Libraries).

curve with roadblocks to overcome. It might have been those experiences that would leave him, like many of his contemporaries from similar backgrounds, with an overwhelming desire to help others. This desire led him to the Milwaukee County government, where he was hired as a social worker with the most difficult assignment in the county. He was immediately responsible for the section of the city called the "Inner Core," the all–black region of North Milwaukee. In this part of town, a small area with houses and apartments stacked on top of each other, was found all of the black residents of the city. It wasn't that they wanted to live there, it was that they had no choice—nobody outside of this area would rent or sell to them. In fact, Mack himself lived there, as did everyone he associated with.

This segregation was the result of a practice called redlining, in which financial institutions graded neighborhoods as desirable or undesirable, literally mapping out the city to determine whether or not to lend money within those areas. Areas with a high concentration of African Americans were considered undesirable, and so people rarely invested in them. In time, their conditions followed this lack of investment, and the housing became more pitiful and run-down, crime increased, and conditions worsened. It was a practice that occurred in cities large and small all over the country, starting in the 1930s, and was especially pernicious in Milwaukee.[37]

Up to this point in his life, and by all measurements, Mack could be considered an unequivocal success. Born in a sharecropper's shack on ten acres of Alabama dirt that his fatherless family was responsible for farming, he had by all rights defied the odds. There's little doubt that most of the other children who also attended his make-shift church-school with him were still back on a farm in Alabama, or otherwise still living in poverty somewhere in the South. But Mack refused to define his life by where he came from, and instead he looked at where he could go, and then he went there. It's hard to say what shaped his fortitude, what made him so set on lifting himself above his past, but whatever it was it pushed him to ever-increasing achievement. By this point in his life, in his early '30s, he had graduated high school, left the slavery of tenant farming in the Cotton Belt, served in the U.S. military, received a football scholarship for a Big 10 college, played varsity football for a private university, graduated with bachelor's degrees, started a career and a family. Anyone would be proud of these accomplishments, but when considering who he was—a black man in America in the late 1950s—these accomplishments are made much more profound.

In the coming years, Mack would prove he was as courageous as he was intelligent and ambitious. He would defy not only the odds, but the law, the authorities, and the power structures of the city of Milwaukee, the state of Wisconsin, and even the United States. His trajectory would eventually take him to Oshkosh and to a small brewery where he would face the biggest challenges of his life. That small brewery would test and fracture all the beliefs he'd formed over a lifetime of struggle.

But that brewery had been testing men for decades. In fact, it started out that way. The brewery, Peoples Brewing Company, was founded as a means of resistance two decades before Ted Mack was even born. It was almost destiny that he should end up there.

2

A Beer Born of Resentment

Nobody is really certain why William Glatz and Joseph Nigl had a falling out. Some suggest there was a face-to-face altercation at Nigl's tavern, while others point to Glatz' new rules and price changes, which most assuredly needled Nigl (well known for his short temper). Whatever the exact cause, it was no doubt Glatz' fault. As the president of Oshkosh Brewing Company (or OBC as it was called locally), the largest brewing concern in Oshkosh, he was known to be hard-nosed and no nonsense. But Nigl, too, had a reputation of being a tough businessman, especially when it came to the business of selling beer. When men as mulish and headstrong as these two crossed paths, a falling out was sure to happen eventually.

The relationship between Glatz and Nigl spanned two decades, back to when their fathers were doing business together. OBC supplied the beer sold at Nigl's tavern, and Nigl sold so much of it that they eventually sold OBC beer exclusively, becoming what was known as a "tied-house" (the tavern was "tied" to the brewery and sold only their beer). In return, OBC paid for the bar equipment in the tavern, and the president at the time, August Horn, would often frequent the place for a mug or two. But all that changed in 1911, and OBC, not to mention the brewery scene in Oshkosh, Wisconsin, would never be the same again.

The Oshkosh Brewing Company was founded in 1894 with the merger of the three largest breweries in town: the Gambrinus Brewery, the Brooklyn Brewery and the Union Brewery. Their respective founders, Lorenz Kuenzl, August Horn, and John Glatz were immigrants from roughly the same part of the world (in and around Germany). Of the three, Horn was the only one who wasn't trained as a brewer in his homeland (Horn was a stone mason, but his brother-in-law had been a brewer and partner in his brewery). Their separate decisions to open breweries in Oshkosh were partly based on a number of factors, like the nearby freshwater source and the abundance of local grain. But perhaps most of all their decisions were primarily based on the local population.

Much of northern Wisconsin had been settled by sweat-stained immigrants from the Germania region of Europe. For these people, beer was a cultural marker, not just a beverage. Each of these areas—from Bavaria to Bohemia—had its own preference and style. Bavaria, in fact, still has a beer purity law dating from 1516 called the *Reinheitsgebot*, which dictates that beer is only to be made from water, barley and hops (later, yeast was added).[1] The people from these areas had grown up drinking beer and had enjoyed it throughout their lives, right up until they immigrated to the United States. When they got to America, however, they found that much of the beer made and sold throughout the country was of the heavy type of ale common in England—dark and sweet. It would do for a time, but they sorely missed the kind of beer they found at home. So, when immigrant brew-masters from Germany started making the crisper, lighter style of lager beer they were used to, they almost literally couldn't get enough of it.

In the early days of beer making, for the three breweries that later merged anyway, business boomed in Oshkosh. Union and Brooklyn Breweries were located on the south side of the city and each saw enormous growth starting from the day they were founded. Gambrinus, on the other hand, located on the north side, had much more moderate growth, but it was still enough to draw business away from the other two. At that time beer was also a much more localized beverage, and so in whatever pocket of the city the brewery was situated, its beer was usually favored by the locals that surrounded it. However, in the 1880s, the Oshkosh breweries started to feel pressure from their competitors in Milwaukee, only 90 miles away. The larger of the three Oshkosh breweries—the Brooklyn Brewery—was capable of turning out 40,000 barrels of beer a year, while Union capped at about 30,000 barrels, and Gambrinus at only about 10,000.[2] Pabst in Milwaukee, by comparison, was producing a million barrels per year and distributing nationally. Schlitz and Miller were not far behind.[3] Luckily the citizens of Oshkosh seemed to be loyal to the local beer producers—for the time being, anyway, but little by little the larger brewers were making inroads.

Those larger breweries, the ones that would eventually threaten Oshkosh brewers (indeed small brewers around the nation), also had their own humble beginnings. Like Oshkosh, Milwaukee was settled by European immigrants, and many of them from Germany, Bavaria and other beer loving regions. Jacob Best, who immigrated to Milwaukee in 1844, was from such a region (Rhenish Hesse, west of the upper Rhine River), and had learned to brew at an early age. He founded his brewery upon arriving to Milwaukee and produced only 300 barrels in his first year. But through steady growth and smart management, his small brewery grew until it was producing over 100,000 barrels by 1874, and by 1898 it was brewing over

2. A Beer Born of Resentment

one million barrels per year. By then it was owned by Frederick Pabst, the husband of Jacob Best's granddaughter, and the name had been changed to Pabst Brewing Company.[4] Joseph Schlitz Brewing Company had a similar story. In 1849 the brewery produced only 150 barrels (it was still known at this time as the August Krug Brewery), but by 1886 it was renamed and brewing over 500,000 barrels per year. And lastly, Miller Brewing Company, which produced 300 barrels its first year, brewed more than 80,000 barrels per year by 1888.[5]

The output of these breweries, despite having origins comparable to the Oshkosh brewers, dwarfed their competitors to the north. As the Milwaukee brewers demonstrated exponential growth and nationwide distribution, their eyes turned to Oshkosh, one of the few cities in which they weren't outselling the local beers. By the late 1880s, though, Milwaukee breweries had built distribution centers in and around Oshkosh. Their intentions were clear—they were going to battle the local brewers for control of Oshkosh beer sales.

Seeing this, and in the interest of self-preservation, the three Oshkosh breweries made the decision to merge in 1894. There was another brewery in the city, Rahr Brewing Company, but it was small and excluded from the new organization. The breweries that did merge were the largest and most notable—perhaps they thought that because of Rahr's size it had nothing to contribute. It didn't matter, Rahr would do just fine for itself for years. But for those merging, the future was going to be very bright. After the merger, they installed Kuenzl as brewmaster, John Glatz as vice-president and August Horn as president.

Horn was a well-known and affable man about town, liked by both politicians and tavern patrons. He could always be counted on for generosity—or perhaps grandiosity. He was known to stop in at one of the many taverns selling OBC beer (like Nigl's tavern) to buy rounds for the customers. He was also known to extend enormous amounts of credit to the tavern owners, and rarely bothered to make timely collections. This was a practice that drove John Glatz' son, William Glatz, company treasurer, to anger. William noted in 1896 that OBC was owed over $20,000 dollars in past due accounts from tavern owners.[6] That bill would amount to almost $600,000 today. But despite William Glatz' insistence that he stop, as long as Horn was still president that was the way business would be done.

When Horn died in 1904, however, OBC's cavalier approach to doing business was finally put to an end and the company was transformed into a disciplined brewery with William Glatz firmly in command. William's father, John Glatz, had died in 1895, making William the de facto vice president (his mother was given the title of vice-president, but everyone knew that William held the position). Now, with William as president, things might run more efficiently, more profitably. And they did. Within four months of Horn's death, OBC announced it would stop the practice of giving beer or anything else for Christmas. Glatz also ended the exorbitant credit extensions and ensured that past-due accounts were collected (tavern owners would now be required to pay in cash for their beer at delivery). And, as a final measure, no longer would the OBC president be buying rounds of beer for the locals at the neighborhood taverns.

The Oshkosh tavern owners, the people who actually sold the bulk of OBC's beer, viewed Glatz' changes with resentment. This was simply another reason to despise the new brewery president. After all, it was due to Glatz that the price of beer was raised $1 a barrel in 1898 (the first price hike in decades). And as he dove headlong into improvement projects for OBC, especially a drive to construct a brand-new state of the art brewery in 1909, tavern-owners started to feel embittered. From their point of view, if a new brewery was going to be built, it would be built based on their hard work. Of those harboring such feelings, there was nobody really willing to do anything about it except an outspoken tavern owner named Joseph Nigl.

A Bavarian immigrant himself, Joseph Nigl made the journey to American when he was just a small boy. Originally settling in the Oshkosh area to farm in the 1870s, Nigl's father purchased a lot in town in 1881 and built a grocery store. The location also proved great for selling beer, and so it was soon a thriving tavern that served thirsty mill workers from the surrounding neighborhoods. OBC beer was popular among the locals, and the relationship between brewer and seller was both profitable and pleasant. So pleasant, in fact, that in 1897, Nigl sold the lot across the street to OBC. There are no records to indicate why he did this, but it's hard to believe he would have made such a sale if he had known what OBC would do with that property in the coming years. As it turned out OBC decided to create a new beer hall that competed directly with their neighboring customer, Joseph Nigl.

So it was that in 1911, perhaps because of the raised beer prices or the decision to stop buying gifts for their customers, or maybe because OBC stopped extending credit to tavern owners and opened the beer hall across the street, Nigl had apparently had enough. He decided he was going to go into the beer business and open his own brewery to compete with OBC's production monopoly. While it's hard to pin down the specific reason behind his decision, the bridge too far might have been seeing the size and scale of the OBC's massive new brewery with a price tag above $90,000 (over $2 million today). Many tavern owners considered the cost paid for by their labor, and the rights of labor were on the minds of many in Oshkosh at the time.

2. A Beer Born of Resentment

In nearby Milwaukee, in fact, the labor movement was in full swing. The Milwaukee Labor Reform Association was agitating for eight-hour workdays, and many industries were forming their own unions, including the lumber and brewing industries, both of which organized the workers in Oshkosh as well. In 1910, most of the Milwaukee city council seats, county board seats, and mayor's office, were won by members of the socialist party. Emil Seidel, newly elected mayor of Milwaukee, became the first socialist mayor in America.[7] And, also in 1910, Victor Berger became the first socialist U.S. Representative when Milwaukee elected him to Congress. The next year, due to legislative activism from the labor unions, Wisconsin even passed the nation's first Workmen's Compensation Act,[8] which required employers provide medical attention for injured workers and compensation for loss of life or limb. Wisconsin, it seemed was a hotbed for socialist action and thought. Perhaps no better illustration of this is found than in the example of the union that ultimately ran the breweries, both in Milwaukee and Oshkosh, of course, but far beyond as well.

The National Union of United Brewery Workmen was first organized in New York City in 1886 through the establishment of Brewers' Union No. 1.[9] The membership was comprised primarily of those who labored as skilled and unskilled workers in the many brewhouses of the city and surrounding area (with the exception of the foremen, who were considered part of management and, therefore, against the efforts of labor). Prior to organization, brewery workers experienced a pretty dismal life (as many laborers did in those days). Workdays could start as early as 5 a.m. and would not end until 10 or 11 at night. Sundays also required work, just like any other day, wages were low, and physical abuse (even to include beatings and whippings) were regular occurrences. Brewery owners included room and boarding in the arrangements they had with their employees, but the living conditions were equally comfortless, with rickety shacks crowded with cots in which to sleep, and flavorless food on which to dine.

Also, while the workers were effectively destitute, the "beer barons" as the brewery owners were called, were sometimes shamelessly wealthy. In 1890, Pabst, the largest Milwaukee brewery and second in size nationally only to Anheuser-Busch, made net profits of over $1.5 million dollars,[10] or the equivalent of over $50 million dollars today. Just like the Oshkosh tavern owners seethed as they watched the building of OBC's new goliath brewery, so too did the tired, sweat-stained laborers working for Pabst Brewing Company clench their fists every time the owner and president, Frederick Pabst, appeared in his horse-drawn carriage wearing a finely tailored new suit. To the people who actually made the beer he sold to get rich, the inequality was inexcusable.

New York's fledgling Brewers' Union fought such conditions as these in late 1885 with boycotts and strikes of the city's breweries, and, by early 1886, had won for themselves shorter working hours, higher pay, and better general conditions. Seeing this success, within no time, the workers at breweries throughout the U.S. began unionizing and agitating for similar outcomes. Cincinnati brewery workers organized in January 1886, then Chicago in March, and then a torrent of cities followed over the summer, including Milwaukee.[11] In fact, Milwaukee was the second largest local union in the organization, registering 811 members by the spring of 1887. What's more, organizing seemed to genuinely help the state of affairs for the breweries' many workers. Before organizing the average wages for skilled and unskilled brewery labor in Milwaukee was $40–50 per month, while afterwards it had increased to $50–60. Working hours also improved, falling from 14 hours per day to only 10, and work on Sunday's was stopped completely.[12] It would be a decades-long struggle for brewery workers to maintain their successes, but within no time, the union would become a very powerful organization in the country's breweries.

And so, in this spirited age of unionization and organizing, Joseph Nigl began talking to fellow tavern owners about OBC's reign as the city's primary source of beer. What he found was that a number of them were harboring similar feelings—a sense of abuse by OBC and lack of appreciation by the company that was getting rich off of their efforts. By early May 1911, Nigl had recruited a formidable group with which to start the new brewery. They included men like Reinhold E. Thom, a fellow tavern owner who, like Nigl, had previously been a loyal customer of the OBC brand, but who also found himself in direct competition with OBC when they opened a slew of taverns in his neighborhood to directly compete with him.

Nigl also found local affluent businessmen who weren't associated with OBC directly, but who saw an opportunity for a profitable enterprise. Lastly, Nigl enlisted William Kargus who had worked for OBC as a bookkeeper before running afoul of Glatz and leaving the brewery in March of that year. Apparently, there was some lasting animosity between them, because Glatz tried to withhold stock options that were owed to Kargus after their separation (after threatening to sue, Kargus got a little less than half of what he was owed, which would be $140,000 today). Kargus, young and intelligent, and possessing not only an insider's knowledge of OBC operations, but also a massive grudge against Oshkosh's largest brewery, promised to be an important ally for Nigl and his new business.

From the start, Nigl and his associates had decided to organize their brewery's structure much differently than that of OBC (which was controlled by just a few). It was a structure that apparently drew inspiration from the socialist movement in local politics. Calling it at first the "Cooperative Brewing Company," they decided to sell stock in the brewery to

2. A Beer Born of Resentment

A postcard dated 1912 showing what would be the completed Peoples Brewing Company in Oshkosh, Wisconsin. The brewery would not be completed and making beer until 1913, but would go on to challenge Oshkosh Brewing Company for beer dominance in Oshkosh (author's collection).

the public, and they further decided that no one person or business could hold a majority share. What's more, stockholders and tavern-owners would share the profits among them, making the business a truly cooperative affair. When they filed paperwork with the Wisconsin Secretary of State, they proposed 11 different names for the brewery, including the initial choice, Cooperative Brewing Company. The Secretary of State, however, chose a different one: Peoples Brewing Company.

By the beginning of 1912 the project had received promises from enough area taverns to ensure the business would be immediately profitable. They had also issued shares to almost 200 stockholders, named their officers (making Nigl president), and picked the location for the brewery. Whether it was designed to annoy Glatz or not, the place they chose was directly across the street from OBC. Every day, traveling to and from work, Glatz would get to view the competition he helped create through his own policies. However, it would take another year and a half before Peoples would actually make any products.

In June of 1913, after a series of delays brought on by a shortage of funds, labor issues, and Wisconsin's bitter winters, Peoples Brewing Company finally started making beer. By November there were 25 taverns selling Peoples Beer, and many of them were selling it exclusively. Joseph Nigl's plan was quickly seeing success, and tavern owners throughout

Oshkosh were able to provide an alternative to the domineering practices of OBC. For their part, though, OBC had already decided to become the leader in locally bottled beer, so while they were losing some tavern customers, they were still safely selling more beer for home consumption. Peoples, on the other hand, was bottling also, but just not in the magnitude that OBC was. Instead, Nigl's aim (as a tavern owner himself) was to focus on taverns and to sell them mainly beer kegs for draught sales. This strategy would see Peoples through some of the most difficult times ahead for small breweries.

Neither strategy, though, would help the breweries—any breweries—on July 1, 1919. On that date the Wartime Prohibition Act went into effect, prohibiting brewers from making their product. The intention was to save grain due to the war effort; World War I, however, had ended in November of 1918. But before they could start making beer again, brewers faced the passage of the 18th Amendment, national prohibition, which went into effect in January of 1920. The breweries, with that legislation, were

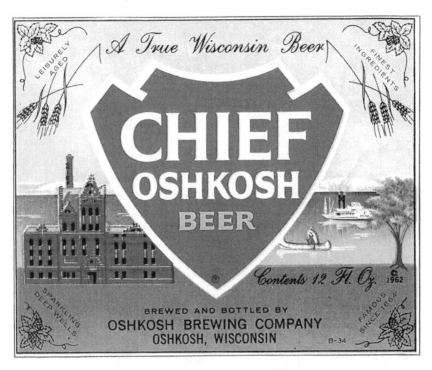

Label for Chief Oshkosh beer bottle. This was Oshkosh Beer Company's flagship beer and once the most popular beer in Oshkosh. From their founding it was Peoples Brewing Company's main competitor and the product Joseph Nigl tried to replace with his own Peoples Beer (author's collection).

effectively shut down. The next 13 years would be difficult for them, regardless of size or location. Most every brewery in the nation searched for ways to stay in business. Almost all tried their hand at making "near-beer," a beverage with the look and taste of beer, but without the alcohol. When this didn't prove profitable, they started making non-alcoholic beverages, like juices or flavored soda.[13] Eventually, they would make whatever they could in order to survive. By the time prohibition was repealed in 1933, the brewing industry in America had been decimated. Of the over 13,000 breweries that had been open in 1915, only 746 actually reopened in 1934.[14] And of those that emerged on the other side of the 18th amendment unscathed, all three in Oshkosh–Rahr, OBC and Peoples—were included.

But when Peoples and OBC began producing their product again, they found that much had changed. Not only did they find less competition, but they also found that consumers' taste for beer had evolved. Thirteen years without commercially produced brew created a generation with a taste for higher alcohol thanks to bootleg liquor, a fact that would benefit Peoples over the others. While OBC was making a light, low-alcohol lager before prohibition, Peoples was making a richer, higher alcohol beer that came to be identified as blue-collar beer. And so OBC had to create a new recipe to appeal to the new tastes of consumers, while Peoples merely picked up where it left off, making beer with much more alcohol and taste.

Once again, Peoples was a favorite of the working class, and the taps at the taverns of Oshkosh again flowed with Peoples. At the same time, the company also returned to their strategy of focusing on kegged beer for bars instead of packaged beer for the home (which OBC renewed their enthusiasm for). They were helped in this effort, although completely by accident, with a by-product of the end of prohibition. With repeal of the 18th amendment came a slew of new laws to regulate the production and sale of alcohol. One of those laws ended the tied-house system that breweries had used for a century to get their beer (and their beer exclusively) into taverns. With the end of this type of system, every bar and saloon in Oshkosh could serve any beer they chose, and often they chose a variety instead of any single brand. Starting in 1934, much to OBC's dismay, Peoples became available at most every tavern in the area.

After prohibition, brewers also quickly learned that consumers had changed their preference for where they drank. Before prohibition most beer was consumed in bars from taps, and only about 10–15 percent of beer was bottled. Beer in bottles—the only viable package you could buy beer in—was simply much more expensive than beer on tap. Plus, keeping it cold with old fashioned iceboxes needing a fresh supply of ice was just not practical for the average household. But then, in 1935, the American Can Company was able to successfully can beer for the first time, and the Kreuger Beer Company of Virginia became the first brewery to sell it in such a package. After seeing their success, many other brewers (including and especially the larger brewers) followed suit. Also, the use of home refrigeration became commonplace in houses across the United States, making it easy to keep beer cold at home. What's more, this new form of packaged beer was easier to ship and distribute long distances, making it more convenient to sell beer outside of a brewer's region. And so, subsequently, packaged beer grew in popularity, and the sales of draught beer fell every year after 1935, from a high of 70 percent of sales to only 14 percent in 1970.[15]

Those breweries that were prepared for this shift prospered and grew while those unprepared were forced to exit the industry. Larger brewers had been laying groundwork for such changes since prohibition went into effect. Brewers like Anheuser-Busch, Schlitz, Pabst and Miller had spent the 13 dry years purchasing refrigeration equipment and trucks, and

Beer label with the Peoples Beer logo and its distinctive arrow and "Hits the Spot" motto. The iconic logo was created in the 1950s by company president Richard Haidlinger and would go on to define Peoples Brewing Company for the rest of its existence (and beyond) (author's collection).

2. A Beer Born of Resentment

perfecting packaging and distribution methods. Such moves were made to bolster the new industries they entered, like soda and near-beer, but when prohibition ended, they were in the position to produce and ship their product far and wide. The result was massive growth for a handful of brewers. The largest five in 1938 were Anheuser-Busch (2 million barrels per year), Pabst (1.6 million barrels per year), Schlitz (1.6 million barrels per year), Ballantine (1.1 million barrels per year), and Schaefer (1 million barrels per year). By comparison, OBC produced less than 50,000 barrels and Peoples produced less than 40,000 barrels.

Smaller breweries simply couldn't compete with these new norms. From the 746 that reopened in 1934, only 468 would survive until 1945. By 1970, that number had dwindled to 154.[16] The regional breweries were doomed. Between huge yearly budgets with which to pay for national advertising and distribution, and the ability to brew millions of gallons of beer every year, not to mention a host of shadier methods they used to sell their products, the big breweries slowly squeezed the Oshkosh brewers, as well as other small brewers nationwide, out of business. The first one to fall was the noble Rahr, starting its production in 1865 and then ending it in 1956. When it first opened it had a brewing capacity of 1,500 barrels a year, making it the largest in the city. By the time it closed it was the smallest, and it just could not turn a profit. The next to go was the proud Oshkosh Brewing Company, which brewed its last batch in September of 1971, and was on pace to brew less than 20,000 barrels that year.

The surprising holdout, the only one that was weathering the storm better than any of the others, was also the youngest, the upstart Peoples Brewing Company. Its strategy of focusing on taverns had continued to help it earn enough to survive. It was not growing, not by a longshot, but the moderation and patience it had practiced gave it the ability to tread the new rough waters of competition while the surrounding brewers went under. If it kept to its strategy of focusing on kegged beer, it might actually pull through. Only a dramatic shift in policy would make the company as vulnerable as the rest, and that's exactly what would happen.

3

Introducing Mr. Mack

When Ted Mack settled into Milwaukee, he was settling into a region with a rich and long African American history. Historically, there had been African Americans in the Wisconsin region since the late 1700s, when they accompanied French, British and Colonial fur traders and trappers, often as slaves.[1] Though there are earlier references to a black-owned trading post, the first recorded black person in the region was a man named Jean Bonga, a slave owned by a British officer during the Revolutionary War[2] and who died a free man in the region in 1795. Through the 19th century, black migration to Wisconsin in general, but to Milwaukee in particular (which was founded in the 1830s), was a slow affair. In 1840 there were reportedly 185 free black people in the entire state, and 15 of these (as of 1838) were in Milwaukee.

Twelve years later this had increased to only 101 in the burgeoning city. While the growth of the black community took time, the general population of the state greatly expanded. Much of this increase was through the migration of white, American-born English descendants, and then later through massive influxes of both German and Irish immigrants. Between 1870 and 1890 the number of foreign-born whites increased from 33,773 to 79,540, while the black population rose from 176 to only 449. This trend continued into the early 20th century as well, with the number of African Americans in Milwaukee in 1910 growing to 980 (versus over 111,456 foreign born white residents).[3]

Starting in the 1910s and ending sometime in the 1970s was a phenomenon called the Great Migration, the term used to denote the era when millions of black residents from the South migrated to areas of the North, the Midwest and the Western states.[4] There were multiple reasons for the migration, such as the opportunity to find jobs in industries needed during the two world wars, or a decrease in the need for Southern farm labor due to the automation of agricultural jobs. And for some locations, the growth was enormous. From 1910 to 1920, Chicago's black population ballooned from 44,103 to 109,458, in Detroit from 5,741 to 40,838, and in New York City from 91,709 to 152,465.[5] In Milwaukee the growth was much more modest, with an increase of black residents from 980 to 2,229 between 1910 and 1920. By the time Ted Mack graduated from college and started to work for Milwaukee County (around 1960), the black population had grown to 62,458.[6]

Since the initial migration of African Americans to the region, numerous early black residents confronted the many inequalities they faced through the same civil right activism that would be carried out much later on. Organizations promoting the welfare of the black population formed as early as the mid-1800s, as did groups founded to promote black labor and employment in Milwaukee, and even organized efforts to bring about suffrage for the disenfranchised black residents from within the black community were taking place in Wisconsin by the 1860s.[7] In 1919, the Milwaukee chapters of both the National Association for the Advancement of Colored People (NAACP) and the National Urban League were formed.[8]

Each of these organizations would become immensely important for the African American population in Milwaukee and the surrounding regions. Founded in 1909, the mission of the National Urban League (originally called the National League on Urban Conditions Among Negros) was oriented towards helping black people find work.[9] They carried out important studies of the local black population, like household salary surveys and skills research, and they hosted workshops and training sessions to better educate African Americans to enter the workforce. And even as early as 1913 they tried working with labor unions (specifically, the AFL) to help get black labor integrated into union shops (though many of their early tries were frustrated by the organization's racially fueled refusal to admit African Americans).

The NAACP, meanwhile, was also founded in 1909, with the goal of shining a spotlight on the "frequently unjust treatment of colored people in the United States and the danger to American democracy of continued and customary injustice."[10] The combination of these resources would help black residents of Milwaukee, especially, in some of their most urgent times, like during the great depression, and in the many battles for equality yet to come. Those battles would be fought by men like Ted Mack, and it would be such a battle that would first introduce the sharecropper from Alabama to the white community of Wisconsin. And as it happened, that introduction was made through a hastily snapped image that would immediately incense the state's white residents who seemed to like things the way they were.

The image in question first ran on the front page of the Eau Claire Leader on March 4, 1964. In it was pictured, in grainy black and white, two men, frozen during what seemed to be a very tense discussion. On the left was a middle-aged man, arms folded tightly across his chest, his eyes behind horned-rimmed glasses, squinting slightly, his mouth turned down in a clear moment of exasperation or perhaps even anger. On the right, standing less than two feet from the first and facing him, was another man, about the same height, his head cocked, looking agitated or maybe frustrated as he said something to the man on the left.

The man on the right had his left hand up, his index finger extended as if making an accusatory jab at the other. The man on the left was white, his name was John W. Reynolds, and he was the governor of Wisconsin. The man on the right, head cocked and finger pointing, was Theodore A. Mack, Chairman of the Milwaukee Council on Human Rights, social worker for the County of Milwaukee, civil rights activist, and black.[11] The image and accompanying story, carried by newspapers throughout the state, would be one of the first published of Mack over the next ten years. And from the perspective of the conservative white majority of Wisconsin, it wasn't very flattering.

The story accompanying the picture provided a small amount of (also unflattering) context. In the words of the United Press International and Associated Press writers who filed the story, Ted Mack and Isaac Coggs (who was one of only two black assemblymen in the entire Wisconsin state legislature at the time) "ambushed" the governor during the dedication of a state government building in Milwaukee. In front of "150 guests and dignitaries" the governor was "lectured by two Milwaukee Negro leaders … and told that if he did not appoint a Negro judge within two months he would lose the Negro vote in the fall."

Mack, who the article noted had been "active in Congress of Racial Equality activities," reportedly told the Governor that "no negro in Milwaukee worked harder" for him to get elected, but that if a black judge was not appointed, "we're not going to ring any more doorbells for you." With the "guests and dignitaries" looking on, Coggs even climbed onto a nearby radiator to address the crowd and voice their demands. In short, the entire scene was textbook direct-action activism that would become increasingly more common in Milwaukee over the next decade. But at the time, before the street marches and picketing by the black community became commonplace, the episode shocked the white attendees (and those who later read the reported account).

For his part, Reynolds, who the Eau Claire Leader was quick to point out was an "outspoken civil rights advocate," stood stoically and silently while Ted Mack and Isaac Coggs made their demands. Later, addressing the event with journalists, the Governor stated that his record spoke for itself and that he would "continue to make appointments on merit."

Clearly, he wasn't impressed with Ted Mack, Isaac Coggs, or their proposition. Neither were the journalists Reynolds was speaking to. While the writers of the article in the Eau Claire Leader (and in other newspapers across the state) were only too happy to paint the episode as an "ambush," the story covered in the *Capital Times* from Madison, was a bit more moderate.

According to that article, Ted Mack and Isaac Coggs claimed they had a meeting set with the governor later that day to discuss the issue of appointing black judges in Wisconsin. However, upon making contact with the governor's team they were told that no meeting was to take place after all.[12] This was a frequently employed tactic of the day to placate the black community with demands—set appointments and then break them—so it wasn't like Mack and Coggs weren't used to being pushed aside by legislators. But this time, once they were told that the meeting was off, they decided to focus on directing the attention of the public towards the issue in question (the appointment of black judges) by interrupting the ceremony that they knew would feature the governor. The press, it seems, were quick to decide that this episode of activism by the black community was unwarranted and, perhaps, insulting.

Indeed, in most of the articles that ran throughout the state there was little that made the two men look like concerned citizens advocating for civil rights. Instead, they were transformed into scary examples of "negro agitators" with headlines written to give a slanted and incendiary view. The *Eau Claire Leader* exclaimed, "Reynolds Told to Pick Negro or Lose Votes," while the *Wisconsin State Journal* reported, "Governor Told: Negro Judge or No Votes."[13] In each case the reporting implied the civil rights advocates were threatening the governor, and the picture seemed to confirm that: a large, irritated black man in the face of the patient, white governor, remaining calm and measured while the other aggressively shoves his finger at him. In fact, the description of the picture reinforced this. In the article from the *Eau Claire Record*, Mack "shook his finger" at Reynolds, and even the picture itself was titled, "Warning Finger." Likewise, in the *Wisconsin State Journal*, Mack "wags finger to emphasize warning" to the governor.

The message could not have been clearer: the black man was out of line by threatening Mr. Reynolds. The responses to this story affirmed the message was received as such. In an opinion piece by the editorial board of the *Racine Journal-Times* on March 5, 1964, titled "Wrong Way to Go at It," Ted Mack and Isaac Coggs were castigated for what the article calls "racist politics at its worst." The editorial board claimed that the two "broke into a ceremonial program" to "make their demand," and admonished them for what the article called "crude and insolent" behavior. But, lest anyone consider the editors unfair, they also made clear at the end of the opinion that they "hope some day to see a Negro ascend the bench in Wisconsin," but that ascension should take place based on the merits of the individual, not his color[14] (an echo of the governor's exact words).

Likewise, on March 11, Madison's newspaper, the *Wisconsin State Journal*, ran a letter from a reader named Harley Jensen who also addressed the episode. Interestingly, his letter, titled "No Governor Should Be Subjected to Threats," was printed two columns to the right of an opinion piece titled, "How About Civil Rights for White Kids?" Clearly, civil rights was a popular topic of conversation for the *Wisconsin State Journal* readers. In any case, Jensen stated in his letter that "constructive criticism is one thing, but the intimidation [the governor] received in Milwaukee from one Theodore Mack ... is too much to stomach."[15] The implication is that because John Reynolds was governor he shouldn't be subjected to such aggressive behavior by others. Harley Jensen seems careful not to address race or the fact that Ted Mack (the only one he mentions, and the only one who was pictured in the article) is black. It begs the question: Would he have written the letter if a white man was pictured talking to the governor. Also in his letter, Jensen echoes Governor Reynolds by suggesting it should not be the color of one's skin that determines the selection of a judge, but his merit. "Just who is this Theodore Mack," he wonders in closing, "that he can demand appointment of a person from one particular race to be a judge in Milwaukee county?"

The surprise and outrage by conservative white residents would have been typical for the time and region, as such episodes (a black man making such direct demands from a white power figure) were relatively new. Though, as previously mentioned, struggles for equality had been occurring in the city as early as the late 19th century, open civil rights activism in Milwaukee really only gained momentum in 1958 when a young black man named Daniel Bell was shot in the back and killed by a local police officer. It was an obvious case of murder—Bell was unarmed and running away from the police when they shot him. But the officers spun a tale good enough to satisfy the white members of their inquest panel and they were exonerated.[16] The case drew protests from black Milwaukeeans who demanded accountability from the city and an end to police brutality. Sadly, the actions of the local law enforcement changed little. However, those who organized in protest found a voice, and slowly but surely, civil rights activism became more and more common in Milwaukee.[17]

This activism especially gained ground as black leaders in the city led campaigns against the many injustices they had been witnessing for years. One leader, Calvin Sherard, a metal finisher at the American Motor Company, organized for better employment opportunities for black men and women, especially in the Inner Core. After establishing an organization called the Crusaders Civic and Social League, Sherard and his supporters picketed an ice cream parlor located in a nearby neighborhood in order to pressure the owner into hiring more black employees. The owner quickly acquiesced to their demands, and the Crusaders got their first taste of victory (albeit a small one). From there, they moved to picket other Inner Core businesses, like the Woolworth and the grocery store chain A&P. Employment became a central issue for Sherard and other, like-minded members of the black community.

According to historian Patrick D. Jones, "the Crusaders believed that expanded black business ownership and increased African American employment in white-owned businesses were the keys to black success in Milwaukee."[18] This was an echo of Mack's sentiments as well that "if the black man were going to survive he would have to get into the corporate structure." In fact, just over a month after "ambushing" Reynolds, Mack would give a talk on this very subject in Sheboygan, about an hour north of Milwaukee. The April 10, 1964, edition of the *Sheboygan Press* announced that Ted Mack would be co-presenting on "Employment opportunities with special reference to Negroes" as the second part of a four-part series on human rights at the Beth El Synagogue Social Hall.[19] The subject was a very important one to the black community in general, and more specifically to Ted Mack himself.

But in addition to expanding black employment opportunities, the Crusaders also worked to end police brutality and agitated for changes to the justice system. Sherard was joined by other prominent Milwaukee-based black leaders through the early 1960s, and different groups were formed, and protests organized for numerous causes. Mack was a part of many of them. As the episode with Governor Reynolds from 1964 demonstrated, he was willing to take the lead on activism. Though always energetic and enterprising, he didn't turn that energy towards activism until 1963, when he answered the call from Dr. Martin Luther King, Jr., and organized Wisconsin's buses for the March on Washington, D.C.

The March on Washington for Jobs and Freedom was organized by civil rights leaders A. Phillip Randolph and Bayard Rustin. It initially began as a march for black employment but as public knowledge about it grew, it attracted other civil rights leaders and organizations, such as Martin Luther King, Jr., and his Southern Christian Leadership Conference (SCLC), the NAACP, and the Congress of Racial Equality (CORE) to name a few. It also evolved from agitating for employment opportunities to advocating more generally for civil rights for the black community. The leadership's goal was to attract at least 100,000 participants to march on the country's capital in a planned, nonviolent demonstration of solidarity and unity (they would eventually attract more than 250,000).[20] To carry out this goal, the groups created a well-organized network of activists to recruit marchers from cities throughout the South, the Midwest and the northeast. Mack was one of these activists.

As co-chair of the United Milwaukee Committee for the March on Washington, Mack's job was not only to recruit and organize marchers in Milwaukee and Madison (and beyond), but to also figure out the logistics of getting them there. It wasn't at all easy. According to an article in the *Kenosha News* from August 26, 1963 (two days before the March), the committee had been able to scrape up enough donations from locals to secure two buses, but were still $800 short from renting a third bus (despite having enough marchers to fill it).[21] The article noted that none of the donations came from businesses or unions, but instead from church collections and even through soliciting door to door. An article the next day noted one little girl donated two cents.[22] Every penny counted.

In the end, three busses would be filled. In total, 108 people from Milwaukee alone would make the journey, plus more from Racine, Madison, Kenosha and elsewhere, and all paid for and sent to Washington, D.C., through small, local donations that Mack was able to procure. The oldest marcher was 81, and the youngest was 14, and Mack led them all.[23] Much later in life, he told an interviewer that organizing the buses and marchers to Washington was the proudest moment of his life.

That achievement came with a price, however. Many of the activists and organizers were threatened or intimidated as they tried to make the march a reality. Mack himself experienced such threats. In an interview years later, he spoke of receiving phone calls at his home in the days leading up to the march. On the other end of the line Mack would hear, "you're going to be dead if you go to Washington, nigger"[24] and there was nothing he could do about it but hang up. These threats had the effect of spreading terror in the ranks and instilling fear in Mack himself. He was afraid (as many were) of the potential for violence at the march.

The feeling that something terrible would happen was so pervasive that hospitals in the Washington, D.C., area cancelled elective surgeries and put their entire staff of doctors and nurses on duty—waiting for an influx of injured marchers. Every police officer in the area was put to work, while reserve officers were called up and firefighters were deputized—all to handle the impending riots so many of them thought would materialize.[25] For Mack's part, he made the decision to go on the march without his family—they would instead stay safely back in Milwaukee.

Fortunately for all, the fear was unfounded, and the event was peaceful and remembered as a watershed moment in the struggle for civil rights.

It was a moment Mack had a part in shaping, but he was far from finished. His next campaign would be directed towards the bigoted practice that kept him from attending the University of Alabama. Ten years after it was supposed to end, Mack was going to march against school segregation in the Midwest.

Though *Brown vs. Board of Education*, the seminal case that appeared before the Supreme Court to end school segregation, was settled in 1954, segregation in the U.S. education system still existed. In fact, the Supreme Court had to rule again the following year (Brown II) to require that states actually desegregate (the first ruling said that segregation was unconstitutional, but never actually suggested anything be done about it). But despite this, many states and municipalities still chose to ignore the ruling and continued operating segregated schools, especially in the deep South where such local actions were often ignored or went unreported. However, it wasn't just the deep South that suffered from some form of de facto segregation, reports from throughout the United States at the time suggested that school segregation in some form was alive in small towns and large cities nationwide.[26] And this included the city of Milwaukee.

While the city did not have explicit school segregation, Milwaukee schools were segregated, nonetheless. Because of redlining, black residents could not find rental units or even property to purchase outside of the Inner Core. So, because of the dense population of black residents, the lines of school districts were drawn to ensure that children from this area went to schools that were only populated with black children from the area. And when these schools became too crowded, it became clear to the Milwaukee Public Schools administration that black students would have to be transferred to different schools (that is, white schools). But, to make sure the two groups (black and white children) didn't mix, they came up with a system called "intact bussing."[27] The plan was to send Inner Core (black) students by bus to white schools, but keep them together in their classes and recess without white kids—thus keeping them "intact." They would even bus them back to their original schools to eat lunch instead of allowing them to eat lunch at the white school, then after lunch they'd board the buses yet again for the trip back to school. Black children were kept isolated and apart, as if they carried some dangerous disease and needed to be quarantined.

In 1963 the practices of the Milwaukee Public Schools (MPS) caught the attention of an attorney and civil rights activist named Lloyd Barbee who had only recently moved from Madison, Wisconsin. He'd already led a movement to pass a fair housing bill in the state legislature and had worked for various human rights causes in the state's capital. After moving to Milwaukee and opening a law practice, he began working with local activist groups to end de facto school segregation in his new city.[28] Though he knew that eventually it would take legal action to get the situation changed completely, he also believed it was worth carrying out a direct-action campaign to bring attention to the issue.

With support from the membership of the Milwaukee chapters of both the NAACP and CORE, Barbee began organizing. He started by creating a single group, called MUSIC (Milwaukee United School Integration Committee), that would oversee all other organizations for school desegregation activities. In 1964, with its headquarters at Saint Matthew's Christian Methodist Episcopal Church in north Milwaukee, MUSIC and its supporters began planning a citywide school boycott in which they would keep their children from attending MPS schools for a week.[29] They carried out their boycott in May, with astounding results (Barbee estimated that about 15,000 students stayed away from MPS schools during the boycott).

More direct action soon followed the boycott, with protestors arriving at schools and surrounding the buses so they couldn't take their cargos of black children to the white schools. A number of protestors were arrested during these actions, and eventually the activists shifted their energy to other important causes, and direct action against de facto segregation would end. However, Barbee filed a lawsuit against MPS, and

March 1, 1964; Milwaukee, WI, USA; Organizers Lloyd Barbee, from left, Theodore Mack and Thomas Jacobson discuss plans for a Milwaukee Public Schools boycott March 1, 1964, at St. Mark AME Church, 1876 N. 11th St. Barbee ultimately sued MPS over continued segregation in the district (© Milwaukee Journal Sentinel–USA TODAY NETWORK).

that lawsuit would wind its way through the courts for a decade, ending in 1976 when federal judge John Reynolds (the same Reynolds that Ted had "wagged" his finger at) found that MPS had indeed enacted segregationist policies. Reynolds would eventually oversee the full integration of Milwaukee schools.[30]

Having already proven that he could organize during the march on Washington, D.C., Mack's skills were gladly received. He quickly rose to oversee the United Milwaukee Committee, one of the groups responsible for organizing the boycott against MPS.[31] His contributions to the cause were substantial.

Mack was a member of both the Milwaukee NAACP and CORE, but became especially active with CORE. He once noted that if CORE was organizing against something, he was most likely involved.[32] Ultimately, CORE found much to protest during the early 1960s. From organizing to desegregate a bowling alley to picketing businesses to force them to hire black employees, the members were kept busy. Through all of it, Mack found himself inevitably leading or organizing much of it. And it made sense that he would find a leadership position in CORE as well as other local civil rights groups. After all, he was a military (and war) veteran, a college athlete, a highly educated college graduate, and he hailed from the South. He would have had much in common with the other black leaders he surrounded himself with, like Calvin Sherard who was also from the South (Atlanta), and Lloyd Barbee, from Memphis who, like Mack, served in the military before going to college and eventually law school.

This was a type of black leadership unique to the early days of civil rights activism in Milwaukee. Those who led the protests of 1963–1965 were often older, in positions of authority in their communities or professions, and frequently considered conservative by the younger, more militant activists who followed them. Mack and many like him who attended the march on Washington, D.C., remembered the feeling of dread during the event, hoping against hope that violence would not break out. They wouldn't have dreamed of starting any confrontations and risking violence. But the activists who succeeded them, however, had no qualms about getting physical with counter-protesters or even the police. The activism more often seen during the second half of the 1960s was much more provocative, much more aggressive. The new breed of militant protestors directly challenged anyone who stood in their way, as if daring them to get violent so they could react in kind.

This approach was avoided by many of the early black community leaders like Mack, who felt that a more measured approach would serve the community much better.[33] Their perspective was not unlike the very earliest activists from Milwaukee's history, a group that historian Joe William

Trotter labels the "professional elite" that became prominent during the late 19th and early 20th century. This group used its ties with the white upper class to affect political and socio-economic change for the African Americans of the time, and in essence, worked within the system.[34] In fact, Lloyd Barbee knew from the beginning that it would take legal action to force MPS to stop de facto segregation, not the more direct types of confrontation. His goal in the street activism was merely to bring attention to the problem, not to solve it.

Following the protests against the intact busing and school segregation, people in the black community began organizing around a number of other issues. They protested the Milwaukee Eagle's Club, a private social club that played host to a number of prominent, local politicians and leaders, but which also did not allow black people to join. Demonstrating against this policy, activists picketed not only the Eagle's Club itself, but also the homes of many of the notable members, like local judges and aldermen. They also wrote letters to members and to the local newspapers, attempting to shame those members into quitting or otherwise becoming active against the Eagles.[35] None of it had any measurable effect.

Another major movement came against unfair housing. Led by a young, white Catholic priest named Father James Groppi, the Milwaukee NAACP Youth Council (YC) organized protests against housing discrimination, which amounted to landlords and homeowners refusing to rent or sell to black people outside of the Inner Core. North Milwaukee was crowded with dilapidated buildings that owners refused to fix for their (often) poor black tenants suffering from miserable poverty and crime. If they *could* find someone to rent or sell to them, black professionals or families moving to another part of town were subject to price gouging or racism in the form of hostile neighborhoods.

Pushing back against these practices, Father Groppi and the YC demanded a fair housing ordinance be passed in the city of Milwaukee.[36] To achieve their demands they began a new, even more aggressive direct-action campaign. They took to the streets and marched into the white suburbs of Milwaukee, and then through the southside of the city, full of working-class white residents. The southsiders proved to be hostile towards the marchers, and pelted them with beer bottles, rocks, and racist epithets. To protect themselves, the YC formed a group they called the "Commandos," young black men who were willing to confront the hostile crowds (including the police) and fight back.[37]

And fight back they did. The second half of the 1960s saw escalating violence and confrontation between civil rights protesters, local white citizenry, and the Milwaukee police department. The pressure caused by the tension of the city, the marches, the injustice of police brutality and housing discrimination was simply too much to bear. In the "long hot summer" of 1967, these elements converged in the Inner Core with disastrous results. On the night of July 29, a fight broke out between two black women outside of a local community center. When police responded they found a hostile crowd, fed up with their treatment at the hands of the white authorities of the city, who began throwing bottles, rocks, and anything else they could find. The crowd quickly grew, and the police called in reinforcements to control the hundreds of hostile locals, who would eventually disperse early in the morning.

The next day, reports circulated that the police had beaten a teenage boy, and crowds began to gather in the streets once more. By the time night fell, the crowd had become violent. Throughout the Inner Core, windows of white-owned businesses were shattered, buildings were set on fire, and there were even reports of gunfire and snipers. By 2 o'clock the next morning the mayor had declared a state of emergency, imposing a citywide curfew and activating the National Guard. By late morning the streets were empty, and it would take another few days for the curfew to be fully lifted. But the city would never fully return to normal, and the riots would live on in the memory of Milwaukee residents for decades.

Some in the black community watched these events with a sinking despair, a feeling that all the hard work and progress made in the first half of the 1960s amounted to nothing in the wake of such turmoil. From their point of view, the type of confrontational activism seen in the latter half of the decade, and the violence such activism begged, would discourage potential white allies. This view was especially present in older, more conservative members, who instead encouraged people of the black community to work within the system—to enter the white power structure and change it from within instead of trying to destroy the power structure completely. It was a different belief in the definition of Black Power. While to some, the term meant that black people didn't need any white allies— that they should instead take care of themselves—to others it meant they should simply see themselves as completely equal to the white community, deserving of anything and everything that could be achieved.[38]

While never stating this overtly, Theodore Mack intimated it throughout his life. On more than one occasion he said that he believed everyone was created equal, and that black people must enter positions of leadership within white industry to improve their lives. And, after fighting for civil rights in his community for half a decade, after serving the black community as a social worker since graduating from Marquette University, he decided it was time act on his beliefs. He decided to enter the white man's "corporate structure."

4

United Black Enterprises and the Famous Beer from Milwaukee

Simply put, the Valentin Blatz Brewing Company (also known as Blatz Beer) was a symbol of Milwaukee. Founded in 1851, only five years after the founding of Milwaukee itself, Blatz grew to become the third largest brewer in the city and the ninth largest in the country. Its history actually had much in common with the breweries in nearby Oshkosh—its founder, for example, Valentin Blatz, immigrated from Bavaria, where he learned the craft of brewing from his family. When he moved to Milwaukee in 1849, he quickly found a job at Johann Braun's City Brewery, which had only opened three years earlier. After saving enough money to venture out on his own, Blatz built a brewery next door to Braun's, and when Braun died in 1852, Blatz married his widow and took over the City Brewery, merging it with his own.[1]

Slowly but surely, Blatz expanded his brewery operations from the 500 barrels per year he was making in 1852, to tens of thousands by 1870. He expanded his distribution as well, entering the Chicago market in the 1860s. In 1873 the brewery burned down, amounting to almost $150,000 in losses (over $3 million today). Luckily for Blatz, while the fire destroyed much of the operation, it didn't destroy his beer, so he was able to continue distributing and selling his product. And while the fire did cost him thousands in rebuilding, it turned out to actually be a fortunate event because it allowed him to build new facilities and modernize his operation (prior to the fire the brewery was a ramshackle collection of add-ons and expansions).

Once completed in 1874, the modern brewery rebounded with a capacity that eclipsed the previous operation, and in 1875, Blatz became the first brewery in the city to begin bottling beer. This allowed him to significantly expand distribution beyond the growing city of Milwaukee, and that year he bottled and shipped 6,000 barrels (or almost 130, 000 bottles) of his beer, and became the first brewer in the region to ship beer nationally.[2]

By the 1880s the Valentin Blatz Brewing Company took up three city blocks and was producing over 100,000 barrels of beer per year. While it didn't own many taverns around the region like its competitors Schlitz, Pabst, and Miller, it was shipping massive amounts of its bottled product out of the area. Blatz had also built a large beer garden and hotel in Milwaukee, both of which served cold Blatz lager. Eventually, the operation grew big enough to gain the attention of British investors, who bought the company in 1891 (though Valentin, and then his son, would stay on as presidents). When prohibition began, the brewery was sold and then sold again in 1943 to Schenley Industries, which grew the company to be the 9th largest brewery in the country. Much of this success was due to national advertising, including sponsorship of the popular "Amos 'n' Andy" radio show, and television ads featuring cartoons that sang melodies about the "famous beer from Milwaukee."

The success wouldn't last, though, as the trend in the 1950s for brewers became one of expansion and modernization, or, alternatively, consolidation. In July of 1958, Schenley Industries sold Blatz to Pabst Brewing Company for $14.5 million dollars in cash, a relief of debts, and 200,000 shares of stock in the Pabst Brewing Company.[3] Though the Blatz brewery was small and in need of updating, it was still at the time a significant beer producer for the area, and the 18th largest in the country. However, Pabst seemed to have no interest in running or remodeling its previous competitor, and instead ceased the brewery's operations in 1959. But while the brewery itself fell silent, the Blatz story was far from over. On October 1, 1959, the United States Government filed a complaint in Federal Court, alleging that the Pabst Brewing Company bought the Valentin Blatz Brewing Company for the sole purpose of shutting it down to eliminate competition and bring about a monopoly, and Pabst was therefore in violation of Section 7 of the Clayton Act.[4]

The Clayton Act was passed in 1914 as a measure to strengthen previously passed antitrust legislation. In brief, the Clayton Act outlawed anti-competitive business strategies, including price-fixing among competitors (Section 2), sales of goods or services that forbade the buyer from dealing with competitors (Section 3), mergers and acquisitions that could substantially reduce competition (Section 7), and the practice of persons sitting as directors for two or more businesses in direction competition with each other (Section 8).[5]

The government argued that by purchasing Blatz, and then by ending its operation, Pabst was eliminating competition and reducing the number of suppliers for the market. In their complaint they stated that through this acquisition, Pabst controlled 4.49 percent of the beer market in the United States, 11.32 percent in a three-state area (Wisconsin, Illinois, and Michigan), and 23.95 percent in Wisconsin.[6] In truth this was by no means the first such case the federal government pursued against a brewer for such violations. There were actually two other cases in the 1950s (*U.S. vs. Lucky Lager* and *U.S. vs. Anheuser-Busch*), as well as five more in the 1960s, and all of the violations and cases were very similar.[7]

The *U.S. vs. Pabst* case amounted to a long, drawn-out, court battle, with each side winning and then losing at times. It was initially dismissed in 1964 in District Court by Judge Robert E. Tehan, who said the government failed to demonstrate that the acquisition would lessen competition. He also found that the three-state argument (that it would specifically lessen competition in Wisconsin, Illinois, and Michigan) was too narrow a geographic region. Pabst was initially vindicated. However, both these rulings were then reversed in the Supreme Court which sided with the federal government, and found that Pabst had indeed violated Section 7 of the Clayton Act, and then sent the case back down to District Court for a new trial. The Supreme Court's opinion expressed their concern for what it saw as an increased concentration in the brewing industry of the United States, and it further indicated a desire to ensure production was in the hands of as many brewers as possible.[8]

After a second trial that ended on February 28, 1969, the District Court, again with Tehan presiding, finally sided with federal government this time and ordered that Pabst divest itself from the Valentin Blatz Brewing Company. In July 1969 that's just what it did. And that's when Theodore Mack decided to enter the white man's corporate structure for real.

By 1964 Mack had left his position with Milwaukee County and was himself working for Pabst Brewing. The company was headed by a very progressive business leader named James Windham, who was by all accounts an impressive man. Before his tenure as president and CEO of Pabst Brewing, he had been the president of a bank, an executive officer at a retail store chain, and a major in the U.S. Army during World War II with duties that had him reporting directly to President Truman (and he later had a high-profile position with the Democrat party). In 1954 he became an officer of Schenley Industries, the company that owned Blatz Brewing Company. He was made president of the struggling brewery and two years later brokered the deal that sold them to Pabst. In the acquisition, Pabst kept Windham on, eventually making him CEO, and he steered the brewery to nationwide dominance, making over $500 million for Pabst in 1976.[9]

Though for years it was impossible for anyone from the black community to gain employment at one of the major breweries in Milwaukee, by the time Mack began working for them they had already, officially, integrated,[10] though it took some time to get that way. While breweries had hired black sales personnel for years, the much more sought after and lucrative production jobs in the breweries, like bottling or packaging, were always out of their reach. In fact, in 1951, African Americans made up only one-half of one percent of the entire brewing industry nationwide.[11] The primary reason black labor was not welcomed at U.S. breweries in the early to mid–20th century had to do with the brewery workers' union. In the first half of the 1900s most unions were either segregated, meaning they had different organizations for black and white members, or completely exclusionary.[12] Much of this was by design. Organizations within the American Federation of Labor (AFL), for example, often had prohibitive "constitutional race bars" that explicitly excluded African Americans from getting employment at businesses with AFL representation.[13] In 1887 the National Union of United Brewery Workmen affiliated with the AFL, so suffice it to say their policy reflected the sentiments of the larger group.

In a city like Milwaukee, home to the biggest brewers in the country, these discriminatory policies were especially painful to the black population. As early as the 1890s, the prejudices of labor unions within the city kept blacks from entering the industrial force.[14] Likewise, these attitudes persisted decades later when, during the great depression, African Americans still couldn't find brewery work after prohibition ended in 1933.[15] Struggles against such practices were certainly carried out in Milwaukee, but also in other parts of the country, like New York City, where local black leaders threatened boycotts and activism if hiring policies weren't changed.[16]

Back in Milwaukee, though, change eventually did take place. In 1946, the National Union of United Brewery Workmen, by then known as the International Union of United Brewery, Flour, Cereal, Soft Drink, and Distillery Workers of America, had dissolved its connections with the AFL and instead affiliated with the Congress of Industrial Organizations (CIO). Although much smaller, the CIO was known as being much more friendly to black workers, and often courted African Americans and invited them into their ranks.[17] By 1948, CIO representatives were working closely with officials from the Milwaukee branch of the civil rights organization, the Urban League, and the major area breweries. In 1950 they were able to announce a major victory for black labor. On July 29, 1950, a headline on page 3 of the *New Tribune* newspaper announced that three Milwaukee breweries, Pabst, Blatz, and Schlitz, had lifted a 50-year ban against hiring black production workers.[18] By the time of the headline there were already 25 black employees working the production lines. The breweries were integrated, and Mack was now going to take his position in one of them, and that would change his life forever.

Mack was hired initially as a production manager, a role with a myriad of functions at a large brewery like Pabst. If one wanted to learn everything there was about brewing beer on a large scale, then production manager would be the right position to be in, as they might do everything from oversee the brewing schedule and beer quality, to directing packaging and shipping. They could also be responsible for raw materials, personnel schedules, maintenance and safety. In short, it was a middle manager position that oversaw the brewery and every part of its operations.

Such a job would give Mack a crash-course in brewing and would indeed teach him everything from the ingredients used (and where they came from), to different methods of large-scale brewing, to the distribution of the product after it had been produced and packaged. He held this job for two years before being made manager of the Industrial Relations Department, the department overseeing relations between employees and the company. This job may have been even better suited for him than production manager, because while he had a degree in sociology, he often told people that his background was in psychiatric social work, a role he would have gained experience in while working for the county three years earlier. This experience would have in turn facilitated a position in employee relations quite easily, as it deals with understanding people, their needs, complaints and personalities—all traits he would have honed while working in Milwaukee County's Welfare Division.

While learning the corporate structure of Pabst, the enterprising Mack was also busy selling life insurance in the Inner Core of Milwaukee. In a 1965 issue of *Ebony Magazine*, New York Life Insurance Company placed a full-page advertisement featuring professional headshots of 28 of their insurance agents, all black, with a slogan at the bottom of the page that read, "What kind of man is your New York Life Agent?" Below the images were the agent's name and city, and below a smiling, business-suit wearing Theodore Mack was "Milwaukee" (he was the only agent listed for that city).[19] Over the next five and a half years he would spend his days at Pabst, and would then hit the sidewalk to make house calls selling insurance at night. His natural charisma and charm, not to mention the fact that he knew so many people in the area, helped him excel with New York Life, and in his first year he sold over a million dollars of insurance, something he would repeat.[20] Before he was 40 years old, he had not only entered the white corporate structure as he'd been telling his own community to do, he'd done so successfully in two different industries.

But then, on March 25, 1969, Mack saw a chance to do more than just *enter* the white corporate structure, he saw a chance to *own* it. On that day,

4. United Black Enterprises and the Famous Beer 49

Advertisement for New York Life Insurance from the October 1965 issue of *Ebony Magazine*. Theodore Mack, fifth from the left in the third row, was selling millions of dollars in policies in the mid-1960s while working days as a manager at Pabst Brewing Company (author's collection).

lawyers for both Pabst and the U.S. government met with federal Judge Robert Tehan to discuss the resolution to the Court's ruling against Pabst. Government attorneys proposed that Pabst sell the Blatz brewery so that it could begin making beer independently once more. Pabst's attorneys said they "might not appeal Tehan's decree if agreement could be reached on the type of relief."[21] But as it turned out, they really had little say in it at all. The Court ordered them to divest themselves of Blatz completely and that they (the Court) would decide on conditions. And so, on June 26, Tehan began a hearing on the sale of the Valentin Blatz Brewing Company. Almost immediately there was interest from regional brewers, but only from a handful of them.

As it turned out, one kink in the transfer was the insistence from the government that the sale not continue to concentrate or consolidate the beer industry. In other words, it couldn't be sold to another big brewer. This hampered a number of interested parties. For example, an idea introduced at the beginning of the conversation in March was that Pabst sell Blatz back to the company it purchased it from: Schenley. However, that idea was nixed by the U.S. Government, which noted that Schenley was acquired by a different corporate conglomerate and so would simply be another case of brewery concentration. What they wanted was a company free from relationships with other corporations to take over not only the Blatz brand, but also the brewery itself: to rehabilitate it and start making beer again.

But this was going to be a difficult deal to make. The Blatz brewery was shut down in 1958 and had been used as a warehouse for storage since then. Brewing technology had progressed quickly in the ten years since it had been purchased, so much of it would need to be replaced. It was a brewery in name only, and any company that bought it would be looking at tens of millions of dollars to bring it up to date. The Court knew that selling Blatz—all of it, including the abandoned brewery—would be a longshot, so they noted other possibilities. One alternative option (and the second most favorable) was to sell the Blatz brand along with one of Pabst's many other breweries. Pabst had a number of regional breweries that could be used immediately (they were already in production), so this would allow a company that wasn't already into brewing to begin making and selling beer immediately. The final option, the one Tehan liked the least, was selling the Blatz brand and associated assets along with the right to brew under the Blatz name—but not the brewery.

The first two options would meet the Court's desire to make the brewing industry more competitive. They meant that Blatz would necessarily be sold to a company that wasn't already making beer—that the beer industry would not become more consolidated. The third option, on the contrary, would almost certainly mean that Blatz would be bought by an existing brewer and would continue the concentration of the beer business that Tehan found Pabst guilty of. It would make sense that if faced with the prospect of selling not only the Blatz brand, but also its brewery, to a buyer that intended to restore the dilapidated brewery, versus just the

4. United Black Enterprises and the Famous Beer

brand to another existing brewery, it would lend serious consideration to the former.

Unfortunately, there were few wanting to invest the money in the old brewery. The first interested party, an existing brewing company, approached both the Court and Pabst in early April 1969. Associated Brewing Company offered one of the first bids of $11.5 million. Next came an offer from Heileman Brewing Company in May, which was followed by a bid from Grain Belt Brewing Company out of Minnesota. In their conditions, none of these companies wanted the old brewery, just the name and rights to brew Blatz. Perhaps for this reason or maybe to create more time for other bidders, the Court refused all of these bids, and instead scheduled a hearing for July 8 to hear from these and any other potential buyers, and to quiz them on their plans for Blatz' future and their ability to fulfill the Court's desired conditions.

That was the plan anyway. But between the meetings in April and the planned hearing in July, Judge Tehan started to get nervous. He was increasingly concerned with the amount of time that had passed since his initial ruling against Pabst. Since that ruling in February, Pabst had stopped production of Blatz altogether, which meant brewery lines were sitting idle, distributors were without beer to distribute, and consumers were moving further away from the brand. With each day that passed, Blatz beer was becoming just another one of yesterday's obsolete beers. In August of 1969, Tehan wrote in an Opinion:

> During the conferences it became increasingly apparent that prompt action was essential if we were not to have here a situation like that in other anti-trust cases involving the brewing industry where the Government's success under [Section] 7 appears to have resulted not in the restoration of competition but in substantial dissipation of the brands to be restored.[22]

In other words, if a beer brand isn't producing anymore, people forget about it and move away from it. Though the case might have been won, the brand was still lost because it took so long for the court to move to restore the brand to the market. Expediency, then, finally trumped most other variables in Judge Tehan's eyes, and so the original hearing for July 8 was moved up to June 26. At that hearing, the Court and attorneys for Pabst and the U.S. Government heard official bids from Associated Brewing Company, Heileman Brewing Company, and Grain Belt Brewing. But then, on July 9, Grain Belt withdrew its bid, and the newspapers reported that official inquiries to submit bids had also been made by the Duquesne Brewing Company of Pittsburgh and Stroh Brewery Company of Detroit. They additionally reported that an organization called United Black Enterprises was expressing interest in submitting a bid for Blatz.[23]

The president of that organization, they reported, was a black Milwaukee insurance agent named Theodore A. Mack, Sr.

United Black Enterprises (UBE), according to the Milwaukee Journal Business News, was an organization "composed of Negro businessmen" who had raised $7 million dollars towards a bid for Blatz.[24] It was Mack who had brought these people together and who had hatched the idea to buy the brewery. And not only had he drawn together local, successful, black business people, he had also assembled some of the more notable community leaders in the area. Four of these in particular were Henry S. Crosby, Robert Peeple, Ray Alexander, and Harold B. Jackson. All four were college-educated in addition to being successful, and they all had different skills and backgrounds. Crosby attended Florida A&M and received a business administration degree from a private university in Milwaukee. He was also a co-owner of an independent insurance agency and of a local Milwaukee nightclub called Alfie's. Peeple, like Ted, had attended Marquette University and was the assistant branch manager of the First Wisconsin National Bank in Milwaukee. Ray Alexander (whose wife was also a member of UBE) was the Community Relations Director for the Northtown Planning and Development Council, a community-based organization that conducted such programs as social work, job training and economic development for mainly black neighborhoods.[25] These men were all Ted's friends. They all lived in the Inner Core of North Milwaukee, they all attended the same church, and they were all active in the same civil rights organizations.

And then there was their spokesman, Harold B. Jackson.

Jackson was an ambitious and smart 1967 graduate of Marquette Law School and had been a prosecutor for the County of Milwaukee's District Attorney, Hugh O'Connell. His father was a famed New York radio broadcaster named Hal Jackson, who had broken racial barriers in music and sports (he once owned the Washington Bears basketball team).[26] Harold Jackson himself was also active in civic and racial justice, becoming the county's only black Assistant District Attorney before leaving the government sector in 1969 to pursue private practice. In 1970 he would become the first black School Board President in Milwaukee, and that year also led an effort to end the "intact busing" that Mack and others had protested against only six years earlier. Then, in 1973, he was appointed to the Milwaukee County Court, making him only the second black judge in the state.[27] But it was his statement to the press in early July 1969 on behalf of UBE that really got everyone's attention.

At a press conference on Wednesday, July 9, 1969, Jackson told the reporters in attendance about United Black Enterprises and about their intention to bid on Blatz. He also told reporters about the $7 million in commitments they had so far raised from various sources. But what they really seemed to focus on were his statements made at another press conference on Monday, July 7. At that discussion, Jackson made clear that a UBE-owned Blatz would only hire from the black community, and that all management positions would also be black.

When reporters pressed him on this during the July 9 event, Jackson clarified that they intended "to establish qualifications for the positions (which) by their very nature would make it difficult to serve. It does not mean we will not hire white people at all. It means that any persons we hire must be able to give the physical and spiritual support (to the company) that we demand of an employee." He then clarified that further, saying that personnel must be dedicated to the idea of "making the Black man a producer and not just a consumer."[28] The statements definitely raised eyebrows at the presser, and Jackson was questioned repeatedly to elaborate and clarify, causing him to irritatedly wonder that "a white employer could set the qualifications for his employee with little notice being taken, but as soon as a black enterprise did the same, it caused an overreaction."[29]

Mack's group, UBE, and especially their plans to turn Blatz into a "black brewery" quickly became a topic of discussion in the local papers. It's not like it should have been a complete shock to reporters that a group of black businessmen would pursue a plan to hire an all-black workforce, after all, other ventures had carried out similar strategies, even in the beer industry. In 1937, for example, Reuben Gray, Grady Jackson, and Everett Watson, all of whom were black, founded the Paradise Distributing Company in Detroit, distributing a limited selection of beer brands to black outlets in Paradise Valley, the city's mostly black area filled with nightclubs and saloons serving primarily an African American crowd. Since its founding, Paradise Valley Distributing Company's mission was to provide opportunities to the local black population, and as of September of 1941 had 30 all-black (and no white) employees in roles like sales, truck driving, delivery and office staff.[30] UBE's plan was not so different at all, except this time they were hoping to make the beer, not just distribute it.

In the July 9 hearings, Tehan gave UBE until noon on Friday to submit a formal bid. So, that Friday, July 11, they delivered a bid for $9 million dollars for the purchase of Blatz. The bid was not only for the beer brand, but for the brewery itself and its equipment, which they planned on using to brew their beer.[31] According to various reports, the money in the bid was being promised by five "eastern banks," including New York City's Freedom National, and Philadelphia's First Philadelphia Bank & Trust Company, both black-owned banks that Mack himself courted and made agreements with.[32] By that Saturday, July 12, Mack told reporters Carole Malone and Dave Novick from *The Milwaukee Courier* that commitments and pledges for funds had exceeded $17 million. However, he also stated that "some offers were being considered carefully because UBE wants the Milwaukee Black community to retain the major controlling influence."[33]

The theme of a black-owned, black-run brewery had been noted from the start. In another article from July 12, a "member of UBE" (it doesn't indicate which) said that "United Black Enterprises is primarily Black people who want to see positive change in the economy for Black people. UBE is Black people who have a strong design to be producers, and not merely consumers, Black people who want to decide what they want by making what they want."[34] This was an echo of a position paper issued by UBE on Monday, July 7, which stated:

> Of the 500 major corporations in America today, none are under Black ownership or control. As a result, a major area of economic leverage and political influence is not available to the Black man as a means of bettering his condition.... What is necessary is that the Black man move deliberately, imaginatively and expeditiously at every opportunity to breach this gap and become a part of this country's major corporate structure. The ownership of a major brewery presents us an opportunity of such magnitude.[35]

In other words, this wasn't just the purchase of a brewery by entrepreneurs and business people, this was an opportunity to better the black community. This was a *cause*. This was *civil rights activism*.

The UBE bid was joined by Associated, Heileman, Stroh (which had bid in partnership with Grain Belt), and Bankit, a Milwaukee credit corporation. However, while the bids from the others were more or less matter of fact, UBE's had a special request attached to it. Though offering an initial amount of $9 million, UBE also asked for a six-week (later amended to three-week) extension of the hearing to "allow potential backers to examine the physical and financial assets of Blatz."[36] This was important because unlike the others bidders (save Bankit), UBE was interested in the brewery itself: they wanted to make beer there. They insisted that the time delay was a necessity to understand how much the entire enterprise would cost. In one article, Jackson estimated it would take at least $45 million to buy, overhaul and operate Blatz and its brewery.[37] However, to be sure, UBE needed more time to figure this out.

But time, as Judge Tehan had noted before, was of the essence. According to him, every day that the Blatz decision stood in limbo was another day closer to shrinking the already concentrated beer industry. In court, referencing the request for postponement, Tehan stated that "the uncertainty caused primarily by this case is imposing severe strain on the Blatz operation, and delay can adversely affect not only Blatz but offerors who have previously appeared ... my sole concern at this time is

4. United Black Enterprises and the Famous Beer 55

to insure, as far as possible, that Blatz is restored to a competitive position, and delay can only jeopardize that possibility."[38] This sentiment notwithstanding Tehan seemed still willing, at least for a brief moment, to help UBE. On Wednesday, July 16, he deferred UBE's request for adjournment and said he would consider the request after UBE was called on to support its $9 million-dollar bid. He also, an article noted, had decided to place UBE last in the hearing to give them more time to prepare their case.[39]

On Tuesday, July 22, Jackson made his argument on behalf of UBE in support of their bid and adjournment request. The bulk of the rationale for their bid was spelled out in a statement released on July 9.[40] First, they argued that they were the only bidder that would create competition instead of concentrating it (that is, they were the only bidder, aside from Bankit, that was not at the time already making beer under a different name). They argued that the lawsuit against Pabst was started because of the elimination of competition, and that they would increase competition as an independent brewer. Secondly, they stated that their bid would keep Blatz and its production in Milwaukee, while others would move the beer production to another city. Lastly, because they were not already a brewer, they would offer innovation and new methods of conducting business.

Despite these points, Tehan was not moved, saying "while I am impressed with the sincerity of the spokesman, Attorney Harold Jackson, with the efforts made, and with the task facing the group, I can only conclude that its plans are only in the embryonic stage, and that the 30 day extension could not realistically cover its needs."[41] This was a major blow for UBE, which had, with their bid, even attached a request for postponement from one of their investors to demonstrate its need.[42] Without more time, their financial backers would back out.

By the next day, Wednesday, July 23, UBE had already called for a rally in a northside park on Sunday to discuss the situation with concerned residents and to garner support from the community. Mack himself was completely dejected by Tehan's decision, saying sullenly that "as I sat there in the courtroom, I realized how a brother on the street must feel. He steals a loaf of bread in order to eat, and the police put him in jail. There are millionaires stealing a brewery and patting themselves on the back for making good corporate deals."[43]

The future was uncertain, and none of UBE's members would say for sure what the next step would be, despite wanting to fight the outcome. While an article titled "UBE will fight Tehan decision"[44] started out by saying "United Black Enterprises president Theodore Mack announced late Wednesday UBE intended to fight Federal Judge Robert Tehan's decision," it later stated "he [Jackson] said he didn't know if UBE would seek an appeal." Likewise, in a Milwaukee Courier article, titled, "Beer fight goes on," Jackson said that "the future activity of UBE is now indefinite."[45] While the will called them to fight on, their energy just didn't seem to be there. Eventually, Blatz—both the brand and the right to brew its beer—was sold to Heileman,[46] and the old brewery never again produced the beer that was Milwaukee's favorite. Blatz is now just another forgotten American beer brand that used to be.

It's safe to say that the decision by Judge Tehan is puzzling. On the one hand, the whole reason why the lawsuit took place and the order for the divesture given was because the brewing industry had been concentrated by the sale of Blatz to Pabst. But then in the end, Blatz was bought by another established brewer, Heileman, which, essentially, made the situation no different than had it still been owned by Pabst. Heileman simply used the name and formula to brew Blatz from its own breweries. Pabst did the same thing. So, what's the difference? It can't be understated how much stir was caused when Harold Jackson revealed that the employees of their brewery would be black. This was in 1969, only two years removed from the riots in the Inner Core. "The Long Hot Summer" was fresh on the minds of the people in Milwaukee. Father Groppi and the Youth Council were still marching in the street about fair housing (and other issues), and civil rights activism was mentioned almost daily in the local newspapers. Whether there was political pressure on the Court to make sure that UBE didn't come away with Blatz isn't clear. But what is clear is that Mack and his group, from their point of view, suffered yet another episode of bigotry by the white power structure.

Of note was that Mack believed they would be successful if they used "traditional methods" to carry out their campaign. He told reporters that "we did it your way. We didn't have any spectators, because we didn't think that was the way."[47] He's specifically referencing the direct-action type of activism he and most of the other members of UBE were involved in during the mid–1960s. As noted these types of methods—rallying protestors to march and picket—were still in use in the region, though much less frequently than before. But Mack's statement implies he and his associates were making a *conscious* choice about how they took action. It was, perhaps unnatural to them to carry it out the way the Court had forced them to; this was the "white man's world" and foreign to these businessmen from the Inner Core. But it also indicates something else—this was activism as they had come to define it. While the early and mid–1960s had them marching in the streets, they had come to recognize direct-action as working within the system for a specific cause, and to believe that changing the system from within was more practical than staging protests.

Also of note is that while they never discussed any definite courses of action they would take after Tehan's decision (despite the headlines of the local newspapers), they indicated that UBE was still pursuing options. Jackson told the *Milwaukee Courier* that "UBE is still investigating obtaining a brewery; possibly buying or building one themselves."[48] As it turned out, it would be the former, and not the latter.

5

Buying Peoples Beer

United Black Enterprises didn't really go away after losing out on the Blatz purchase, and in fact their desire to own a brewery refused to ebb. In Mack and the others, it may have been even stronger than before. He later said that during the campaign for Blatz, they learned that black people in the U.S. were one of the country's largest groups of beer consumers.[1] After finding that out, they were resolved to "somehow ... own a brewery"[2] and so they actively started looking for one to purchase. By November they had found the one they wanted. The UBE spokesman Harold B. Jackson confirmed in a November 8, 1969, article that they were preparing for negotiations to purchase a brewery. He wouldn't say which one it was or where it was located, only that "preliminary discussions had been held with a smaller firm—located outside of Milwaukee."[3]

The one that UBE had settled on was a small brewery in nearby Oshkosh. It was small, stable, and was well maintained, meaning it would not take much to rehabilitate (unlike Blatz). And, best of all, it would cost a fraction of the price. If Mack was going to insist they make beer, this might be their best shot at doing so. Over the course of the next year, Mack made many trips to the small city in the Fox Valley, and by spring of the next year, UBE was ready to seal the deal.

On April 14, 1970, the *Milwaukee Sentinel* broke the news that members of United Black Enterprises planned to purchase the Peoples Brewing Company in Oshkosh, Wisconsin.[4] Though they were unable to reach any member of UBE, the paper's reporter was able to track down the president of Peoples, Harold Ziegenhagen. When asked about UBE, Ziegenhagen would neither confirm nor deny any pending sale to the group. However, he teasingly said that, "if anyone comes along with the right amount of money we will sell."[5] Importantly, though they never interviewed him, the article also recalled and then highlighted what Jackson had said about the plans for Blatz management if UBE had been successful in buying that brewery. Quoting him out of context, the article stated that "Jackson has said if the black organization acquired a brewery, management jobs would be filled by blacks and the policy would be to hire blacks."[6]

This was undeniably false, however. Jackson never said "*a* brewery" (as if his statement or their policy applied to *any* brewery), instead he was specifically talking about Blatz and the situation of the Pabst divesture. Blatz was an empty shell, a product name. And, crucially, in that particular situation, Blatz had no employees and UBE would have been hiring a completely new staff had they acquired the brand and former brewery. In other words, they could have hired whomever they felt like hiring and nobody would have suffered. The situation at Peoples was different. Very different. At Peoples there were 21 employees, white employees, and according to the *Sentinel*'s article, they might soon be fired and replaced by black workers instead. This accusation would come to haunt Ted Mack and Peoples for a long time.

But nevertheless, the Sentinel was right about the purchase. As it turned out, on that Tuesday, April 14, Theodore Mack, Henry S. Crosby and Ray Alexander were not available for interview because they were attending the stockholders' meeting of Peoples Brewing Company in Oshkosh in order to formally make an offer on the brewery. The newspapers reported that it was a long day of negotiations, but that by the end of the day, 80 percent of the 160 stockholders had voted in favor of selling.[7] In truth, this was actually the end of a long process that began almost a year earlier. The end to the campaign for Blatz left them disheartened, but instead of wallowing in depression they found determination. They took calculated and measured steps, rushing nothing, but spending the time necessary to ensure this venture succeeded.

By November 1969 they had set their sights on Peoples. In March, Mack had approached Ziegenhagen about buying the brewery. And now in April, they had finally accomplished what they set out to do the previous July: they'd bought a brewing company. The picture carried in the newspapers of the press conference after the meeting showed Mack sitting at a table with faces familiar from the Blatz campaign, specifically, Henry S. Crosby and Ray Alexander.[8] One person quite obviously missing was Harold Jackson, the young, brash attorney who'd spoken about the black-only hiring policy at Blatz. Instead, sitting as attorney for the group in the picture, was a Michael B. Laiken, a white lawyer from Milwaukee.

An Oshkosh paper reported on the numbness felt by Mack, finally achieving his goal after a year of hard work. To the press gathered, he admitted exhaustedly, "I worked so hard, I don't have any feelings yet. Maybe I'll have some reaction tomorrow."[9] His elation, though subdued from fatigue, was real. He'd finally accomplished something everyone said was impossible, and at the same time he'd shown that entering the

April 15, 1970; Oshkosh, WI, USA; Theodore Mack, center, and his associates in purchasing Peoples Brewing Co. meet the press after shareholders approved the sale of the Oshkosh-based brewery on April 14, 1970. Flanking Mack, from left: Henry S. Crosby, an owner of Carter-Moody & Associates; Ray Alexander, community relations specialist at Northtown Planning and Development Council; Attorney Michael B. Laikin; and Fred Gordy, real estate broker (© Milwaukee Journal Sentinel–USA TODAY NETWORK).

white corporate structure was indeed very possible. Although weary and drained, Mack and the others still had a long way to go before they actually took control of Peoples. The next step was to arrange financing.

The purchase price wasn't revealed to the reporters on the night of their press conference, but the Wisconsin Manufacturers' Association directory listed Peoples Brewing Company's net worth at $500,000.[10] The bank that was providing the loan for the purchase valued the brewery's assets a little lower, at $365,000 plus another $70,000 in inventory (or $435,000 total).[11] Through negotiations, however, the stockholders and Mack's group settled on slightly more—$440,000.[12] That amounts to a little more than $2.89 million today, a sizable sum for anyone, but especially for a group of black Milwaukee businessmen (though it was substantially less than the amount they were bidding on Blatz a year earlier).

The purchase was truly unique—black business people really didn't exist outside of black neighborhoods in 1970.[13, 14, 15] And for a group of minority men to spend that kind of money on a business outside of the black community was unheard of. Mack, Henry Crosby, and the others were breaking new ground. But unlike the Blatz campaign, this time they were prepared. In fact, they'd spent the time since their bid was rebuffed the previous year to lay all of the necessary groundwork for the purchase.

5. Buying Peoples Beer

Mack was able to negotiate a loan of $390,000 from Marshall & Ilsley Bank,[16] a local Milwaukee institution. And while a staggering amount to get from a local bank by a black businessman, it was still $50,000 short of what he actually needed. To make up these funds, Mack and his associates decided to raise the money internally. First, certain members of the board bought 24,500 shares of the new company at $0.83 per share for a total of $20,335. Of this stock, Mack bought the lion's share—22,000 shares (amounting to $18,675). The remaining $1,325 was contributed by the other men.[17] Finally, to make up the rest, Mack himself provided an additional $30,000 loan to the company,[18] completing the required payment that Peoples' stockholders had asked for in negotiations.

Consider this amount for a moment. Theodore A. Mack, Sr., at 40 years old, a black man who was born a sharecropper in Jim Crow Alabama, had $48,675 to provide to this venture. Adjusting for inflation, that equals over $320,000 in cash he had available. This is telling about the man. The most obvious (and most flippant) thought about Ted Mack is that he was one hell of a life insurance salesman. But also, he must have believed in this campaign with all his heart and soul to be willing to sacrifice so much. This must have been much more than just the purchase of a brewery to him: this must have been a cause. And by signing a check for over $48,000, he was proving his dedication to that cause—and his community.

After providing the seed funding and getting a promise from the bank, he just had what might have seemed to them like some loose ends to tie up. These consisted of a guarantee from the Small Business Administration (SBA) and an additional $200,000 cash for operating capital, which were both required by the bank before they'd provide the loan to Mack and his associates.[19]

The SBA loan guarantee turned out to be alarmingly easy to get considering they were asking the federal government to back $390,000 for a group of men who had never managed or run such a large enterprise before. But in order to get it, the SBA asked Mack and four other members of what would become the Board of Directors (plus their wives) to personally guarantee the loan (thus making them personally liable for it). This should have been a bright red, flashing warning sign to them, an ominous indicator of things to come. But, ultimately, perhaps owing to the enthusiasm of the SBA officials that were helping them, or maybe because of their own jubilance at the prospect of what could be, they all acquiesced and signed. According to Congressional testimony Mack gave much later, the SBA told them they were eager to help them apply for the loan because their brewery would be a minority-owned business.[20] Again, this shouldn't have been a surprise, but it also should have sent out more warning flares about what was in store for them. The SBA, after all, had its own shady past to beware of.

The SBA was formed in 1953 as a concession to Democrats in Congress in a deal put together by President Dwight Eisenhower. After being elected in 1952, Eisenhower set about trying to dissolve a Depression-era federal program called the Reconstruction Finance Corporation (RFC).[21] Created in 1932, the RFC was charged with the mission of providing taxpayer-funded loans to struggling banks and large corporations on the verge of failure. The program was kept and expanded through World War II, and then again through the Korean War. In both of these wars the RFC's mission transformed into providing funds for defense contractors manufacturing arms and equipment for the U.S. military. Eisenhower was keen on getting the federal government out of the business of providing loans to private companies, especially big ones, and so the elimination of the RFC was a year-one priority. But Democrats in Congress would only agree to dissolve the agency if there was another program created in its place with the mission of helping small businesses, and so the deal reached was the formation of the SBA.

As an agency, though reportedly working to help mom and pop businesses across the U.S., the SBA was created and then run with political purpose. Though Eisenhower wasn't fond of the government's getting involved in private finance, he knew that the appearance of helping small businesses would make the Republican party, at the time considered allies of big business, look much more attractive to the average American. Kennedy, too, when he took office understood that the agency could be used to help him appear friendly to small businesses, thereby bolstering his support from Main Street as well as from Wall Street. And so he, too, supported the agency because of political expediency. But when Lyndon Johnson came to the Oval Office, the agency took on a much more ideological mission than the one it had previously pursued. Some in the administration, namely Eugene Foley, the director of the SBA, recognized that the agency could be used to further Johnson's civil rights and social reform agendas, and so loans and assistance were intentionally funneled specifically to black borrowers.[22] Such policies would kick into overdrive in the next administration.

In 1968, then presidential candidate Richard Nixon started touting an approach to solving African American poverty through a philosophy he called "black capitalism," devised as a response to the civil unrests and riots in large cities in 1967 and 1968.[23] Nixon was expected to include in his platform a way to help the black community, yet he also had to come up with something that would please both moderate Democrats and his staunchly conservative Republican base. As Nixon saw it, black capitalism was a way for the black population to lift themselves up through betterment programs instead of through welfare programs. To facilitate this Nixon created a new agency called the Office of Minority Business Enterprise (OMBE). Through the focus of the OMBE, and with added assistance from the SBA in the form of grants, loans and expertise, black capitalism was intended to help the African American population by creating new businesses in black neighborhoods, businesses owned by black entrepreneurs, serving their own communities, and hiring from within their own population.

The plan would see both praise and derision. While the plan appealed to white conservatives who appreciated it for its "pull yourself up by your own bootstraps" solutions, and to some in the black population who appreciated the empowerment the plan would seem to earn them, others felt that it smacked of segregation.[24] Black business people were not being asked to compete as equals, but only in their own communities.

Since the passage of the Small Business Act in 1953 (which created the SBA), there had been a certain class of contracts called "set aside" contracts, also known simply as "set asides." Set asides were federal contracts reserved for small businesses and were specifically to be used for military contracts, as many were concerned such contracts were only going to large corporations. Increasingly, however, set asides became mechanisms to restrict contracts to minority-owned businesses. Then, only three years before Mack walked into Milwaukee's SBA office, Howard Samuels, SBA's briefly serving director at the end of the Johnson administration, introduced a program called the Section 8(a) Business Development Program.[25] This program consisted of special resources specifically created for small and/or minority-owned businesses.

Through this program, Mack and the others were told that if they bought the brewery, they would be provided technical assistance and training, and, even more important, set-aside federal government contracts. This meant they would have little or no competition (as there were no other minority-owned breweries at the time), which would prove a very lucrative advantage over any other brewers, especially (so they thought) the larger ones. The prospect of this was immense—the opportunity to get government contracts with no competition sounded almost too good to be true. So, with these thoughts in mind, and with the expectation of help from the SBA, Ted Mack, his friends Ray Alexander, and Henry S. Crosby, all signed the SBA application as guarantors. With their signatures they were promising the U.S. Government they'd pay back the $390,000 they were getting from the bank should Peoples ever fail. But, with the promise of guaranteed contracts they wouldn't have to compete for, they felt they had little to worry about. Their application was subsequently approved

July 24, allowing them to focus on the remaining $200,000 that the bank required.[26] To raise that money, they would do for Peoples what Nigl did for it almost sixty years earlier: sell stock.

Formalizing the company, along with selling stock in it, would completely occupy the next few months for Mack. Less than a week after the purchase agreement, on April 20, he formally incorporated the United People's Brewery Ltd. with the Wisconsin Secretary of State, and then filed papers with the register of deeds office in Winnebago County three days later.[27] United People's Brewing Ltd. would be the name of the company that would buy and own the 59-year-old Peoples Brewing Company until the purchase had been completed, after which the company would change its name to Peoples Brewing Company. The name they chose seemed to be a deliberate nod to their earlier organization, United Black Enterprises. Also, of note was the use of the possessive in the word, "People's" where there is none in the name of the original company. It was never noted why either of these variations existed (the lack of possessive in the original or the inclusion of the possessive in the later name), but it is an interesting difference.

The next step was to get approval for the sale of stock to raise the required $200,000. To do this they would have to sell 40,000 shares at $5 per share (their hope was to raise more than required by selling 65,000 shares to give them a safe buffer from which to operate). Their agreement with the bank gave them 60 days from the day of approval to sell the required amount and raise the funds.[28] The requisite approval to sell shares came from the regulatory agency in late July, and so on July 27, United People's Brewing Ltd. began distributing their prospectus at the Marshall & Islay Bank (the same bank providing the loan).[29] With all they'd already been through over the past year and a half, Mack and the others were supremely optimistic about the enterprise, and so this step just seemed like a minor, but necessary, complication.

But it wasn't. For starters, the prospectus really didn't paint a very positive picture about the company Mack was trying to create. In fact, financial journalist Ray Kenney noted at the time that "there are high risks involved"[30] in investing in United People's. Prepared by the Milwaukee law firm, Laiken, Swietlik & Laiken, the prospectus was required to spell out these potential risks to investors, and unfortunately there were many, starting with competition. Highlighted in that section was the amount of beer brewed by Peoples in 1969, which was 25,033 barrels.[31] This put it third from the bottom in the list of 14 other breweries in Wisconsin. The top two spots were taken by the Milwaukee favorite, Pabst (1,379,603 barrels), followed by their cross-town rival, Schlitz (571,910). This was a stark indicator of Peoples' almost insignificant place among other brewers in the state.

5. Buying Peoples Beer

The section also argued that the beer industry was both fiercely competitive while at the same time tyrannically dominated by only three brewers (Anheuser-Busch, Inc., Schlitz Brewing Co., and Pabst Brewing Co.), and that there "can be no assurance that the Company will be successful in its efforts to expand markets and sales."[32]

Another section further discussed management ownership in the company, pointing out that Theodore Mack purchased 22,500 shares, Diane Williams purchased 335, Henry S. Crosby 665, and Ray A. Alexander 1,000, all for only $0.83 per share. The price for these purchases was in exchange for the work each of them carried out on behalf of creating the company (and in Mack's case also for the $30,000 "loan" to the company). Additionally, Mack was given the option to purchase another 9,000 shares within five years at the introductory price of $5.00 per share. If exercised, the options would give Mack 35 percent of the company, and therefore controlling interest in Peoples (they had obviously dropped the collectivist philosophy Nigl embraced to ensure no one person could control enough stock to control the company). The point of the section, and legitimately bad news for potential investors, was the fact that because 24,500 shares were already sold at significantly less than the offering price, anyone buying stock going forward would immediately lose money. While the original shares sold for $0.83 per share, the bank counted the "book value" of the stock (the value after paying off all the company's current liabilities) at $3.89 per share. Thus, those members who bought stock at $0.83 per share would see an appreciation of $3.06 per share, while anyone who buys shares for $5 would see an immediate dilution of $1.11 per share.[33] In other words, investors would go into United People's losing money.

Next, the prospectus dissected the humble background and education of the company's management—with close attention to its *lack* of experience in the brewing industry. Mack's employment at Pabst was emphasized, but in general the conclusion of this section was that "the officers of the Company have had little or no business experience, especially as it relates to management of a substantial enterprise."[34] An uninspired endorsement to be sure.

But perhaps the worst news of all came on page five, the Pro-Forma Statement of Earnings. This was designed to relay to potential investors how well the company had done financially over the past year. Through this section they could tell quickly whether Peoples was making money or not. Sadly, it was the latter. For the first four months of 1969 (the time period used to be comparable with the date of sale for 1970), Peoples *lost* $4,130.01. For the first four months of 1970, Peoples had lost over three times that—$15,853.95.[35]

In general, the prospectus did a magnificent job of affirming the opinions of financial writer Ray Kenny by making clear all the reasons why people shouldn't invest in Mack's company. The industry was too competitive, and the brewery's place in it was too low. The management had woeful little experience, especially when it came to the product they were proposing to sell. The company itself lost barrels of money just the year before, and as soon as someone bought stock, the value of that stock cratered, leaving the buyer in the hole. If someone decided to invest in this venture, it wasn't because they were looking for a sure thing, they'd invest for a different reason, and that's what Mack was banking on.

But despite the doom and gloom, there were some bright points in the prospectus, a reason or two to be optimistic about investing in this venture. One of those reasons was a particular group of consumers that Mack and his associates knew a lot about. In Ray Kenney's article about the stock sale, despite derisively accounting the risks involved, he also pointed out the potential for high rewards. He specifically quotes two lines from page eight of the prospectus, which read: "The Company intends to develop a market within the Black communities in major population centers. A slight shift in consumption to the Peoples beer brand would result in significantly improved sales."[36]

Of the potential elements that would lead to the company's success, this was, according to Kenney "an interesting one." In the prospectus, Mack was flat out telling potential buyers that if they could get the black community to buy Peoples Beer, they'd have a lucrative business. And according to the section titled "Minority Opportunity; Employment Practices" on page nine, that community was the entire reason for purchasing Peoples in the first place, though that reason wasn't to make money. Rather, it states that "The primary purpose for the organization of the Company and purchase of the brewery was to provide additional economic opportunities to minority groups, through improved employment opportunities and equity ownership of business ventures."[37]

This was activism as Mack and his associates—Ray Alexander, Henry S. Crosby and others—defined it. It was no longer a matter of marching in the street, it was about entering the industrial sector of the United States; about becoming producers and not just consumers. This activism—this mission—was indicated throughout the prospectus. In its "Terms of Offering," it clearly states that the "Company intends to use its best efforts to sell as many as possible of the shares offered hereby to members of minority groups."[38] It said further on page 17 that the "intention of the Company is to have it controlled by members of minority groups."[39] On page 13, under "Management" the prospectus points out that they intend "to provide opportunities for 'upward mobility' to members of minority groups" and that "every effort will be made to hire minority and 'hard-core' unemployed persons."[40] Similarly, on page 14, when discussing the Board of Directors, it states that "it will be the policy of management to have a majority of the positions on the Board of Directors held by qualified members of minority groups."[41] This was a movement to create a company owned and run by minority investors, managers and employees. And Mack was looking beyond just Peoples and was instead hoping that they could inspire others to do the same as they had done, saying after the purchase that "what keeps me going is the knowledge that if this is successful all the minorities will be able to move in the same direction."[42]

So, by the end of July, they just had the matter of selling the stock. While the prospectus painted a necessarily grim picture of Peoples Brewing Company and any investment into it, the ever-outspoken Ted Mack was brimming with cheerful confidence, which he, of course, exuded to potential investors. "We're here to tell you that if you want some (stock), you'd better get it in a hurry, because it's going like hotcakes,"[43] he told a gathering of people at the Project Breakthru community center in Racine. He and Ray Alexander were visiting the small city 30 miles to the south on a trip around the state to promote interest in the Peoples stock offering. While he wouldn't say how much had been subscribed up to that point, he remarked that "it will be oversubscribed soon." It's unclear whether he was exaggerating or not (though he probably was), but his strategy was quite clear. Just as the prospectus foretold, the group that he was focusing on was minorities—especially members of the black community (the Project Breakthru community center was primarily used by the black population of Racine).

He even affirmed this, telling the Racine newspaper that he "wants to reach the working classes, particularly blacks first," but then after a moment's thought was quick to clarify, saying that stock wasn't "restricted to blacks." His focus was on black investors in Milwaukee too. When shares were offered for sale there, Mack organized a public rally at Garfield Park (located in the primarily Black Inner Core) to "explain the stock sale and prospectus"[44] for community members who might be interested. Afterwards he hit the road again, and during a swing through Appleton he talked about the success of the rally in Milwaukee and said that, while he didn't know how many shares were sold, "I do know they're going fast."[45]

The people he was selling stock to seemed to understand that this wasn't a typical investment. Instead, they realized the importance of supporting the struggling, black-managed brewery in Oshkosh. In an article written that October, a "white woman doctor" who'd bought shares said that "investing in Peoples Brewery is not like watching the stock market, it's watching a venture in which we are all concerned."[46] And in that same article, a black man who'd never before invested in anything bought stock in Peoples because he said "the black community has an obligation to support black ventures." This wasn't about making money, this meant something more to everyone involved, especially to Mack, who, through countless hours on the road and in front of crowds, was able to bridge the black and white communities and get them both to support his campaign.

They were given 60 days to sell the 40,000 shares, but it only took them five weeks. On September 16, 1970, United People's Brewing Ltd. closed its sale on Peoples Brewing Company and Theodore Mack officially took over as president. Officers of the company included Henry S. Crosby, vice-president, Barbara A. Bender, secretary, Willie Ousley, treasurer, and Robert Peeple, Ray A. Alexander, and Samuel Ross, all directors of the Company, and all of them black. Many of these people were from the original United Black Enterprises group, though some were added (and there were some from UBE who were not a part of Peoples). But all were from the riot-scarred Inner Core of North Milwaukee, and all had enjoyed success in their respective communities and professions. And, finally, they were all successful leaders in their community.

It is an easy observation to say they had been working at this goal for over a year. However, in truth, this goal—the ownership of a significant business—was more than likely a goal they had in mind for years, perhaps even decades. The ownership of industry, a company that produced a product in the United States of America, was something they had probably desired more than most could imagine. This goal had certainly been on Mack's mind for a long time, so surely it would have been the goals of the others as well. Ownership meant, to borrow Ted Mack's own words, that they were no longer mere consumers, they were producers. They had entered the white man's corporate structure, and they could stand on their own.

On October 10, 1970, they celebrated their hard-fought victory. On that day, they invited the public of Oshkosh, as well as stockholders, students from the local college, city and state government officials, and anyone else who was interested in touring the brewery, enjoying free beer, and eating some locally-made food (no doubt bratwurst and sauerkraut). By all accounts the day was a success, with plenty of beer enjoyed by all[47] (though perhaps enjoyed a little too much, as it was later reported that two half-barrels of Peoples Beer were stolen from a loading dock during the festivities[48]).

Theodore Mack, his wife Pearlie Mack, and U.S. Representative William Steiger together cut a green and gold ribbon at noon to celebrate the ownership.[49] Ted was recorded as saying "with this symbolic ceremony, we open the door to an unlimited future of expansion and growth for this

5. Buying Peoples Beer

Oshkosh made product."[50] The day began with a buffet lunch and brewery tour for a reported 2000 shareholders and guests including local business people and government officials from 11 to 1, and then at 2 p.m. another 5000 showed up for public tours (which included more free beer). During the ceremonies a number of dignitaries spoke, but one of note was Representative Steiger, who said

> We are seeing here today not an example of black or white capitalism, but an example of a man, Ted Mack, with the courage and initiative to find a product he knew something about and then secure the cooperation of banks, financial institutions, the Small Business Administration, and people with enough faith to invest their money. This is a tribute to the city, the people who worked with Mr. Mack, and to the American system.[51]

Steiger was right. The story of the Peoples acquisition had many names attached to it—Harold B. Jackson, Henry S. Crosby, Ray A. Alexander, and others—but the entire venture was planned, organized, and carried out by Theodore Mack himself. In the company's prospectus, in the section titled "Interest of Management in Certain Prior Transactions," the writers explain why Mack and the others (but especially Ted Mack) were permitted to buy stock in the company at $0.83 a share. After divulging the loan that he had provided to the company, the section reads:

> Mr. Mack, and to a lesser extent, the other present shareholders, have devoted a considerable amount of time and money in their efforts to find a business suitable for the purposes for which the Company has been organized.
> Most recently, these individuals attempted to acquire the Blatz Brewing Co. when it was for sale pursuant to federal court order. Legal and related expensed were incurred.
> These individuals, and especially Mr. Mack, traveled extensively to examine potential businesses, to consult with government agencies for guidance and availability of financing, and to have prepared feasibility studies of the various businesses under consideration.
> These activities this past year materially interfered with their regular employment. Mr. Mack's income in 1968 and 1969–70 was reduced approximately $7,000 and $10,000, respectively.
> Since about March of this year, Mr. Mack has devoted virtually all of his time to matters attendant to the negotiations for the purchase of the brewery. From the date of this offering to closing of the purchase, Mr. Mack will be spending most of this time in Oshkosh at the brewery.[52]

It was clear who's venture this was: it was Ted Mack's from start to finish.

At the end of the dedication ceremonies on October 10 at the brewery, it came time for Mack himself to say a few words. He got up and thanked the dignitaries who were visiting and the bank who had given them the loan to make the purchase possible. Then he spoke briefly about the journey he'd just completed.

> All the stockbrokers said it wasn't possible to sell this stock. They said blacks were too poor and whites had lost all their money in the stock market. I called Mamma and told her to pray hard again. Five weeks after the sale started, you made it possible to buy this brewery.... For a man born in Alabama on a farm where you weren't sure there would be anything to eat, to be standing here today as the first black president of a brewery, I have to say I'm proud of my country.[53]

Mack's sentiments were recorded and published in newspapers throughout the region, and they were truly a moving tribute to all he had achieved and all he was able to achieve in the U.S. Sadly, though, there was much he was going to face that would test those sentiments and make him question his feeling towards his country, perhaps even his faith. The most insidious of these things would be the torrent of racism that broke over him upon the initial announcement he was buying Peoples. But considering the history of Oshkosh, maybe it shouldn't have come as such a surprise.

6

Race in Oshkosh

The number of African Americans in Oshkosh in the early 20th century topped out at 98 residents in 1910, and then, when the rest of the North and Midwest experienced the influx of black newcomers as a result of the Great Migration over the next 20 years, the number of African American residents in Oshkosh sharply dropped. From the high of 98 in 1910 to 39 in 1920, and then to 33 in 1930. Compare this to Milwaukee, which saw 906 black residents in 1910, then 2346 in 1920, and 7,501 in 1930.[1] In fact, most cities in the state would see their African American populations grow significantly, but not Oshkosh. The next 30 years would see even more black residents flee the small Fox Valley city until only a handful of them remained by 1960.

By all accounts there doesn't seem to be any reason for such an exodus. Oshkosh was very much like Milwaukee in its early days: filled with European immigrants with few pretenses. Milling and lumber—perhaps the bluest of blue-collar pursuits—were the common industries.[2] In Milwaukee, in the early 1900s, black residents were not only found in the unskilled, menial types of jobs seen in the trades (similarly like mill-work and chopping down trees), but also in service jobs—waiters, bellboys, and housekeepers—as well as in entrepreneurial positions, as owners of hair parlors and small retail stores.[3] It's not a stretch to think the black residents of Oshkosh, a mere 90 miles away, shared the same professions, and, indeed, very similar lives. So, what was the difference?

There is no specific event, person, or phenomenon to point to, just theories. It could have been, for starters, the lack of work. In the case of Milwaukee, World War I provided jobs to black migrants moving from the South because the white factory workers enlisted in the military and went off to fight in the war. Then, once the war was over, many of them returned and the black workers found themselves out of jobs as they were fired to make room for the white laborers instead.[4] It makes sense to believe this happened in nearby Oshkosh as well. In such a situation, black workers wouldn't have even found help from labor unions, which at the time were segregated and often actively discriminated against them.[5] It would definitely make sense that the black population of the city would decline if they couldn't find any employment, so this idea certainly has merit. However, there might have been another reason for the sustained exodus of African Americans from Oshkosh, Wisconsin.

On December 24, 1920, a headline in the *Daily Northwestern*, Oshkosh's main newspaper at the time, read "Revived Ku Klux Klan Grows Rapidly."[6] Beneath an image of perhaps nine white-robed and hooded individuals, one holding what looks like a cross arrayed with burning candles, the reporter states that the "once extinct" organization was reformed to "aid the cotton growers in the price depression period and correct other 'evils' in the southern states." The image is apparently one of a member initiation, in which they "must take oath beneath the firey [sic] cross and American flag to work for country, home and each other."

The Ku Klux Klan had been revived in Georgia five years earlier by a man named William Joseph Simmons. Apparently, Simmons got the idea while serving in the Spanish-American war and saw a wispy puff of clouds in (according to him) the shape of robed men, galloping on horses across the sky. Somehow he took this rather subjective interpretation of an everyday meteorologic occurrence as a sign from God that his mission was to reform the old, secret organization in order to put right the many wrongs he believed his country was facing. While the Klan of the South during reconstruction was an instrument primarily of terror for the sake of white supremacy, Simmons saw this incarnation as one meant to defend America, and specifically to pit good, white Protestants against pretty much everyone else, including "Catholics, Jews, blacks, radicals, immigrants, bootleggers, and evolutionists" according to researcher Robert A. Goldberg.[7] In the fall of 1920, about a month before the story announcing the Klan's reinstatement ran in the *Daily Northwestern*, a chapter was created in Milwaukee. Over the next few years there would be branches of the organization formed in every county in the state of Wisconsin.

Because the Klan's stated mission was to preserve the fundamental, perhaps old-fashioned values of America, the organization had much more appeal in rural areas than in large cities.[8] Their recruiters spread quickly through the state and within only a few years had a sizeable membership in Wisconsin. Though an exact number of members for the state is hard to find (it was a secret organization, after all), it is reported that at a "konclave" (that is, a Klan gathering) in Madison, Wisconsin, in which the members of branches from eight of the state's 72 counties participated, there were well over 2,000 attendees (in fact, 250 were even initiated at the gathering).[9]

Oshkosh, of course, also had a branch of this organization,

membership of which was kept stocked by a man named Pat Malone, a particularly gifted preacher who spewed hate from the pulpit against all the segments of society that Simmons blamed for the country's ills, especially Jews, blacks and Catholics.[10] In July of 1927, Oshkosh was even picked to host the organization's, multi-state convention. The local newspaper declared that an "Elaborate Program" was being planned for the event taking place at the fairgrounds.[11] It was also reported that officials expected 6,000 attendees from Wisconsin, Minnesota, Illinois, and Iowa, with "representatives" traveling from Texas, Alabama, and Michigan. Events included live bands, speakers, a bugle corps, and even a fireworks display to top off the festivities.

The accumulated effect of all of this going on in Oshkosh—the lack of jobs, the active discrimination and segregation from labor officials, and the groundswell of support from city residents for a group as despicable as the KKK—was to chill the migration of black people coming into the city. And so it was that Oshkosh and the surrounding area gained a reputation as being unfriendly to African Americans. In a letter written to the *Baltimore Afro-American*, one of the oldest black newspapers with the widest distribution in the country, a letter writer recited a story in which he asked his friend what Oshkosh was like, and in reply his friend had compared the city to hell.[12] Unfortunately, the reputation, whether deserved or not, would be passed on for years to come.

On March 17, 1964, George Wallace kicked off his campaign for the Democratic U.S. nomination for president at the Rotary Club of Appleton, Wisconsin (about 25 miles north of Oshkosh), by railing against the Civil Rights Bill that the Johnson Administration was pushing in Washington. Called the "proponent of one of the most evil systems ever,"[13] by Wisconsin Governor John W. Reynolds, Wallace, the governor of Alabama, once famously said "segregation now, segregation tomorrow, and segregation forever."[14] He advocated releasing police dogs on, and the beating of, civil rights marchers, and in 1963 personally blocked the door of Foster Auditorium at the University of Alabama to prevent black students from attending after the school was ordered desegregated. Generally speaking, he was a vile racist who found a shockingly warm reception in the state of Wisconsin. He even quipped once that "if ever I had to leave Alabama, I'd want to live in the southside of Milwaukee."[15]

People seemed to respond to him in Wisconsin unlike most other states in the north he visited. And, as unappealing as it might seem, he was able to garner 24.5 percent of the Democratic primary vote in the Badger State. In the city of Oshkosh, Wallace took 41 percent of the vote (3697 Oshkosh residents voted for him),[16] and in Winnebago County as a whole (the county in which Oshkosh and a number of other small towns are found), he took 40 percent (a total of 8057 county residents voted for Wallace). Clearly his message resonated with many of the people living in Oshkosh and the surrounding area. That message, delivered across the mostly white, working class, blue-collar state, emphasized a belief that if the Civil Rights Bill was passed, workers would lose their jobs and labor unions would be gutted.[17]

Editors of the *Baltimore Afro-American* didn't find this too surprising, saying that Appleton made "an ideal starting point for a diehard segregationist" because the area is "thickly populated with odd-ball characters who want to do away with the income tax, would like to impeach Chief Justice Warren, want to abolish the United Nations and who nourish inbred prejudices against foreign-born, Jews and colored Americans."[18] Clearly the reputation of the city and its residents lived long past the 1920s. And Wallace tapped into the fears and bigotries of the region's residents perfectly.

And as far as the black community of Oshkosh went, there really wasn't any black community when Wallace courted the voters of the Fox Valley. In 1960, according to the U.S. Census, there were just seven African Americans living in Oshkosh, and only one in Appleton.[19] At the time, both of the towns still shared the same problems that Milwaukee had with regards to explicit (though unspoken) segregation and unfair housing issues. Oshkosh and Appleton were also known as "sundown towns," where black people were tolerated during the day but expected to leave by nightfall (and would risk their safety by staying past dark).[20] But despite its inherit racism, Oshkosh had really never had to confront race dynamics until the fall of 1968, when Wisconsin State University–Oshkosh (WSU-O) saw an enrollment boom of 11,000 students, 116 of them black.

Upon arriving in the Fox Valley, the black students must have felt as if they were walking in an alien world. Little looked like home, and many problems would arise that they would have to struggle with. One of the first of these problems was finding places to live. As in Milwaukee, housing discrimination in the form of redlining was rampant throughout the area, and landlords often refused to rent to black residents—students or otherwise. After a contentious public debate, however, supporters of fair housing were able to push an ordinance through the city council on August 1, 1968 (something that never happened in Milwaukee). But the tension caused by the debate surrounding the ordinance had many city residents feeling on edge, at odds with each other, and particularly sensitive about racial issues in the city.

Unfortunately, the fair housing ordinance didn't really apply to or help students on campus. In fact, that fall, a group of all-black female freshmen were told there were no more rooms in the dorms, and so had to sleep in subdivided dorm lounges instead of getting their own spaces. General harassment and racism were always daily annoyances for black college students at WSU-O; however, race issues on the campus seemed much more pronounced that fall of 1968 than they had been in previous years. Black students had always faced discrimination at the university, like being victims of racial epithets and insults hurled at them from cars or open windows.[21] Sometimes they'd even had rocks thrown at them while walking through campus.[22]

But now that the number of black students had grown—50 had arrived in August as freshmen—some white townspeople, including students and even professors, turned outwardly resentful. That October the student newspaper reported an incident off campus where "a bunch of black women were subjected to insults on High Street near downtown."[23] This became commonplace, and the entire town devolved into a scarily oppressive place for black students to live. And it was clear that this prejudice wasn't isolated to either the college campus or the city of Oshkosh, this was an overall attitude from a large percentage of the population (as Wallace's strong showing in the area demonstrated) in the general region. The area was tense, the residents felt it, the students felt it, and it would take something small to push either side to take some type of drastic action. That would happen in November.

All of the black students at WSU-O were attending with the promise of financial aid funding their tuition, housing, and other expenses. As it turned out, that financial aid was not so easy to get. There were many delays in getting their funds, and the students went for weeks without their promised aid. The situation was frustrating to say the least, and added to the mounting problems they were facing, like the absence of private living spaces and the constant harassment they were being subjected to both on and off campus.

The sentiments of the students were summed up in a November 21 letter to the school newspaper by Rufus E. Finner, a black third-year accounting student. After briefly discussing a recent skirmish on campus between some white and black students (pointing out the black students did not attend WSU-O but were from another school), he then pleads with readers, begging them to end their abuses of students like him. "Just give us our proper respect," he implores, "and stop heckling us from crowds when you see us on campus."[24]

The letter is heartbreaking, and you can feel the weight of his exasperation and anguish—he's tired of the ridicule, tired of the bigotry. But at the same time, you can also sense something a bit more ominous. Before his appeal, as if foreshadowing something to come, Finner (who in his signature calls himself as "A militant junior"), wrote, "your system sowed the seeds of hatred, racism, and evil. Now you are reaping what you have sown. You made the cake, now eat it." At first the line is puzzling, but Finner was referencing what he and 93 of his classmates would be doing later that day.

Just that October, a month earlier, members of WSU-O's Black Student Union produced a list of requests for the school's administration. Many of their requests were intended to help the students cope in the conservative, white city of Oshkosh, brimming with hostile residents only too delighted to hurl insults and rocks at them. They asked for courses in African American history and literature, the hiring of black faculty and administration, and an African American cultural center—a physical place where they could meet and join in fellowship with each other. A month later, after hearing not a word from the administration about their requests, the students grew frustrated and restless. Certain members of the group felt that action, not rhetoric, was needed to sway the administration into moving on their appeals. They needed to meet with them directly.

And so, 94 black students on the morning of November 21, 1968, marched together to Dempsey Hall to confront WSU-O's president, Roger Guiles, in person. Their objective was to hand him a new, more forceful list of requests, and to get him to sign off on them during their encounter, thereby meeting the demands and indicating the administration's willingness to help them. They were confounded, however, when, after marching into Guiles' office, the alarmed president looked up at them and blurted out the only thing he could think of, "Do you have an appointment?"

This set the tone for the rest of the meeting. Guiles refused to sign any list of demands, saying he had no power to do so, and so the students and president faced each other for several tense moments. What happened next has been debated for decades. Some of the students in the group began destroying the offices: overturning desks, dumping typewriters on the floor, smashing windows, and emptying filing cabinets. A photo in the newspaper following the event showed the offices in complete disarray, as if subjected to a tempest.[25]

Guiles, negotiating with the students more desperately now, told them that he could only meet the requests if they were approved by the faculty and administrators, who happened to be meeting that morning. The students agreed to sit in the offices and wait until the meeting was concluded to get their demands met. But that never happened. Instead, a call went out to police departments in every nearby city and town. They began trickling in slowly, and within a few hours they'd all arrived at Dempsey Hall. When the students looked out of the windows and saw a group of helmeted police officers marching into the building, carrying shields and wearing riot gear, they understood their demands were never going to be met. Realizing the grave danger they were in, they lost their resolve. The group dropped their heads, gave up, and quietly filed out the building, escorted by the billy club–wielding officers. They were loaded into rented moving vans that had been brought in for the occasion, and then transported to the county courthouse where they were arraigned on charges of unlawful assembly and disorderly conduct. Because there were so many of them, the students were distributed to town jails throughout the area, not just Oshkosh.

Guiles, disgusted by what he saw as a blatant show of disrespect, began immediate proceedings to expel all 94 students from WSU-O. Ultimately, following a show trial at the university that barred the students from pleading their cases, or from even having someone represent them, 90 of the students were expelled before the end of December, and four were suspended. Only one student had been allowed to actually testify and share his side of the story. There was, in other words, no justice for the black students of WSU-O.

Such was the environment that the all–black team who'd bought Peoples Brewing Company were headed into. And, to make matters worse, they were headed into this environment after a newspaper article announced they would be firing all the white workers and replacing them with black employees (effectively lending truth to the platform that Wallace had campaigned on only a few years earlier).[26]

It's hard to say why the writers who penned that April 14, 1970, *Milwaukee Sentinel* article breaking the story about the Peoples sale (and telling readers that black people were about to take white jobs) framed their article in such a way as to make Mack and his colleagues out to be villains. The crux of their article was true about UBE's plans for Blatz (had they been allowed to purchase it), but it was never part of their plan in the context of this sale. After all, Blatz didn't have any employees to replace: nobody would be out of a job to fulfill Ted Mack's goal of equality for the black worker. Peoples Brewing Company, in contrast, already had a staff of full-time employees, according to the Sentinel article, who would soon be getting fired.

This, combined with the fact that Oshkosh wasn't exactly accepting of the black community, would have made any mention of replacing the existing crew particularly inflammatory. Such a consideration clearly wasn't made, and the article (released in the morning edition while Ted and his partners were locked in negotiation and unable to respond) hit the wire, spreading to other towns throughout the state. And whether it was the writers' intention or not to create concern and, perhaps at some level, to sensationalize the sale of Peoples to a black business organization, that's exactly what happened. Mack's triumph was immediately and suddenly eclipsed by scandal.

The newspaper's article fed rumors that rapidly made their way throughout Oshkosh and beyond. These ranged from speculation about Peoples firing the white employees and replacing them with black workers, to stories about the company making beer just for the black community and maybe even changing its name.[27] In the minds of some residents, they were losing a part of their city, and they were losing it to black men from Milwaukee. After the stockholders' meeting on April 15, instead of discussing how historically important it was that a group from the black community purchased a company in a traditionally white market space, Ted Mack found himself countering the allegations created by the *Milwaukee Sentinel*. The *Milwaukee Star*, to take just one example, reported that "Mack strongly denied a statement which appeared in the Milwaukee Sentinel which said that UBE was completing a purchase transaction and that both work force and management of the new brewery would be all-Black."[28]

Ultimately, because of the *Sentinel* article, the backlash took the form of a boycott of Peoples Beer. An article from April 26 stated that a tavern owner on Main Street in Oshkosh stopped selling Peoples because the customers wouldn't buy it. The paper reported that "he and an undetermined number of other owners pulled Peoples from their taps almost as soon as they heard of the sale."[29] The article's writer found this to be true in most of the taverns in town, where patrons either refused to drink Peoples Beer or the taverns refused to reorder it once their kegs ran out. It was generally accepted that the boycott was because of the perception, given in the newspapers, that Peoples was going to change its name and focus on the black community. But was it really this, or was it something else? Something more sinister? One of the people quoted in the April 26 article, a tavern-owner's wife who was tending bar on the day the reporter stepped in, stated that the idea that black people might move into Oshkosh "seemed to frighten a few persons." In other words, it came down to simple racism.

Within a short time, a more purposeful boycott was carried out, and it persisted at least a month after the news broke that Mack and his associates were purchasing Peoples. In an article written by an Oshkosh Lutheran minister, readers were admonished to face their "sins." Such sins, he wrote, were not the result of a system, but a result of peoples' own traits, including "hatred and fear and prejudice." He then lectured to readers that "it is men who stop buying and selling People's Beer because of new ownership, not a system."[30] Simply put, stop being racist and end the boycott.

Despite his message, though, others felt justified in boycotting because of the new ownership.

In a separate letter to the editor in the May 18 edition of the *Daily Northwestern*, Oshkosh resident Dennis Schmid, in a general rant about the ills of the world and the need to turn back to God, singled out Milwaukee's Father Groppi—the Catholic priest and civil rights leader who had often led boycotts against the unfair hiring practices of local businesses— as reason enough for shunning Peoples. After suggesting that the church (that is, the *Catholic* church) was not doing its job, Schmid asks, "shall we drink People's beer, white man? Well, a certain Milwaukee priest told his Negro following to boycott *white* establishments"[31] (emphasis added). Apparently, it was eye for an eye for Schmid and, perhaps, for others as well.

And, while surprising, such bigotry, out in the open for all to see, wasn't really anything new when it came to Mack's venture. The many articles written the year before about UBE's campaign for Blatz were laced with implicit and sometimes overt racism that was both insulting and demeaning. Most headlines about their pursuit tended to emphasize the color of their skin over anything else. The July 9, 1969, edition of the *Milwaukee Journal Business News* ran an article titled, "Black Group Reveals Support in Blatz."[32] The next day, the *Wall Street Journal* announced, "Negro Business Group Raising Funds to Bid for Blatz Brewery."[33] Two days later, on July 12, *The Greater Milwaukee Star*'s article read, "Blacks Bid for Blatz Brewery."[34] Many of these articles also focused much more on UBE's proposition of hiring black management and employees over anything else. The campaign and what it stood for was trivialized, and the impact and significance of what they were trying to accomplish was superseded by the color of their skin.

The trend continued with the Peoples Brewing Company purchase. The first articles written about the purchase, dated April 14, 1970 (the date of the stockholders' meeting) had headlines that included, "Black Group May Buy Out Peoples,"[35] and "Black Firm Now Seeking Oshkosh Unit."[36] Both of these articles referenced Harold Jackson's statement regarding the hiring of black management and workers for Blatz. Two days later a headline stated that "Blacks Purchase Upstate Brewery,"[37] while four days later one announced that "Blacks Buy Oshkosh Brewery,"[38] and another said "Black Brewery to Open Within Two Months."[39] This strategy of using the word "Black" in reference to news about the Peoples Brewing Company would persist for the next two years, though it wouldn't be nearly as prolifically used as it was when the purchase was first made.

But why this fascination with the racial makeup of the owners of Peoples (or, for that matter, UBE when they were bidding on Blatz in the

MILWAUKEE SENTINEL
Black Group Bidding for Brewery

KENOSHA NEWS

Freeport (Ill.) Journal-Standard
Blacks Buy Oshkosh Brewery

Oshkosh Daily Northwestern
Black Group May Buy Out Peoples

Black firm is now seeking Oshkosh unit

THE CAPITAL TIMES
Blacks Purchase Upstate Brewery

RACINE JOURNAL-TIMES
Oshkosh Has 1st Negro Brewery

Daily Northwestern
Black Businessmen Buy Peoples Brewery

The State Journal
Black-Owned Brewery Dedicated in Oshkosh

THE CAPITAL TIMES, Monday,
Black-Owned Brewery Welcomes the 'Thirsty' Months

Oshkosh Advance-Titan
Black brewer prospers in Oshkosh

A collection of the headlines for stories written about the acquisition and running of Peoples Brewing Company by Theodore Mack and his associates. Each was racialized by identifying the group as "Black" or "Negro." Mack fought for years to be counted simply as a businessman, but the press and culture of the day would insist on tokenizing him instead (author's collection).

first place)? Why was it so important to journalists and editors that readers needed to be constantly reminded that Ted Mack and the others were black? The simplest answer is to say that the region was deeply racist—this was perhaps already proven by their attitude towards such things as school segregation or open housing, not to mention their support for George Wallace or the past legacy of the Klan. The headlines could easily be written off as manifestations of the racism inherent in both the region and its white citizens. And while all this may be true, it's important to acknowledge another factor that might have also played a huge role in the fascination by white journalists and readers—the market that Mack had entered and the product he was going to sell: beer.

Beer, in this region anyway, was very much a Western European–based product, almost a cultural marker for some of the people whose families immigrated to Wisconsin from Bavaria or elsewhere. The story of

Blatz and Peoples (and indeed, the story of ALL breweries in the Midwest region of the United States at the time), was the story of European immigration. Not only that, but beer played a huge social role in the cultures from which these people immigrated.

Consider this: in April of 1855, Chicago Mayor Levi Boone and the Chicago city council began enforcing an ordinance requiring all taverns to close on Sundays. The ordinance was seen specifically as anti-German because families of German immigrants often spent Sundays (their one day off) at beer gardens or beer halls socializing after attending church. While beer was a big part of a beer garden, activities also included bowling and other games, picnics, and even singing or dancing. These were places brought from the "old country," a piece of home that members of certain European communities looked forward to visiting on their very infrequent days of leisure.

The ordinance Mayor Boone and the council began enforcing led to the arrests of over 200 German immigrants found in violation of it. And after these arrests started, the German (and, coincidentally, Irish) immigrants decided they had enough. On the 21st of April, German and Irish immigrant marchers and protestors stormed downtown Chicago, clashing with police and creating havoc for Boone and the city council. Finally, after the subsequently named Lager Beer Riots had settled, the city compromised with the tavern keepers and order was eventually restored.[40]

Boone, incidentally, wasn't the first potentate to feel such wrath by the thirsty and subjugated. Bavarian King Ludwig I famously tried to tax beer in 1844, and the result was similar to Chicago's attempt at closing beer halls on Sundays—riots. The poor Ludwig even had to lower the price of beer by 10 percent to appease his people,[41] and eventually abdicated the throne. Such was the importance of beer in the Bavarian culture, and such were the lengths people from these regions were willing to go to in order to preserve an aspect of their way of life.

Mack was aware of none of this. To him, beer was simply a product and the beer industry was one that looked profitable. What's more, a demographic about which he knew a lot, and of which he was a member, consumed much of this particular product. For him it only made great business sense to become part of this industry. But to the white descendants of immigrants who consumed beer from a social and cultural dimension Ted Mack would never share, a group of black people making and selling a symbol of their heritage was akin to a black family moving out of the Inner Core of north Milwaukee and into the white suburbs. It simply shouldn't be allowed. It was especially egregious that they should buy an established brewery with a history and heritage like Peoples.

Yes, it was racism to be sure, but simple racism was one thing. This was much more complex. And this explains why so much attention was paid to the fact that Ted Mack, Henry Crosby and the rest were black, and why all the headlines kept reminding readers of this fact. It was most likely also why UBE's initial position about hiring black workers was so inflammatory. Had Mack known this, perhaps his pursuit of a brewery might have been tempered, or maybe he would have abandoned it altogether. While he expected some tension, it's hard to believe he could have imagined the reaction his purchase of Peoples would cause.

And sadly, the racist view that many had towards Peoples wouldn't end anytime soon. Even in 1971, when Mack was looking to expand into Milwaukee, he told reporters that his salesmen were being "thrown out" of taverns outside of the predominantly black inner core of the city. He told them that Peoples' salesmen, "black and white, have been told in these places that they are not going to sell any nigger beer."[42] But as he had proven throughout his life, Mack wasn't easily dissuaded from those things he set out to accomplish. As usual he didn't shrink from fear or dejection; instead, when race suddenly became an issue, he immediately came up with a strategy to win over the people of Oshkosh.

7

Overcoming

Mack quickly understood the potential threat posed by the message conveyed through the *Milwaukee Sentinel*. He had obviously read it the day it was published and was prepared to address it once the stockholders' meeting had wrapped that same night. He began the meeting by categorically denying the charges, starting with the accusation that staff would be replaced. Addressing the reporters, he affirmed that management would change, "but that all of the 21 employees would be retained under the new management."[1] He also told those gathered that the name would not be changing, it would still be called Peoples Brewing Company, making Peoples Beer. That beer, added Henry Crosby, would also stay the same, and they'd use the existing beer formula for the product.

This might have seemed to be the end of it; however, there was one more item bothering Mack. An article in the Milwaukee Journal reported that "Mack said he was furious at a report that Attorney Harold B. Jackson, acting as spokesman for UBE, said UBE would purchase the brewery and operate it with black managers."[2] He pointedly denied that Jackson had anything to do with this current purchase—they had most definitely parted ways. But aside from this more personal remark, the remainder of the discussion (the majority of it, actually) then turned to details of the sale, including when Ted Mack would take control, the immediate plans for the brewery, and other minutia.

Though he was perceptive enough to address the allegations in the *Sentinel*, he vastly underestimated how much attention he should give those allegations. He also, perhaps most importantly, underestimated the furor the article would cause and the speculation it would provoke. So, in the interest of brevity, and after quickly countering the charges, he moved on. To his exasperation, his few words would do little to extinguish the fevered gossip about a group of black men from Milwaukee taking over the historic Peoples.

And as it turned out, he also had very little time to tamp down the rumors before they took on an unbridled energy and spread through every tavern in Oshkosh. The article that started the rumors was published on April 14, but the two main exposés about the purchase, which each highlighted Mack's specific denials about the article's points, weren't published until April 18—four days later. That was four days of people talking, gossiping, speculating, and criticizing. As the news spread, the outrage grew. There *were* two articles published in newspapers in distant cities on April 15 and 16, but they were very brief, less than 100 words each, and they were also circulated too regionally to reach the readers in and around Oshkosh and Milwaukee.

A longer article ran on April 15, the day after the press conference, and though it provided more information and was circulated in the city of Oshkosh, it had a very small circulation rate (in fact, the paper switched to a twice weekly, free "community paper" four months later and was out of business the next year). That article also affirmed that the brewery workers would keep their jobs, and that the story published by the *Sentinel* was "unfounded" and "very much irresponsible."[3] Perhaps more than any other article, this one spent time on Mack's reaction to the attack on Peoples' new owners, and made it clear he took it personally, saying that "being a black man I've been subjected to lay-offs ... we will not subject other people to what we've been subject to. All people (Peoples' employees) ... will be retained. I'm staying over tonight to inform them in person of that."

Sadly, though, few would read this statement. The widest circulation was had by the newspapers that didn't carry the story until Saturday. So, by the time the two longer articles (featuring Ted Mack's rebuttals) had been published, the city was already buzzing with stories about the changes that were going to be made to the second oldest brewery in Oshkosh.

For his part, Mack recognized his mistake and the danger in letting those rumors go unchecked, and so immediately called another press conference for April 27 in order to, in his words, "stymie some of the falsehoods"[4] that were circulating in the region about the brewery's purchase. Sitting in the Oshkosh Area Chamber of Commerce office alongside the president of the Oshkosh Common Council, Byron Murken, Mack read an impassioned and forceful statement regarding many of the stories and narratives he saw as threats to his new brewery. In those statements, he denied, once again, that Peoples would be changing the name, the brand, or the formula of the beer, saying that they're "not making any 'black beer'—if you see a beer you like, you should buy it." He also denied, once more, that Peoples would be replacing the current staff with black employees, telling reporters that "we will continue to employ all the personnel that's there. Our board of directors will be integrated and as we increase our production; we will hire whoever wants to work for us."

7. Overcoming 85

Prepared statements aside, it was Mack's abrupt answers to the reporters' questions that made it clear he considered the attacks and rumors as personal jabs at he and his colleagues. In answer to a question about bringing more black residents to work at the brewery, he remarked, "I'm not a black superman that can move people here and there. I'm coming here to produce beer—I'm not here to bring black people here or to bring white people here." When another asked about his concerns in moving to Oshkosh, he told them, "I came here because I thought I liked the brewery ... there are good and bad people everywhere ... we must work together to see that the goodness comes out over the bad."

His responses demonstrate surprise at the circumstances, and a naivete of sorts about dynamics of the brewery's purchase. He simply wanted to buy a business and make a product, which, after all, was what he believed would help the black community. He hadn't expected the racism which held black people to the inner core of Milwaukee to also be so pervasive in American industry. Yet, as had been pointed out by reporters in multiple articles, not to mention by Ted Mack himself, he *was* the first black brewery president in America—there had to be a reason for that. And that reason was most likely because the industry was a *white* industry. The rumors were a symptom of the ownership the white people of the Fox Valley felt towards that industry, probably even towards Peoples Brewery itself. Mack simply wasn't prepared for it. And, so, over the course of the press conference, after an onslaught of patronizing and demeaning questions, he lashed out, placing the blame for any of Peoples' failures on the citizens of Oshkosh themselves, not on his own efforts.

> Myself and Oshkosh are very much on the spot. [Oshkosh] is regarded as one of the most bigoted cities in the country, north and south. If sales are down it will be a black eye on Oshkosh, not on me. I can hold up my end. It's a matter of whether or not Oshkosh can hold up its end ... the brewery will not go out of business ... if it does, it will be a black eye on Oshkosh.

On a roll, he then expanded these points for the (most likely shocked) crowd, saying that their treatment towards the new ownership and to Peoples itself will have far-reaching consequences. He specifically spoke of "black football players," their desire to start businesses in Oshkosh, and the attention they were giving to the Peoples purchase.

> Max McGee, Bart Starr, etc., can have big businesses here, but what did the Fox Valley ever do for Willie Davis, Herb Adderley or Willie Wood? Blacks and whites are taking a hard look at this area ... if they're not drinking our beer in the Valley I'll be surprised if you have black football players up here next year.

Whether any of this reflected fact or mere speculation is unknown, but it was clear that it wasn't something he came up with on the spot, but more likely reflected thoughts he'd been fleshing out in conversations with Alexander, Crosby, and others since the rumors and boycott had begun. This was the first time, though, that he had made such frank comments about Oshkosh and its residents, and reflected a justified frustration with the backlash they'd received by the taverns and beer drinkers of the city.

A calculated interjection from Oshkosh Common Council President Byron Murken redirected the conversation away from accusing local residents of forcing the brewery into failure and back to the matter of the boycott. After answering a particularly terrible question about whether there was "fear" in the city council because of the acquisition (what fear could the reporter have been suggesting?), Murken wisely replied that "it is an economic benefit to the city to have citizens buy local products ... the end result is significant to the city."

The entire discussion was emblematic of the issues facing the black buyers of an established, local brewery in northern Wisconsin in 1970. Ted Mack and the others were outsiders, they were seen as a threat for multiple reasons, they were interrupting the way of life, they were sullying tradition and legacy. For Mack, though, this was an enormously helpful and needed wake-up call about the situation they were facing. And though his answers and attitude may have belied his frustration, even anger, at the situation, he later used the information he gained going forward. Mack and the new board of directors now recognized the importance of winning over the residents and assuaging their anxiousness about the fate of the brewery. They began crafting a strategy to ensure they had the trust of the locals, including the newspapers, and to make sure they weren't taken by surprise again.

They initiated this strategy by issuing a written guarantee that assured readers that all employees would remain with Peoples. On page three of the Prospectus, tacked on at the end of the section titled "The Company" (and directly following the discussion about managements' woeful lack of business experience), was the statement, "All present employees of The Peoples Brewing Company are expected to remain after the purchase of the assets and business by the Company. Three directors of the present Board of Directors of The Peoples Brewing Company and its officers are expected to serve as special advisors to the Board of Directors and officers of the Company."[5]

Mack also decided it would make smart business sense to move to Oshkosh and become part of the community, representing the local brewery as its president. He told a reporter that he wanted to support the city, and that "this [Oshkosh] will be my home."[6] He started by spending two days a week there, eventually moving there completely in May of 1970 (he waited to move his family until the school year ended).

When he announced that the Mack family intended to move to Oshkosh to become full-time residents, more than a few reporters must have lifted their eyebrows. Considering the notoriety of the city's unfair housing issues (the fair housing ordinance was only passed in 1968 after major dissention between the city's aldermen), it's not hard to understand why. Immediately they asked him about housing. One article stated that "Mack said he expects no unusual problems in his move to Oshkosh"[7] without bothering to define "unusual problems."

Another reporter, spending more time on the issue, asked him if he had "attempted" to find housing there for his family, to which he replied that "there is an effort being made on the part of a real estate broker to acquire housing." Then, unprompted, Mack continued, saying "I don't know if there has been any 'static.'"[8] The issue—the problems faced by a black family trying to buy a house in a very bigoted region—was never addressed out loud, but it didn't have to be, everyone there understood what was meant.

To the credit of Oshkosh and its citizens, the issue of Ted Mack and his family, all black and moving to the Fox Valley, never really seemed to matter at all. In fact, Mack publicly stated that he felt Oshkosh had been treated unfairly by the media, who he claimed labeled the area "antiblack" after the 1968 incident concerning black students at the University of Wisconsin–Oshkosh. On the contrary, Mack told a reporter, "I moved my family here ... and we've not had a single incident," and then added "and that's what counts."[9] The area genuinely seemed to accept him with open arms, and he settled into the city comfortably, even joining civic clubs and organizations, like the Oshkosh Newcomers Club,[10] the Oshkosh Area United Fund,[11] and the local Chamber of Commerce.[12]

In return, Mack offered help to his own community whenever he could. In one instance, when one of the many local lumber companies was in the midst of an employee takeover, Mack offered the employees "legal assistance in their plan to continue the operation of their company."[13] Mack himself was apparently a popular presence at the meetings of these organizations, even prompting the women's editor of the local newspaper to remark that when she attends a public function, she likes "to be seated somewhere near Theodore (Ted) Mack, president of United People's Brewery," because, she stated simply, "he's sharp."[14] Mack returned the sentiments and truly seemed happy with his new home, telling a reporter that "Oshkosh residents had been great to him."[15]

Another issue that Mack wanted to address was the quality of the beer, which critics said would be lowered when they bought the brewery and (supposedly) stopped making Peoples Beer and started producing "black beer" (meaning a cheap-tasting beer for the black community).

He put this issue on his long to-do list and finally addressed it the following March of 1971 when he set up a test of their beer by the Siebel Institute of Technology in Chicago. In brewing circles, there could be no more respected entity on earth. The Siebel Institute was founded in 1868 by Dr. John E. Siebel, a physicist and chemist who immigrated from Germany in 1866. The aim of the institute was to train people to make beer, and it soon expanded into classes on chemistry, engineering and malting, all in the pursuit of making a better brew. Their industrial lab, the one that Mack had contracted with for the testing, was used nationally by large brewers to analyze beer and ingredients, and to provide consulting and research services. If he was going to use any organization to attest to the quality of his beer, he would find none more reputable than the Siebel Institute.[16]

After a March 20 phone discussion about what he needed, Ted sent bottles to the lab for analysis, which Siebel began carrying out immediately after receiving them on March 25. After a few anxious days, Ted received a reply from the institute in early April, and it was exactly the news he was hoping for. The report started with a summation of the findings, saying that "the sample makes an exceedingly good impression in almost every respect." It went on to list the different aspects they test for, and the results of those tests. It stated that the appearance of Peoples Beer was "brilliant at room and refrigerator temperature" and still clear after spending 24 hours at sub-freezing temperatures. It had a "slight" amount of sediment that was typical of this type of beer, and a "very satisfactory" foam when poured. The second page of the report provided the chemical analysis of Peoples Beer, confirming in the language of the laboratory what the first page summarized. All in all, the report provided a glowing description of the beer Mack was making.[17]

A very satisfied Ted then turned to making sure beer-drinkers heard this news. Dispensing with press releases or press conferences, he turned to a direct mail campaign, sending to taverns and customers in the Oshkosh region a letter, signed by him, with copies of the two pages of the Siebel Institute report stapled behind it. The cover letter, dated April 21, 1971, read:

Dear Customer:

There has been much speculation on the quality of beer that the Peoples Brewery is producing. This speculation is done by amateurs, therefor, at this time we are sending you a lab analysis of our beer.

You will find that Peoples Beer is a brilliant product.

Respectfully yours,
Theodore Mack, Sr.[18]

It took him just over a year but he had addressed and dispelled every one of the rumors that had been started on April 14, 1970. No white employees had lost their jobs, the name hadn't been changed, and the beer itself remained high-quality and worthy of the Siebel Institute's approval. This should have been the end of it; however, it never really was.

Though Mack at first sidestepped questions about the boycott hurting Peoples (despite its being stated in the company's prospectus[19]), he later admitted it actually did cost them a lot of business (a dip of 25 percent according to his estimate). In March of 1971 he said that they had "met with some order cancellations since becoming black-owned and operated."[20] Likewise in a letter to shareholders sent in May 1972 in which he listed the reasons for a loss in revenue the previous year, Mack listed first the "loss of business in the Fox Valley area due to rumors of all blacks replacing whites in the company."[21] And while business had mostly rebounded by the time he had sent the letter, the effect of the *Milwaukee Sentinel*'s April 14 article, and the bigotry it conjured, lasted much longer. Mack told the *Milwaukee Journal* Business News in September of 1971 that two of the outlets that dropped them initially *still* hadn't put Peoples back on tap.[22] One of those outlets was even across the street from the brewery itself. An understandably frustrated Ted Mack pointed the tavern out to a reporter during an interview and said, "that's a white bar, they refuse to sell Peoples."[23] Even despite all he had done to demonstrate none of the gossip was true, even after sending letters directly to the taverns of the city proving the quality of Peoples Beer, some places still chose not to sell it. There could only be one explanation why: sheer bigotry.

But despite some people and places refusing to view the new owners of Peoples equally, most of Oshkosh treated them fairly, as attested to by the fact that most all of the taverns in town put Peoples Beer back on tap. And in fact, some in the city were excited to see a group of minority business people purchase the brewery. The open house thrown at the brewery to celebrate Peoples' new ownership drew between 5,000–7,000 residents, and the crowd was a diverse mixture of the stockholders of the brewery and the residents of the city. Because the majority of stocks were purchased by the black communities of Milwaukee and elsewhere, many of those in attendance at the open house were black, but others attended as well. In fact, in his opening remarks at the event, Mack told the crowd that "in these days of confrontations, you make a pretty picture standing there, black, white and brown."[24]

The diversity of the crowd was applauded by students at the University of Wisconsin–Oshkosh. In a column called, "Good Stuff," the editors of the student newspaper wrote about the open house, saying "it drew black people from campus, Milwaukee and Racine, and Greek students and freak students and townies of every shape, age and political persuasion. All got drunk together (at least a little). And not a bottle was thrown

Students at the University of Wisconsin–Oshkosh Reeve Union's Draught Board circa 1970. The bartender is pouring from the Pabst tap while the Peoples Beer tap (to the left) is ignored. Mack found that his biggest obstacles were his competitors just down the road in Milwaukee, especially Pabst, Schlitz, and Miller (photograph courtesy UW Oshkosh Archives).

at anyone."[25] This last line was perhaps in reference to the harassment that black students often faced on campus only two years earlier, when insults and even rocks were regularly hurled at them by bigoted "townies" and students alike. Beer, it seemed, brought everyone together (for at least a little while).

Throughout the frantic struggle to rise above the rumors and gossip, Mack held firm to his belief that capitalism and the "corporate-structure," and therefore by extension he and his company, were above the side-street prejudices seen in Milwaukee or Alabama. It was one thing to own a black business that did business in the black community, but he believed that it was entirely different to produce and sell a product for everyone. At one press conference, Mack remarked, "I want to get away from this blackness and whiteness—I didn't buy this brewery for black power ... there is only one kind of power in this country and that's green power—money."[26] At another he said, "we are not making a black beer or a white beer, we are making what the name implies—a people's beer."[27] He couldn't fathom why his purchase of Peoples had caused such a stir. He couldn't understand how he was any different than Harold Ziegenhagen, the last president of the brewery.

The boycott mattered little in the end. The purchase had still gone through and by October he was celebrating with his friends, family, and thousands of stockholders and city residents at the open house. He had worked tirelessly to quell the "falsehoods" (as he called them) of the *Milwaukee Sentinel* that threatened his enterprise. Business was picking up and he was getting back the customers he had initially lost. Theodore Mack was riding high on a wave of success, and not even the movement of naked racism could bring him down. Now that he was in charge, now that he was the president of an American corporation, he set his sights on success. To succeed he firmly believed he would have to dramatically expand his new business. And that's exactly what he did.

8

Growing Pains

"I don't ever sleep."[1] That's what Ted Mack told a reporter for an article in May 1971, and judging from the amount of his activity between the finalization of the purchase in September 1970 and the publication of that article, he wasn't speaking in hyperbole, he meant it. The main bulk of this activity was concentrated on growing his company as quickly as possible. To one reporter he said, "[t]he Future of Peoples Brewing [Company] depends on its expansion."[2] Believing that selling only to Oshkosh taverns and stores (as Peoples had done for the last six decades) would lead to their demise, he set his sights on placing Peoples Beer throughout the state, and then beyond. "To stay in one locale, that's how you get killed quickly," he told his employees; "[we] have to have a bigger base."[3]

Before he had even closed on the sale of the brewery, he began their growth. On September 3, 1970, Peoples announced the hiring of six more employees in Oshkosh, and ten more in Milwaukee, which they said would aid in distribution in both Milwaukee and Racine.[4] Then, on September 28, 1970, only 12 days after closing the sale of Peoples, Mack formally announced they were expanding into Racine, initially starting with 25–30 local taverns and stores, but hoping to grow to many more. In fact, if the demand proved high enough, he said he would be looking for a Racine-Kenosha distributor as well.[5]

Before long, Peoples was also selling in Sheboygan, Milwaukee, and Madison, and was also distributing to North Chicago by the end of June 1971,[6] Memphis, Gary and Indianapolis by mid–September 1971.[7] And though he was already selling at WSU-Oshkosh when he took over Peoples, Mack had his eye on selling to all of the other universities in the state as well. By the end of March 1971, Peoples Beer was found in the student unions of UW–Madison, UW–Milwaukee, St. Norberts College in Green Bay, and WSU–Whitewater.[8] Mack even managed to get Peoples into a number of sports stadiums across the state.[9]

He didn't just limit his changes to territory expansion but also looked at modernizing the brewery and products too. Peoples Brewing Company

8. Growing Pains

was originally founded on the mission of selling kegged beer primarily to the Oshkosh taverns. That was in 1911. It moved only begrudgingly into bottled beer production after prohibition, and even then, what it offered was still a small, almost dismissed part of the company's product lines. Mack set about changing this immediately by moving away from bottles to canned beer instead. A large, November 20, 1970, advertisement in the *Daily Northwestern* announced Peoples Beer was available in "pop-top cans" for the first time. The caption underneath read, "Yes! better late than never."[10] Another caption, however, "available all over the Fox Valley," spoke to the limited availability of the new packaging. In most of its other markets, Peoples was still only available in bottles, though they switched to "non-returnable" bottles, which were thinner, lighter and (most-importantly) less expensive than the returnable bottles the company had used for decades. In addition to this change, Mack also installed new tapping and palletizing systems at the brewery, automated its water, heat, and refrigeration, and bought new delivery trucks.[11] And, in anticipation of the huge demand he foresaw in Milwaukee, Peoples bought a 7,700-square-foot warehouse and office building in the city before the end of 1970.[12]

Another item Mack wanted to work on immediately was a diversity of products. When they bought the Peoples Brewing Company, it only had a single offering—Peoples Beer. It was a high-quality lager beer, not unlike other lagers produced in Milwaukee and elsewhere, and had been their staple for decades. But he wanted to appeal to more consumers and felt that diversity would be a key to future growth. As demonstrative of this, only two months into his tenure, Peoples announced a new, seasonal holiday brew to go on sale later in November and through December of 1970. The beer would have a higher alcohol content than the beer they typically sold, and Mack was sure to tell the papers they'd make it year-round if the demand was high enough.[13] Unfortunately, it wasn't, and so he had to search for other products to diversify with, and as fate would have it, he found them in Peoples' oldest rival.

By 1970 the production of the once dominant Oshkosh Brewing Company (or OBC) was hovering close to Peoples' equally low production, and ranking just above Peoples Brewing in the state ranking of brewery output (11th versus 13th).[14] The problem, however, was that OBC was simply a much larger operation, and so needed a much greater output to survive. While Peoples had focused its business on selling to Fox Valley taverns, OBC's model had been to sell mainly to consumers for home-consumption. The plan worked brilliantly, for a while at least. The 1950s saw enormous expansion of the city's oldest brewery, but in the 1960s it saw a decline that was even more impressive.

At that time, it was owned by an heir to the Milwaukee Schlitz fortune, David Uihlein, a dashing, good looking businessman who darted about town in flashy cars and wore flashy clothes. He was also impatient and didn't want to stand in line to run his family's empire, but instead wanted to run his very own brewery. Most people felt he was running OBC as more of a hobby, something to keep him busy until he was made president of Schlitz. Unfortunately, despite his family's history of brewing, he knew almost nothing about actually running a brewery, and so proceeded to run OBC right into the ground.

Almost as soon as Uihlein took over as owner in 1961, he started fiddling with the thing that made OBC so renowned: the beer. The standard beers of the day were made with more or less the same ingredients, malt barley, hops, yeast and water (with sometimes the addition of corn). The OBC beer was much loved by the people of the Fox Valley, but it wasn't nearly as cheap as the big beers from Milwaukee. So, Uihlein planned to lower costs by using cheaper ingredients, such as corn syrup, which resulted (of course) in a beer of a much lower quality. And, as is always the case, taste usually follows ingredient quality and the customers reacted accordingly by eschewing the beer that had dominated in Oshkosh for decades.[15]

By the end of the 1960s the brewery was a shell of its former self. Using cut rate extracts in their beer instead of natural ingredients reduced demand to practically nothing in the town that used to *insist* on Chief Oshkosh, OBC's main product. Uihlein finally admitted defeat in 1969 and sold the company to a group of employees led by Harold Kriz before retreating back to Milwaukee to claim a seat on the board of Schlitz.

Amazingly though, Uihlein failed to learn any lessons at all from his debacle in Oshkosh. In the 1970s he led Schlitz to its own historic downfall using tactics there similar to what he did at OBC. He once again began adding corn syrup to cut costs and reduced the fermentation time using extracts and chemicals, and then had to add yet other additives to counter the haze and problems the other methods introduced. The result was a bland tasting beer that looked unappealing and simply wouldn't sell. He would go on to ruin the brewing company his family had sacrificed so much for. At one time Schlitz had been worth hundreds of millions of dollars, but by 1981 it was worth so little it was purchased by the mid-size Detroit competitor Stroh's and recognized as the cheapest of the cheap beers.

But back in Oshkosh in 1971, the group of loyal OBC employees who'd scraped up enough funds to buy the aging brewery also had to throw in the towel after missing their tax filing and reducing their workforce to practically nothing. It was too late to save their beer's reputation, and too

8. Growing Pains

difficult to compete with the inexpensive beer flowing into the city from the country's largest brewers ninety miles away. And so, on September 9, 1971, Oshkosh Brewing Company produced its last batch of beer before ending production for good.

It would be another two months before they would tell anyone about their halt in production, although residents started figuring it out much earlier. Two articles published in Oshkosh newspapers in October discussed OBC's status, and whether it had halted production or not. In each article, Kriz declined to comment. However, one of the reporters didn't just stop at interviewing the president of OBC, he also talked to Mack about his competitor's production and asked if he knew what state their operation was in. In response, Peoples' president coyly said, "I think they've got something doing over there, but I don't know what."[16] In fact, he knew exactly what they were doing, because he was doing it with them.

On November 4, 1971, Peoples Brewing Company acquired a $25,000 loan from the same bank they had used to make their initial purchase of the brewery. The next day, after receiving a check for $25,000 from Peoples, Oshkosh Brewing Company announced that its beers, along with the rights to brew them, their labels and rights to sell them, had been bought by Peoples Brewing Company. The feud between Joseph Nigl and William Glatz had finally ended, and it was safe to say that Nigl won. But most importantly for Ted Mack, Peoples Brewing Company now had an additional five beers to produce and market, giving him the much more diverse suite of products he had been after.

Through 1970–1971 most of Peoples' expansion went smoothly, and it demonstrated the ambitious plans that Mack had for himself and for the company. Growing it well beyond the Fox Valley and turning it into a much larger, more productive brewery was the obvious hope of the one-time social worker. But there were some notable bumps along the way, and once again, on the surface, prejudice and bigotry seemed to be the factors responsible. In Milwaukee, where he'd bought an enormous warehouse with office space in anticipation of the demand he assumed he'd meet there, his distributors were being tossed out of taverns in the white sections of town as their owners told them they wouldn't sell "black" beer.[17] Most of the places that agreed to carry Peoples were in the Inner Core, the black neighborhoods of Milwaukee. Little by little, though, he began getting Peoples Beer into more outlets. So, most of these episodes, though a statement on the terrible racial dynamics of Wisconsin's largest city, were still manageable. And none of them were really spoken about in the press. Instead, it was Mack's attempt to bring his beer into Gary, Indiana, of all places that made the newspapers.

On June 28, 1971, three trucks full of Peoples Beer made their way

November 5, 1971; Oshkosh, WI, USA; Photograph of Theodore Mack (left) and Harold Kriz at a press conference announcing the purchase of the Oshkosh Brewing Company by Peoples Brewing Company in Oshkosh. Mack was the president of the Peoples Brewing Company, the first black-owned brewery in Wisconsin. Kriz was the general manager of the Oshkosh Brewing Company (© Oshkosh Daily Northwestern–USA TODAY NETWORK).

200 miles down to Gary, Indiana, where Peoples had purchased a new distributorship. With $5,000 per week in new orders waiting for them, Mack and the others were confident Gary was going to prove a lucrative city in which to sell their beer. And if they did well there, it wouldn't be long before they would find their way to the rest of the state. Even Richard Hatcher, Gary, Indiana's first African American mayor, was reported as being especially pleased to see Peoples enter the city.[18] It seemed a perfect fit.

Other officials in the state, though, didn't see it that way. When the trucks reached the Peoples Brewing Company warehouse, they were greeted by Gary Police, Indiana State Highway Patrol, and agents from the state excise tax agency, all for a few trucks full of beer. As it turned out, Indiana law forbade the producers of alcohol to sell directly to either outlets or the public. Instead, they were required to sell through a middle-man

8. Growing Pains 97

distributor that wasn't connected to the brewery. The problem was that Mack didn't know that. Working with Peoples' lawyers to ensure all ran smoothly, he had purchased the warehouse and created the distributorship, had filled out all the paperwork, and acquired all the necessary permits, and all well in advance of June 28.

When asked about the situation by reporters, the chairman of the Indiana Alcohol Control Board called it a "misunderstanding probably,"[19] and said that Peoples' lawyers were sent all copies of the regulations when they applied for permits, which begs the question: why were the permits given in the first place? Why did Indiana officials let them drive the 200 miles to the warehouse—a warehouse already purchased and legal as far as Ted Mack knew—if they were only going to impound the beer anyway?

Mack was pretty sure he knew the answer. He immediately saw the episode as yet another indicator of racist-fueled resistance towards their venture, telling reporters that "everywhere we go we run into the white power structure."[20] He also indicated it was part of a larger conspiracy against them, saying that "[i]f they can keep us from making any money this summer, they know we'll have to go out of business," then adding that "they'll jump up and down and clap their hands and say 'see the nigger can't do it.'"[21] He didn't tell reporters who was responsible for the conspiracy, who "they" were, but noted that when the shipments arrived at the warehouse, a "white man" met them there, saying that "no Peoples Beer would be sold in Gary."[22] Whether the event was a result of a conspiracy of bigots or not, considering the boycott and rumors he'd already faced in Oshkosh, the actual hometown of the brewery, it's hard to blame Mack for seeing it that way.

The story was picked up and shared first in their two respective cities (Gary and Oshkosh), then their states, and then nationally. Once again, the words chosen to describe the incident really demonstrated what Mack was up against (and added evidence to his conspiracy theory). In Ironwood, Michigan, the *Daily Globe* announced, "Negro Beer Confiscated."[23] In Madison, and Fond du Lac Wisconsin, the articles reminded readers that Mack was president of a "Negro-owned brewery."[24,25] For his part, Mack wouldn't back down. He told the *Wisconsin State Journal* that "Indiana authorities harassed him to keep his company from selling beer in the Gary area."[26] And to the Associated Press he said that "tremendous pressures have been brought to bear to prevent Peoples beer from becoming a viable and competitive factor in Gary."[27]

Though it's hard to prove that it was racism at the core of the event, Mack seemed to be correct in deducing that there *was* a conspiracy to keep Peoples out of the region, but circumstances suggest it wasn't the KKK, it was the Teamsters. The *Milwaukee Journal* reported that "a Teamsters Union strike against other beer distributors in Gary complicated Peoples' attempt to enter the market," and suggested that, "the first complaints about Peoples came from Teamsters officials."[28] Teamsters were ruthless when it came to contract negotiations. In 1969 they shut down Anheuser-Busch for over three months, locking out over 30,000 employees with hostile, even brutal tactics. In Gary, the last thing they would want is another brewery distributing its product while they were in the middle of picketing the others.

So, when Mack rolled into town, the Teamsters could have used the event to keep pressure on other beer distributors by ensuring that Peoples Beer didn't get put on shelves in Northern Indiana. In fact, Indiana officials even said they were tipped off to the Peoples Beer shipments by an anonymous phone call that, they admitted, "could have been some member of a labor movement."[29] Further, and perhaps the most telling evidence of all, was a report that "Mack's truck drivers were approached by some of the striking Gary beer truck drivers," who "tried, without success, to recruit the Oshkosh drivers into their strike."[30]

Whatever spawned the dispute in the first place, Mack managed to clear up the technical and legal problems quickly. Most importantly, he found a distributor owned by Gary residents and began shipping Peoples Beer to them within weeks, and so, Gary then became a regular outlet for their sales. Mack later credited the exposure they received in the press as a major reason the incident was settled so quickly. He told one reporter that "after the news media let the country know what was going on—and after I was contacted by CBS, NBC, and ABC—I went from 'Hey you, boy' to 'Mr. Mack' in 20 minutes."[31]

Despite what seemed an impending disaster, he'd managed to overcome yet one more hurdle, and to all who were paying attention, he seemed destined for success. And coincidentally, many were paying attention. Mack wasn't just appearing regularly in articles from the *Milwaukee Journal*, but also in major African American outlets like *Jet*[32] and the *Baltimore Afro-American*,[33] and even in national newspapers like the *New York Times*.[34] And along with this success, along with the constant coverage in the local and regional papers about his plans and expansion, he was creating a name for himself beyond his circle of Inner Core friends back in Milwaukee, and his presence was subsequently in demand throughout the state.

At the Peoples' stockholder meeting on January 11, 1972, Mack told those in attendance that he "has had more requests for speaking engagements across the country than he can handle." These requests, he elaborated, "come in from business groups, service clubs and colleges."[35] And

8. Growing Pains

while they were more than he could handle, he certainly tried his hardest to be accommodating. Between March 1 and March 10, 1971, to take one small block of time, he made presentations to three different groups, specifically the Wisconsin Governor's Task Force on Commerce and Industry in Milwaukee, the Economic Society at the University of Wisconsin–Oshkosh, and the Oshkosh Rotary Club. When time allowed, there seemed to be no group he wouldn't speak to if they asked. He was only too happy to deliver remarks to the local Optimist Club,[36] the Lions Club,[37] and even a local Catholic CCD class.[38]

His schedule would grow even busier as the year drew on, but luckily, he seemed to enjoy the opportunities he was presented with, a fact that's spawned criticism by some. In fact, it's been insinuated in the only book written about the history of breweries in Oshkosh that Mack craved the spotlight and that what he really wanted was to stand in front of crowds and make clever remarks.[39] But critics who suspect this, however, miss one important fact about each of the presentations he gave—not a single one of his many presentations was ever about himself. Instead, whenever he was in the spotlight and had the opportunity to speak to an audience, he always spoke to help his community.

When he was to give a lecture to the Economic Society at UW–Oshkosh, for example, Ted announced that his topic would be "Destroying the Myth of Black Capitalism," and began by stating, "I am not a black capitalist; I am a businessman."[40] His remarks expanded on this point, saying there was no difference between black businessmen and other businessmen in the country save one: no major corporations were run by black businessmen. "There are 500 major corporations in this country," Mack said to the professors and students in attendance, "and not even one of them is under the control or even the management of blacks."

He was speaking from a moderate position of equality, one that insisted, as *he* had always insisted, that he was every bit the businessman a white person was, and this was not the position of black capitalism. In a 1969 paper presented to the American Economic Association meeting in New York, Federal Reserve officials Andrew Brimmer and Henry Terrell pointed this out explicitly:

> [black capitalism] has an intuitive appeal to varying shades of political opinion. To the black militant, it is appealing because it promises community ownership of property and an end to "exploitation" by outside merchants. At the other extreme, the strategy is appealing to white conservatives because it stresses the virtues of private enterprise capitalism as the path to economic advancement instead of reliance on public expenditures, especially for public welfare.[41]

While Ted argued for equality, and not segregation, he also recognized that equality didn't exist in America. He told the attendees that "the economic system in the U.S. deprives not only minorities, but all private enterprise." This argument was bigger than himself, it was an argument against the current philosophy he felt was being pursued in error by those in authority. Sure, the frame of reference he was using was his own, but the lecture encompassed equality for all in the black community.

Likewise, a year later he was invited back to speak at the university for Black History Week, and this time discussed "the role of black Americans."[42] Once again he focused his remarks on the plight of the black community, not on himself. He gave a passionate speech, comparing the black man in America to the mule, the lowliest of farm creatures.

> The Negro and the mule have traveled parallel roads. Soon after the Negro came to America they were combined as a team and began to clear the land. Along came Whitney and his cotton gin, and suddenly the Negro and the mule became very important. But it wasn't until the machine age that the parallel reached its highest and most tragic peak, it was during this age the mule was put in his pasture and the Negro was put in his ghetto. Not only that, but ever since the Negroes have not been fully employed, America grew richer, while the Negro and the mule were left behind.[43]

A favorite speech of his seemed to be one called "Changing of Priorities," which he gave to a local meeting of the American Association of Retired Persons in June 1971,[44] to the annual convention of the Wisconsin Retired Teachers Association in October 1971,[45] and then yet again to a meeting of the area Lions Clubs in November.[46] In it, Mack suggested that America was divided thanks to "cheap politicians." He suggested that all citizens, the young and old, black and white, should work together to make our country better. In ending he quotes Dr. Martin Luther King, telling the audience, "'Let no one make you stoop so low that you hate.'"[47]

Mack's remarks always circled back to the same topics, like the black worker, the black businessman, the black community, and about how these people are not *choosing* to live in the ghetto, but were instead relegated to the Inner Core of Milwaukee and elsewhere against their will. They were forced there by the inequality of America. His lectures consistently pointed out that the black man yearned to work, yearned to produce, but that for some reason, the American industrial system didn't want this to happen, or in his words, "there's a conspiracy to keep black folks out of business and off of welfare, too."[48]

Mack's sudden notoriety caught the attention of state politicians,

8. Growing Pains

and in particular the Wisconsin governor, Patrick Lucey, who said that the Peoples Brewing Company was "one of the really shining examples of minority owned capitalism in the whole United States."[49] In January of 1971, Lucey appointed Mack to a statewide blue-ribbon business panel called the Commerce-Industry Committee. The committee consisted of 26 members in total, and was chaired by James C. Windham, president of Pabst Brewing Company. The panel's charge was to investigate "a possible reduction of the manufacturer's inventory tax and possible creation of a State Department of Commerce."[50] Noted in one article was that the committee was filled with "prominent Wisconsin business executives"[51] who were drawn from throughout the state and included the owners, officers, and presidents of businesses large and small. Mack recognized that he was in distinguished company, noting that some of the other members of the committee "pay more taxes each year than me and my employees earn."[52]

Despite their status, Mack was far from intimidated. In fact, he continued advocating for his community every chance he got, even to his fellow committee members. At one meeting in March 1971, they focused on issues faced by the black business community. Taking the podium, Mack gave an impassioned speech about the many problems faced by minority business people like himself, specifically informing them that such problems "put the aspiring business candidate out of the market before he can get started."[53] There's little doubt that these business leaders would never have really been exposed to the struggles of the black businessman had it not been for Ted Mack.

As his company expanded, as his notoriety grew, and as more and more focus was placed on him, Mack's message never wavered, and nor did his mission. His civil rights activism was on full display through the example of what he was doing. Through the action of buying and running Peoples Brewing Company, he had gained a platform to advocate for others like himself, for the aspiring black entrepreneurs in the Inner Core of North Milwaukee and elsewhere who longed to escape their circumstances, but who felt they lacked the opportunity. Mack was showing them how to make their own opportunities. He was demonstrating that the black community could produce, not just consume. He was demonstrating that black business people were simply business people, not "black capitalists."

But despite all this fervid activism for his community, Mack still had a company to run. He was often fond of saying he didn't believe in black power or white power, he only believed in green power—money. But it was exactly that kind of power he was sorely missing by the end of 1971 when Peoples' accountants delivered the year-end financials. The news wasn't good, neither was the balance sheet, but Mack merely shrugged, saying, "I think everybody expected some red ink." Maybe he was right, but the article, titled "Peoples Brewing 1st Year Loss $100,000"[54] still didn't paint a flattering picture of the new management or owners. And to be honest, the article really didn't show how distressing the first year's loss really was. According to their accounting firm, Milwaukee-based Philip J. Siegel & Co., Peoples Brewing Co. had a net loss of over $160,000 the first 12 months of new ownership.[55] (Adjusting for inflation that's a loss of over $1 million in 2022.)

Mack told reporters, stockholders and the Board of Directors that the loss was caused by three factors, a "loss of business in the Fox Valley area due to rumors of all blacks replacing whites in the company, expanding into new areas, and making improvements in the physical plant."[56] It's unclear how much sales were really hurt by the boycott against Peoples, but the cost of sales and delivery was noted at over $326,000. Each time they entered a new city they had to send beer there. That meant paying delivery drivers, paying for fuel, and paying to store it at a distribution point in the new city. All of that added up quickly and wiped out the $206,000 profit they made from sales in that first year. But, undeterred and ever optimistic, Mack told stockholders at their annual meeting in January, and again in the company's annual report in March, that the brewery was now on the right track and that the first quarter of 1972 was the best quarter they'd had since the new management had taken over. "In fact," he confidently said, "sales have increased by twenty thousand dollars per month over last year."[57]

What he didn't tell them was that despite the increase in sales, the first year's loss completely wiped out the capital Peoples' acquired from the stock sales—the capital that the bank required before granting the loan for the purchase of the brewery in the first place. True, that money could be lost—was meant to be lost, in fact—but it could be lost only once. Any funding they needed after it was depleted would have to be earned from sales going forward, unless they incurred even more debt. And taking on more debt would be a move very few on the board would be willing to make. After all, they had spent over $38,000 the previous year alone for the interest on the loans they already had (plus had added to that loan amount to buy the Oshkosh Brewing Company recipes and trademarks for $25,000).

So, needless to say, 1972 started with the promise of difficulty for the small brewery. But, as usual, Ted Mack wore a smile and spoke with enthusiasm for the coming year as if they were flush with cash. Underneath the optimism, though, he knew that Peoples was in a precarious position. They needed to increase sales to stay alive, especially with the competition from the beer barons in Milwaukee and St Louis. He had a strategy for success, one that he'd been thinking about since 1969. It was a simple one: get the black community to buy Peoples Beer. As the prospectus for their stock pointed out, even a slight shift from black beer consumers towards the Peoples' brand would prove a major payoff. It was a gamble that they'd asked stockholders to make, but it was a gamble that would never pay off and would leave Ted Mack bitterly disappointed.

9

Black Beer

When United People's Brewery officially took over Peoples Brewing Company in late September 1970, Ted Mack and company threw a party for the entire community—opening the brewery's doors to neighbors, stockholders, politicians, and townspeople. Giving a speech after the ceremonial ribbon cutting, a pensive Mack stood before those assembled and reflected on all they went through to accomplish their goals. In ending his remarks, he told them, that "for a man born in Alabama on a farm, where you weren't sure there would be anything to eat, to be standing here today as the first black president of a brewery, I have to say I'm proud of my country."[1]

The question of whether or not he was in fact the *first* black brewery president has been a subject of debate among those interested in the history of beer in the U.S. Although there's little doubt that the production of beer, and even its consumption, was squarely dominated by white European immigrants, there is still a strong legacy of black brewers in this country. Thomas Jefferson's household beer was made by an enslaved chef named Peter Hemings, who Jefferson raved about to James Madison, saying his maltster and brewer was "uncommonly intelligent"[2] and even offering to have Hemings apprentice a pupil for the fourth president (it's unknown whether Madison took him up on this).

But the first recorded evidence of a black American taking an interest in owning a brewery happened much later. In 1955, a black, blind entrepreneur named John Randolph Smith announced, through a single newspaper article, that he was founding the Colony House Brewing Company in Philadelphia, PA. Printed primarily in black newspapers of the day, like the *Jackson Advocate* and the *Roanoke Tribune*, the story reports that Smith, a businessman from Atlanta, made the announcement at a "huge banquet" attended by nearly 200 civic leaders, distributors, and tavern owners. Apparently, he made samples available to all 200 dignitaries, as the article goes on to say the attendees, "rated the brew favorably with the best premium beers on the market."[3]

The article is rife with optimism and big dreams. Smith said that he'd already selected 50 metro areas to distribute to (implausible at best, considering the difficulty Mack had just getting into the small towns of Wisconsin), that he'd traveled 7,000 miles creating and testing his new formula, and that his new company would be a great opportunity for black entrepreneurs who wanted to invest their money (this last item, it seems, might actually be the catalyst for the article in the first place).

What's curious about the account of Colony House Brewing Company is that there never seemed to be any follow up to this single story. No other articles extolling the quality or taste of Colony House beer were even written, there were never any newspaper ads for their product, and there's also no mention of a brewery by that name in the Philadelphia City directories of 1955 or 1956. John Randolph Smith, brewer, simply vanished, and there's no knowing what ever became of his national aspirations. It's pure speculation to say that Smith's brewery ever really existed at all.

Another episode, much closer to Mack's day, had a few odd and unusual (but entertaining) twists. There is a single article in a 1970 volume of the *Brewer's Digest* that tells a fantastic story about a Reading, PA, brewery called Sunshine Brewing Company. The article highlighted the brewery's spectacular—almost magical—newfound success under a management team of black entrepreneurs from Philadelphia, led by their new brewery president—also black—named A. Bart Starr.[4]

But the story of "black entrepreneur" A. Bart Starr's tenure in the brewery's management has a few unexpected sidenotes that actually begin in 1964. In that year, a man named Leo Israel Bloom put together a group of investors to purchase Sunshine. Bloom had just come off of bankrupting his family's furniture business, and now set his sights on making the same impact in the beer industry.

And this he did. Within three years of his purchase, he'd drained the company of every dollar it had and was finally forced out as president of the brewery in late 1967 by his investors through a court order. But by that time, though, Sunshine was in receivership, owed money to nearly 300 different creditors, and faced almost $200,000 in government tax liens.[5]

Bloom, ever creative, talked the brewery's employees into buying thousands of dollars' worth of company bonds to keep Sunshine afloat. But instead of paying off creditors and improving the place, he pocketed most of the money. Then in 1969 he organized a small group of black businessmen from Philadelphia who took out a $400,000 SBA loan to buy the brewery and get him off the hook. This is where A. Bart Starr comes in: he was named the president of the company and, with his group, spent the next year selling off every last asset Sunshine had (while at the same time pocketing loans against the brewery). Starr, the smart, young, black entrepreneur touted by the brewing journal, went by other names as well, like

Gordon F. Andrews (his real name), and Alexander Scott (by which name he was indicted in 1973 for impersonating an SBA loan officer).[6]

With such an unseemly character, it seems curious they were able to purchase the brewery in much the same way Mack had, through the SBA. But, for some reason, they were granted the loan guarantee and set about dismantling the once proud brewery bit by bit. By late 1970, Sunshine had reverted back into bankruptcy again and the black "entrepreneurs" celebrated as the first to own and run an American brewery had up and vanished (though Andrews' name would once again make headlines in 1977 when he was indicted by federal law enforcement officials on 20 counts of mail fraud, aiding and abetting fraud, and conspiring to distribute heroin).

Bloom, for his part, was arrested, and turned State's evidence in an organized crime trial in 1971,[7] while the brewery was finally seized by one of its creditors and sold off piecemeal (what was left of it anyway). What Bloom and his colleagues left in their wake was an empty brewery, drained of all assets and virtually worthless.

Neither of these stories were familiar to Mack or really anyone else at the time. In both cases there were only single articles written about them, and then they both seemed to be quickly forgotten, their characters and memories lost to history. When Ted Mack declared himself the first black brewery president in America, a claim echoed by most regional newspapers, he was most likely right.

Ultimately, though, he never really dwelt on this subject, he was too busy trying to make Peoples a success, something that was proving more difficult than he thought. And though he might have had a ready set of consumers in the black community, he seemed conflicted about his plans for selling beer to them. On the one hand he often asserted he wasn't selling a "white beer" or a "black beer," but on the other hand the company had made it clear they were pinning their success on black beer drinkers. As pointed out on page eight of the stock prospectus, "the Company intends to develop a market within the Black communities in major population centers."[8] But since the announcement of the purchase, Mack refused to vocalize this plan, instead insisting that Peoples Beer was for everyone.

This incongruence was noticed by reporters, too. In July 1971, the *Daily Northwestern*'s Joseph H. Sayrs pointed out that "Mack has denied running a 'black brewery,' but has stressed new markets where there are a lot of blacks."[9] Maybe it was because of the initial reaction to their purchase, or maybe because deep down inside, he really wanted to make a product for all consumers (not just the black consumers), but whatever the case, Mack's courtship of black beer drinkers was tepid at best.

9. Black Beer

And this community—the community of black beer drinkers—was certainly one Peoples would have liked to get a toehold in, just as others were trying to do. While Mack refused to call his beer a "black beer," other companies didn't have such reservations. In 1969 a small group of black leaders from Chicago banded together to form Black Pride Beer, a beer specifically aimed at the black beer drinker. Like Peoples, Black Pride beer was funded by stockholders, 75 of them who each raised and invested $1000 apiece. Unlike Peoples, however, the group who owned Black Pride didn't brew their own beer (though they hoped to one day own their own brewery). Instead, they contracted with a small brewery in northern Wisconsin called West Bend Lithia Company, which was owned by white people (something that was pointed out in most articles about Black Pride Beer).[10]

Interestingly, there are an astounding number of similarities between the stories of Peoples Brewery and Black Pride Beer. Like Ted Mack, Edward J. McClellan, the man who came up with Black Pride Beer and led its founding, was a military veteran, a community leader, and ranking member of a civil rights organization (the NAACP of Chicago). He was highly educated and believed that members of the black community needed to lift itself up and do things for themselves instead of waiting around for the white man to help them.[11] Also, like Mack, McClellan said one of his motivations for starting Black Pride Beer was the revelation that black consumers made up a large portion of the beer drinkers in the U.S. Naturally, living in a city like Chicago with such a large black population, that knowledge motivated him to create a product targeting that demographic. But, as with Peoples, there was much more to Black Pride Beer than simply a product meant to generate income from the black community. As explained in an article from 1969:

> It is not enough, they say, for the black simply to give up this psychology of dependence on white magnanimity, for where a self-defeating mood of despair does not supplant it, an equally self-defeating concept of presumptive "black power" will be likely to prove most attractive. Rather, what is needed on the part of the black is self-respect, a proper pride in himself. This is difficult to achieve and impossible to sustain unless, to speak in reverse chronological order, blacks have tangible evidence of personal achievement (among which would be upward mobility within a corporate structure) and the opportunity for such upward mobility and achievement. Thus, Black Pride, Inc., in the best tradition of the free enterprise system, seeks to provide a means of such achievement for its stockholders as well as for its employees and for those with whom it does business.[12]

This philosophy closely echoes that of Mack and the stated mission of Peoples Brewing Company under his leadership. It wasn't just about selling beer, it was about helping his community, or at least about showing his community what was possible.

The founders of Black Pride Beer were ambitious and optimistic and envisioned their beer becoming a popular product in Chicago and beyond. They spoke of franchising distributorships, about opening their own brewery one day, and about expanding nationally. But within three years of founding their company, it had closed. When McClellan and the others founded the company, they had assumed that, because they themselves were black, because of the message they were selling along with the product (that is, that the black community should support black businesses), and because of how they branded their product, support from the black beer drinkers of Chicago should be an easy get. But that simply never happened. The enthusiasm they assumed they'd receive for Black Pride Beer just never materialized. It wasn't only frustrating, it also felt immensely

Black Pride Beer label created for the short running beer out of Chicago that was created to capitalize on the Black pride movement of the 1960s. Like Theodore Mack's vision for Peoples Beer, Black Pride wanted to create a product for and by the Black community and to offer an example of what that community was capable of (author's collection).

9. Black Beer

painful to see their own community turn their backs on them. Why would they do that?

Mack was once asked why it was so important to place Peoples Beer in areas with a high percentage of black residents, to which he simply stated, "Blacks drink a lot of beer."[13] In planning their ventures, both Mack and McClellan leaned on studies stating that black beer drinkers were responsible for a large amount of the beer sales in America, but neither one seemed to dig deeper into the details. Rather, they most likely read the statistics about the amount of beer the black community bought, and stopped there. They should have addressed other important questions. What sort of beer did they actually buy? What motivated them to make a decision about the beer they consumed? Studies conducted more recently—from the 1980s until the present[14,15]—do a better job of answering these questions, and the answers may have tempered the enthusiasm to court the black beer drinking crowd (or at least changed the trajectory of their products and marketing). One set of statistics in particular show that black consumers were one of the biggest groups buying a very particular kind of beer: malt liquor.

Malt liquor was invented in 1937 when Michigan brewer Clarence "Click" Koerber introduced Clix Malt Liquor to the market. It was pretty simple to make—Click merely added extra sugar to a typical beer recipe to give the brew extra alcohol. Though most beers of the time were anywhere between 3 and 4 percent alcohol by volume, Click's new beer was closer to 7 percent. His trademark application referred to the new brew as "a pale, light bodied, *malt liquor*,"[16] which according to most sources was the first use of the term. Clix was soon joined by Sparkling Stite malt liquor made by Minnesota's Gluek Brewing in 1942, then by Goetz Brewing which introduced Country Club Malt Liquor in the early 1950s. Even Peoples Brewing Company came out with Old English 600 Malt Liquor (though it didn't brew it long before selling it to a different brewery). What was similar across all of these brands—other than the method of making beer with a higher alcohol content—was the consumer they were trying to appeal to, and that consumer wasn't black.

As the names "Country Club" or "Old English" suggest, each of these brewers was trying to reach the young, white, suit-wearing set. Much of their marketing budget was spent trying to convince consumers that these types of beverages were replacements for champagne or cocktails. Their advertisements, found in periodicals like *Life* magazine, included images of young, white couples playing tennis or golf, or attending cocktail parties and having a grand old time. This wasn't the type of beer slurped by the masses; this stuff was sophisticated. Even brands that would later focus on very different marketing demographics started out trying to appeal to the young white professionals. Colt .45, introduced in 1963, and Schlitz Malt Liquor with its iconic blue bull, were initially aimed at white urbanites, not black consumers.

But surprisingly, it was the black beer drinker who began enthusiastically buying the various brands of malt liquor being placed on shelves. Statistics for how much malt liquor they bought range, but generally speaking, while black Americans made up about 12–14 percent of the population, they purchased 30–33 percent of the malt liquor in the U.S.[17] A 1964 article even remarked that "Negroes have shown a strong preference for malt liquor over regular beer."[18] The reason why is speculated but generally comes down to two theories, the first is value.[19] With regards to the amount of alcohol contained, each can of malt liquor was equal to about 1½ cans of normal beer. People could buy and drink less for the same wobbly effect as drinking more, normal-strength beer, and they could do it for a lower price. The other reason it could have been so compelling might have been the fact that the marketing campaigns defined the products as high-brow and sophisticated. Drinking malt liquor was a gateway into the upscale life that the white, middle class was already enjoying, and the black consumers wanted to join them.[20,21]

After these consumption rates were reported, brewers had no choice but to take notice of their new group of consumers, a group they'd overlooked for a very long time. In the late 1960s, ads for malt liquor, this time featuring pictures of black beer drinkers, began showing up in *Jet* and *Ebony* magazines—both of which were written for and sold mainly to the black community. An ad in *Ebony* from 1971 for Champale, a malt liquor that billed itself as an alternative to champagne ("but costs only pennies more than beer" according to the ad), featured a black man painting a white picket fence. The tag line read, "Champale. Some people just know how to live."

Likewise, in 1971 the smiling white yuppies drinking Country Club Malt Liquor at their cocktail party had been replaced by former Boston Celtic great Bill Russell. With lightning bolts striking a "half quart" can of Country Club and Russell staring intensely into the camera, the ad tells you that Country Club is "A lot to drink without drinking a lot." A bit late to the game but still relevant was Budweiser, which ran ads in *Ebony* in 1972 proclaiming its malt liquor was "the first malt liquor good enough to be called Budweiser." The indication was clear: the demographic that Mack and McClellan were relying on was also being targeted by the largest brewers in the country, but for a different product.

But Mack was relying on this demographic in a very specific place: Milwaukee. And according to the 1970 census, the city had a black population of over 105,000. If he could just tap into that community and get them to buy *his* beer, it would make a huge difference for Peoples. But this was the same plan that Black Pride Beer tried, and they didn't last three years with an even bigger black community of 1,102,620 in Chicago. Mack had already rolled the dice on Milwaukee, though. This was the city he was living in when he planned his venture into the beer business in the first place. This was the city he knew, with the neighborhoods he'd walked as a social worker. He knew the churches here, the community centers, the black leaders. And what's more they knew him. They knew him from the rallies he'd organized with CORE. They knew him from the picket lines he'd walked to protest the segregation of the schools. They knew him from the pictures in the paper, like the one where he's jabbing his finger in the face of the white governor and demanding that black judges be selected for the Wisconsin bench. They also knew him from his attempt to buy Blatz beer. And, of course, they should have known him as the president of Peoples Brewing Company.

After all, how could they not? Ted Mack's name had been in the paper at least once a month, if not more, since April 14, 1970, the day of the infamous *Milwaukee Sentinel* article. The media had a keen interest in every move he made, from selling stock to opening up distributorships. Most every headline that ran since the moment he started negotiations with the old leadership of Peoples was some variation of "Black Group Buys Brewery." The black community had to have known that he and other prominent residents of north Milwaukee's Inner Core had bought the old brewery only 90 miles away. Even a year and half after taking over Peoples, In March 1972, an article ran with a headline that read, "Black Brewer Prospers in Oshkosh."[22] How could they not know that Peoples was owned and run by people just like them?

But then again, if the black community of Milwaukee didn't pay attention to those headlines, if they didn't read those articles, if they didn't know what Ted Mack, Henry Crosby and the rest were up to, then they'd never know that Peoples was a brewery they should support. That was doubly true because Mack really didn't seem willing to tell them. In that article of March 1972, Mack made it clear that he "does not capitalize on the fact that [Peoples is] a black-owned product." In fact, clarifying further, Mack said that "it might make good sociological reading, but it doesn't necessarily mean that it would be good for business." Instead, he said he'd rather "emphasize that I'm selling a quality product." He'd even said before that he wasn't making a "white beer" or a "black beer," he was just making beer.

Despite this sentiment, though, he *did* seem to expect the black residents of Milwaukee to support his company. But a year after opening, he bitterly admitted, "it just hasn't turned out that way."[23] The sales he was counting on from Milwaukee never took place. Sales there were so bad, in

Though Mack consistently denied they were making a "black beer," his strategy from the beginning was to appeal to a population of Black beer drinkers. Despite a minuscule advertising budget, he had ads created specifically for the Black community like this ad from 1971 (author's collection).

fact, that they were being dwarfed by sales in much smaller cities with little to no black population. Madison, with a population of just over 170,000 compared to Milwaukee's 740,000, tripled the sales of Milwaukee. And in one week the sales to Gary, Indiana's 175,000 residents, matched Milwaukee's sales for an entire month. And to top it all off, Oshkosh and the surrounding Fox River Valley, the places that initially spurned him because he was black, the area that only seven years earlier had voted at a rate of 40 percent for segregationist George Wallace, became his best market. Mack was left scratching his head. "I've been studying human behavior all of my life," he vented, "but since I've been in the brewery business, I have found out that I don't know a damned thing about it."[24]

Every assumption he'd made about black support turned out to be wrong. "It just doesn't make sense,"[25] he said in exasperation, "the whites are saying that they don't want no nigger beer, and I don't know what the Blacks are doing."[26] What black people were *not* doing was buying Peoples Beer, and he couldn't understand why. "The best way I can put it," he told a reporter from the *Daily Northwestern*, "[is] bigotry on the part of the whites and complacency on the part of the blacks."²⁷ It wasn't just in Milwaukee that he witnessed such complacency. He told another reporter about a recent trip to Gary, Indiana. There he overheard a conversation in a tavern, where "a Black man was insisting to a white man that whites must offer their assistance to other races. The white man was saying that Blacks must help themselves too. I happened to order a round of beer. The Black man spoke up and said, 'I'm from Milwaukee. Don't give me any of that Peoples.'"²⁸ All Mack could do was shake his head in wonder.

By September 1971 Peoples was looking to leave Milwaukee to focus on the other markets and was trying to sell the warehouse they purchased the year before. Milwaukee had three delivery trucks, which meant Peoples was paying labor for drivers and salesmen, as well as the maintenance and gas for the trucks. They had also purchased the warehouse and were paying to staff that as well. All told, the Milwaukee distributorship was his second biggest expense after the actual brewery in Oshkosh, and it wasn't even paying for itself.²⁹ In frustration, Mack placed the blame for their failure on the residents of the Inner Core. Just like he had told reporters in Oshkosh that if Peoples failed it would reflect badly on Oshkosh, he told them a year later that if they failed in Milwaukee, it would be a "stigma on the black community."³⁰

And from his point of view, this bitterness was justified. He didn't get into this business because he loved beer, he got into this to help his people. "Unlike other breweries that only leave a few (economic) crumbs in the black community," he explained, "black people in Milwaukee must come to understand that not only will Peoples provide jobs but most of the profits will come back to the community. If we don't support ourselves, how can we expect anyone else to support us?"³¹ His philosophy, though, simply wasn't shared by the black consumers. "Here you have over 100,000 Black people saying we want to do our thing," he said in frustration, "and when you give them this opportunity, they don't respond."³²

But why didn't they respond? Why was Milwaukee such a bust for Peoples? There is no doubt that a number of factors contributed to the failure, but not all of them were because of the black community's apathy. One of those factors was no doubt Mack's reticence to exploit the fact that Peoples was managed and controlled by a group of black business people. He was relying on it being common knowledge since so many newspaper articles had highlighted this fact. He had even told one reporter that "he believed that the beer would sell very well in Milwaukee's black community because it was well known that Peoples was black controlled."³³

But what if it *wasn't* "well known"? Mack's refusal to market on the black leadership of Peoples' might have been a major contributor to the miserable level of sales to Milwaukee's black community. Then, on the other hand, it didn't seem to help Black Pride Beer at all (and they were trying to sell to a population 10 times the size that Mack was trying to sell to). Black Pride Beer was also much more upfront about which demographic it was trying to appeal to, it was right there in the name. They made a product for the black community and emphasized that fact. Ultimately, though, they failed, so, it's difficult to say how much it really hurt Peoples to not market on the basis of being a black-managed company.

Price sensitivity could have been another reason for the lack of interest in Peoples Beer. The population that Mack was relying on was historically much poorer than the white beer consumers in the city, and Peoples wasn't cheap. "One of the complaints in the black community is that [Peoples Beer] was priced too high" an article claimed. Mack brushed this aside, saying, "you can't make a quality product and give it away."[34] He also pointed to the report from the Siebel Institute, telling reporters that "Peoples Beer was found to be 'exceedingly good' in almost every technical respect."[35] In other words, it wasn't just that the manufacturing cost of their beer demanded a premium price, it deserved it because of the quality.

Be that as it may, consumers might have had a point. In Oshkosh, at Ray's Beverage on West New York Avenue, Peoples could be found for $2.70 a case (24 bottles) or $.99 a six pack (cans). This wasn't by any means the most expensive, that would be Budweiser at $4.03 a case, followed by Schlitz and Hamm's at $3.79. But it wasn't the cheapest either. You could buy a case of Buckhorn (an inexpensive beer made by Olympia Brewing in Washington) for $2.44 and Bohemian Club (another inexpensive brand) for $2.29.[36] At the Beverage Mart on Main Street, though, Peoples was a bit more, going for $2.81 a case while a case of Rhinelander was only $2.29.[37] Two hours to the south in Kenosha at the Town 'n' Country Liquor Store, a six pack of Peoples (or Falstaff) could also be had for $.99 while Gettlemans (made by Miller) was only $.89.[38] If you wanted something a bit stronger, you could also pick up a six-pack of Budweiser Malt Liquor (as advertised in Ebony) for just a little more at $1.19.[39]

So, Peoples was priced somewhere in between the premium brands and the cheap stuff and consumers still didn't buy it. You'd have to assume then that the price point wasn't necessarily a turn off. It had to be something else, something more important than the cost. Maybe they weren't drinking it in Milwaukee because Mack simply didn't give them a reason to. He wondered aloud why the Fox Valley region was the source of his highest sales, but it makes complete sense considering the residents of that area had been drinking Peoples Beer since 1914. They knew the brand, knew its history, and had a connection to it. Beer drinkers in Milwaukee, in contrast, simply didn't. They had grown up in the one U.S. city that was

9. Black Beer   115

most identified with beer, the city with brands like Schlitz, Pabst, Blatz and Miller.

Those were the brands they knew. They had been driving by those sprawling breweries and watching the steam belching from their boilers all their lives. They knew people who worked in them and had relatives who wouldn't drink anything else but their favorite Milwaukee beer brand. Peoples Beer had no significance to them, especially when Mack refused to sell on the one advantage he had over the large brewers with their white board of directors and presidents. What's more, while all of those brands had long ago made inroads into the taverns and markets of Oshkosh, Peoples had remained stationary, staying close to home and never trying to distribute into Milwaukee or elsewhere.

Mack was losing out on the city and population he most counted on to help his venture's sales. Without them he knew it would be a lot harder to make Peoples Beer successful. His instincts told him that he needed to give the beer significance and that consumers needed to know about it. "I see everybody on TV but Peoples," he told stockholders during their annual meeting in January 1972, "we have to get more money for advertising. I hope we can let the people know about our fine beer. Peoples Beer is rated one of the finest beers in the country."[40]

Peoples Beer was advertised in both the Black and white communities of Oshkosh and Milwaukee, with specific ads made for each audience. Here is the same look, style, and theme of two of their ads from early 1970–1971 meant for the two different communities (author's collection).

In mid-1971 until early 1972, they carried out some advertising in the black communities through billboards and posters, but little in the newspapers, on TV, or on radio. Their marketing also tried to present Peoples so that it appealed to the black beer drinker specifically. One ad featured a young, smiling black couple lying in front of a fireplace playing a card game. Next to each was a bottle of Peoples Beer and the tagline that read, "People who know their beer drink Peoples." Another featured a young black woman wearing eye shadow, lip gloss and a very revealing top. She stares intently at the reader while holding a glass of beer. Next to the Peoples Beer logo the tagline read suggestively, "Had it lately?"[41]

The message of these ads was fine, the problem was they simply didn't have the resources to spread them consistently or at the level they needed to. Mack told the board of directors that he needed at least $100,000 just for marketing, and they said they'd consider selling more stock to raise the capital. What he didn't realize, what he couldn't have realized, was that it would take a lot more than that to compete for the market he was trying to enter. His competition, all but one based in Milwaukee, had much deeper pockets, and they didn't play fair.

10

The Hidden Truth About Big Beer

"[T]he big brewers did not exactly say 'welcome to the fold,'"[1] Mack said in 1971 when asked about the reception he received from other Wisconsin beer producers. It was true, the big brewers didn't let anybody feel welcome, they hated competition. Instead, they wanted to dominate, to squeeze their rivals out any way they possibly could until there were fewer and fewer of them left. And over time, the win-at-all-cost approach proved to be working. In 1950 there were 407 breweries in the U.S., but by 1971 that number had shrunk to just 134.[2]

As some breweries got bigger and bigger, others just couldn't complete and had to close. And those that wouldn't close, those that refused to die, were simply bought out and then shuttered, as Pabst did to Blatz before it was sued by the federal government. The big brewers were ruthless, always trying to edge out their competitors at every turn, no matter how small those competitors might have been. As far as big beer was concerned, it was war, and casualties happen in wars.

By 1970 the chasm between the biggest brewers in the U.S. and the smallest was truly absurd. Anheuser-Busch, the largest brewing company in the country, produced over 22 million barrels of beer per year, dwarfing the next two competitors, Schlitz, which made a little over 15 million, and Pabst, which made 10.5 million. By comparison, in 1969, Peoples Brewing Company had made just 25,033 barrels that year, hardly enough to put a dent into the sales of the big brewers. But that really didn't matter to them. Every beer sold by a small company like Peoples was one less bottle of Budweiser, Schlitz, Pabst or Coors being bought by a thirsty public. And they didn't like that. Each of them wanted to grow and acquire even more market share, even though those four brewers alone already sold 46 percent of the beer in the country by 1970. To make matters worse for Mack, of the 10 biggest breweries in America in 1970, three of them—Schlitz, Pabst, and Miller—were only 90 miles away. While some smaller breweries could count themselves as relatively safe against the big brewers because they were very regional (like Yuengling in Pennsylvania), Peoples had no such advantage. The three big brewers in Milwaukee were unfortunately in the same region as Peoples was, and they had no intention of helping their smaller neighbor out, no matter how noble its cause may have been.

One major front in the beer war these big brewers waged was in the area of marketing. In its first year under the new leadership of Ted Mack, Peoples Brewing Company spent a total of $31,768 on advertising. That amounts to over $200,000 in today's dollars, which is certainly nothing to dismiss for a small brewery. The total included $9,500 for signage that was hung in sales outlets, like taverns and package stores. They spent $5,100 for newspaper advertising, like the ad announcing Peoples' new availability in cans. There was a little over $10,000 in "general advertising," which most likely included everything from logoed pens and stationery, to billboards, shirts, bottle openers and anything else they could slap their name on. Finally, they spent a little over $6,200 on radio and TV, which was the second lowest amount they spent on anything in their budget.[3]

Compare these numbers to the largest brewer in the country, Anheuser-Busch. In 1974, just two years after Peoples had spent the above amounts, the Saint Louis beer goliath spent $17,840,000 on "6-media" advertising (newspapers, magazines, spot radio, network TV, spot TV and billboards). Of that, $10,649,000 was spent on TV alone (over $55 million in 2022 after adjusting for inflation).[4] By these numbers, even the $100,000 Mack had requested from the Board of Directors seemed pointless. It was like an army using bows and arrows against tanks and machine guns. And besides, even if Peoples did ratchet up their advertising and steal away a little market share, the big breweries had still nastier tactics to use. And use them they did.

Mack was at first innocently oblivious to those kinds of strategies—the underhanded kind that wasn't talked about in public. His background was in social work, and despite his years at Pabst, he most likely wasn't privy to the conversations had by upper management behind closed doors. He understood competition, but he could never have imagined how cut-throat it really was among the big brewers, especially when it came to distribution. Instead, he found out the hard way how the big breweries operated when he tried to expand across his own home state of Wisconsin. After months on the road, going from town to town, the only new outlets he was able to secure were a limited number of taverns and stores in Milwaukee, Kenosha, Racine and Madison (plus Peoples' hometown of Oshkosh). That was it—five cities in the entire state. He wondered aloud on more than one occasion why he couldn't get into more than that. But then, on two of those trips, the truth of the situation was revealed to him. On a visit to a liquor store in the northern part of the state, the owner told Mack that he wouldn't be able to sell his beer there because "major companies" were selling to the liquor store at cost. "They make money" the store owner explained, "by getting [people] used to drinking [their beer]."[5]

The combination of cheap beer and an exclusive market was, in effect, freezing smaller breweries out. And likewise, while trying to sell to an outlet in Woods, Wisconsin, Mack was told, "you cannot stand a chance here because [big brewers] are selling [beer] at less than cost."[6] He was stunned. He never could have guessed that selling something as simple as beer could have been so sullied by the corruption he was finding in the towns of America's Midwest. But, as it turned out, this was just one of the common practices the big brewers used. It was also one of the dirty secrets of how they got so big in the first place.

And Peoples wasn't the only brewery experiencing these problems either. In November 1972, Grain Belt Brewing Company in Minneapolis filed an antitrust suit against the two biggest brewers of the time, Anheuser-Busch and Schlitz.[7] In the third quarter of 1971, Grain Belt's earnings were $198,000, but a year later that amount had dropped to only $20,000. They placed the blame on the unfair pricing and marketing tactics of Anheuser-Busch and Schlitz, which, Grain Belt claimed, had hurt its business. The unfair pricing tactics they accused the brewers of were the same ones Mack was discovering in locations around Wisconsin. The large brewers simply reduced the price of the beer to cost or below, not necessarily for the consumers, but for the outlets selling them. The outlets, in such cases, had no incentive to sell other brands when their largest profit was with the bigger ones. And of course, unlike small firms like Grain Belt or Peoples, Anheuser-Busch and Schlitz could survive this cost cutting, at least until there wasn't any more competition to worry about, at which point their prices went up again.

Then in 1976 the big brewers' laundry was more completely laid bare. An ex-agent for the Securities and Exchange Commission (SEC), attorney August Bequai, testified to a U.S. Senate Subcommittee about a three year-long investigation (begun in 1972) into the unfair business practices of the biggest brewers in America, including Anheuser-Busch, Schlitz, Pabst, Miller, and Falstaff among others.[8] The story about the agent's testimony monopolized headlines for months as Congress, the SEC, the Bureau of Alcohol, Tobacco, and Firearms, and the Federal Trade Commission all began investigations into the American beer industry. The meteoric rise in growth for the biggest brewing companies suddenly made a lot more sense after Bequai's revelations were publicized.

One of the first things that the investigation revealed was that price-fixing was indeed a common practice, confirming the experiences had by Peoples and Grain Belt Brewing.

Wholesalers were instructed to sell their product at near cost, cost, or even below cost to ensure that it would get on the shelves while other brands wouldn't. And if other brands did share shelf space, retailers were sure to place those brands at the back of the store and keep them at full price. In a scheme like that it's easy to see why liquor stores, taverns, restaurants and other outlets were only too happy to push certain products while ignoring others. They could also discount the prices to consumers through sales that undercut any of the other brands (those brands that didn't also take part in the same practice, that is).

Such a revelation shouldn't have been a total surprise, either to Congress or the public, as there had been incidences stemming back years. In 1960, for example, a full decade earlier, the Federal Trade Commission (FTC) won a case against Anheuser-Busch for similarly fixing prices. The FTC charged the colossal brewer with lowering the wholesale price of its beer for the St. Louis market, while keeping the price higher in other regions. The U.S. Government called this price discrimination, which had been illegal under federal law going all the way back to 1914 (the Clayton Act, incidentally, the same law that forced Pabst to divest from Blatz).[9]

But while such practices had gone on before, what Bequai was exposing was the extent to which they were taking place at that time. Such pricing schemes left little room for competition, and companies like Peoples Brewing and Grain Belt Brewing were left wondering why they couldn't get any traction in certain regions of the state. It wasn't that consumers didn't want their beer, it was because those consumers just weren't presented with their beer as a choice.

Another common practice, according to Bequai, perhaps the most nefarious, was one that had been invented years before, perfected during Prohibition, and then continued afterwards: payoffs (though the brewers themselves actually called the practice "black bagging,"[10] a name that traces its history to a time when distributors and wholesalers would actually tour beer outlets while carrying a black bag of cash to hand out to the owners). Payoffs were made to distributors and retail outlets to guarantee exclusivity. In return for the bribe, the outlet owner agreed to sell only certain brands of beer, and no others. Bequai noted that military bases, especially Army and Air Force bases, were popular targets for the payoffs, and distributors and big brewers ensured that the servicemen and women only drank the beer they wanted them to drink.

Also important to the brewers were restaurants, hotels and gas stations. Bequai specifically named the hotel chain Holiday Inn as well as the restaurant chains Pizza Hut and Emerson Limited (which ran a number of limited menu restaurants), and the Seven-Eleven convenience stores as all taking payoffs from Schlitz (Schlitz reportedly had a $1 million-dollar fund specifically for such practices).[11] Each business denied these payoffs, of course, but corporate spokesmen also admitted it was ultimately up to each local hotel, restaurant, or store to decide which beers to serve or sell at their locations.

If the local owners or managers were taking bribes and keeping certain beers off their taps, the parent company would never have known. Sometimes, though, even while other beers were available, retailers would only promote the single brand that was paying them off, ensuring that was the one that sold. Ted Mack once claimed to a reporter that "Peoples Beer is one of four beers available at Milwaukee County Stadium, [but] only one is being pushed."[12] This would certainly be in line with the type of black bagging practices Bequai was exposing before Congress.

The distributors and wholesalers were themselves also "taken care of" by the brewers. These people were the ones who actually approached the retail outlets to offer the payoffs in exchange for the exclusivity (at the brewers' directive). Most of these distributors and wholesalers were independent franchisees, and so they were responsible for getting the beer to the stores and bars in their respective distribution areas. Selling cases of beer to a package store at or below cost wouldn't earn them much money, so the breweries compensated the distributors and wholesalers in the form of cash payoffs, loans, or gifts. These gifts were often extravagant and costly, like Rolex watches, and were given under the pretense of "prizes" for top distributors. In other words, distributors and salesmen were handsomely rewarded for the methods they used to make sure only certain beer brands were found in as many outlets—and with as little competition—as possible.

But what if a distributor had a conscience and decided not to "play ball?" Well, then they simply wouldn't be a distributor very much longer. Bequai told the Senate subcommittee about a businessman who owned a Schlitz franchise in Florida. The company ordered the man to make the customary payoffs to a local military base. If that wasn't bad enough, they also directed him to sell his beer at a price close to his cost. Afraid of being prosecuted for the activity he thought was probably illegal, the man refused, and Schlitz, in turn, revoked his franchise. The message was clear, Schlitz didn't have time for distributors who wouldn't help them ensure their market dominance.

After the news broke with Bequai's stories of illegal activities, other distributors with similar tales stepped forward. In Wausau, Wisconsin, a distributor told the newspaper there that he was ordered by a Schlitz executive to cut the price of beer he was selling to a racetrack by a dime a case. Schlitz promised to reimburse him if he carried out the directive, but like the franchisee in Florida, the Wausau distributor refused to make any bribes or to unfairly undercut the competition. And so subsequently, also like the franchisee in Florida, he had his license pulled by Schlitz.[13]

All of this activity was, of course, quite illegal and broke a number of different laws. Due to the bribes and payoffs, the big brewers were foremost in violation of the Federal Alcohol Administration Act, which forbade such exclusive sales arrangements. And while there were the more obvious schemes, like the cash bribes paid to restaurants and taverns (most of them against the law), these bribes sometimes took different forms. Miller, for example, was found to violate the law when it paid $100,000 in advertising costs in exchange for gaining exclusive accounts in Chicago. For this they were fined and paid $20,000, though they still denied any wrongdoing.[14]

The FTC, meanwhile, also made it illegal to engage in predatory pricing for the purpose of knocking competition out of the market (which was the sole reason for offering to sell beer at cost). This was the catalyst for Grain Belt's lawsuit against Anheuser-Busch and Schlitz. Of the two, Schlitz settled with Grain Belt, paying them a $375,000 settlement. Anheuser-Busch was also sued by Canadian Ace Brewing Company for much the same reason in 1977, while Miller and Schlitz were sued in 1977 by three San Francisco brewers for illegally discounting prices to hurt their business. And in addition to federal actions, there were also different state laws that regulated discount pricing, the revocation of franchises, the payoffs and other activities, many of which the big brewers found themselves in violation of.

The investigations of Bequai also brought about a number of federal charges, not just lawsuits, for many of the large brewers, the biggest of those (once again) being Anheuser-Busch. The SEC accused the beer giant of making payoffs amounting to $2.7 million over a two-year period, from 1971 to 1973. Before the case could be resolved in court, however, Anheuser-Busch negotiated a settlement for $750,000 and escaped penalties.

Another of the largest of cases was against Schlitz, Peoples' next-door neighbor. The company with "The Beer that made Milwaukee famous" was charged with making extravagant bribes and payoffs totaling at least $3 million. The Securities and Exchange Commission additionally slapped charges of tax fraud on top of the bribery charges because of the complicated scheme that Schlitz used to launder payoff money through distributors and wholesalers (trying to avoid a direct connection to them). Unlike any of the others, Schlitz initially fought the charges, appearing in court to dispute the U.S. Government's case, but eventually, like Anheuser-Busch, agreed to an out of court settlement of over $760,000. Ultimately though, the SEC, the FTC and the ATF had all determined that there was enough evidence to prosecute many of America's biggest breweries for unfair practices that put competition—especially smaller brewers—out of business.

This was the environment in which Mack had unwittingly decided to make his stand for civil rights. Not only was he woefully outgunned and outspent when it came to advertising and marketing, but he also stood no chance against competitors who were willing to break the law and at the same time actually lose money to put him out of business.

Companies like Anheuser-Busch and Schlitz could nonchalantly spend upwards of $3 million dollars just in bribes to make sure their products, and not Mack's, ended up on the shelves of liquor stores and the taps of taverns. When found out, they simply did a *mea culpa* and wrote a check. Big checks to be sure, after all, $750,000 in 1975 amounts to about $3.5 million dollars in 2022, but that was only slightly more than they had budgeted to actually pay people off, so they were definitely willing to lose that kind of money in the first place. Perhaps more perturbing is the realization that the fines they paid–$760,000 and $750,000 for Schlitz and Anheuser-Busch, respectively—were almost double what Ted Mack had actually paid for his entire brewing company. They could literally buy his company for the simple cost of reconciling their own criminal activity.

For better or for worse, Mack was unaware of most of this. While the SEC was behind the scenes investigating big beer, he actually had direct experiences with liquor store owners who were bought off, either through bribes, price-fixing, or both. But other than the isolated events he ran into while trying to sell his own product, he knew nothing about how crooked the big brewers really were. He was still, in all respects, a pragmatist. He had counted on the black community, and they had let him down in spectacular fashion. He had banked on expanding throughout his home state of Wisconsin, but big beer had made that path likewise very difficult and his expansion was stuttering to a stop by the middle of 1972.

It was time, he decided, to turn towards the one trump card they had. They were themselves, after all, black. And when they visited the Small Business Administration in Milwaukee back in 1970, the administrators there had practically fallen over themselves to get Ted Mack, Henry Crosby and the rest signed to a loan, gushing about the federal program call Section 8(a) and promising the businessmen that there would be a lucrative future for Peoples Beer, simply because they were black. They were told they wouldn't need to compete with other businesses for government contracts, because the contracts were theirs for the taking. This was a guarantee by the U.S. government, by the U.S. president himself, all they had to do was find a program, agency or department that bought beer and the brewery would be saved. As it turned out, it was not nearly as easy as the SBA had made it out to be. In fact, it was impossible.

11

Government Contracts

When he first talked to the officials at the SBA in Milwaukee about getting a loan to purchase the Peoples Brewing Company back in early 1970, Mack was struck by how enthusiastic the loan officer had been about their loan. He told Mack that he'd "come in at the right time now because the federal government is really going to push minorities getting contracts."

This stunned Mack, who at first had no idea what the man was talking about. But the SBA officer continued, specifically bringing up their situation and suggesting how favorable circumstances would be for them, saying they'd be eligible for Section 8(a) contracts, where (as he later recounted to Congressmen) "you will not have to go and compete with the big companies, this is kind of a set-aside thing over here that you will not have to fight for." Neither he nor his associates had expected this bit of news when they walked into the office that day, but as the official kept talking, their own enthusiasm began to grow. "You mean I am going to get government contracts?" Mack asked, a bit incredulously.

"Yep" the official replied, "you should be able to get that also, so it is all written down from the President of the United States and the Congress...."[1]

Ted Mack, Henry Crosby and the others had just gone to see about getting help to buy the 60-year-old brewery, but now their imaginations were swimming with the success that could be (but, sadly, would never actually turn out to be).

The contract program that the official was referring to, the Section 8(a) contract program as it was called in the SBA, was fairly new; however, its roots can be traced back to 1941 when Franklin Roosevelt required federal agencies to forbid defense contractors from discriminating on the basis of "race, creed, color, or national origin."[2] The first official version of the program was instituted by the Johnson administration in the late 1960s. In this first form, the program provided incentives to businesses willing to open in urban areas and employ members of minorities, or, alternatively, it provided financial assistance directly to minority-owned businesses. In either case, the program didn't require the businesses actually be minority owned, but that changed in 1970.

In the year that Mack and the others decided to pursue the purchase of the brewery, the Nixon administration, as part of the president's black capitalism agenda, mandated that the Section 8(a) program be used specifically to "assist small concerns owned by disadvantaged persons to become self-sufficient, viable businesses capable of competing in the marketplace."[3] The way it assisted those small concerns was by helping them get federal government contracts, either through set-aside or sole-source awards.

A set-aside award is a contract for which only other minority-owned businesses are competing (therefore, only small businesses that wouldn't otherwise have the chance when competing with larger, more established contactors). Sole-source awards were given directly to a small, minority-owned business without any competition at all. Either prospect would be a boon to whoever got the award. Another important item that 8(a) businesses were eligible for was assistance, technical and managerial assistance to be exact. When requested, the SBA was to aid the Section 8(a) organization by dispatching experts to help train them to run more effectively and efficiently.

All these things should have been made available to Peoples. They were promised by the loan officer, by the Small Business Administration, and by the President himself. The problem, though, was that nobody really knew how to carry out the details of the Section 8(a) and make those promises a reality, at least not in Milwaukee anyway. Although he didn't start looking for help from the SBA until well into 1972, Mack quickly found himself facing a legion of bureaucrats who themselves didn't understand how to administer Section 8(a) assistance. They didn't know where he might go to look for contracts, set-aside or sole-sourced, and they also didn't know how to provide the technical or administrative assistance and training they had offered him.

Frustrated, unable to get help locally, Mack hammered out a flurry of letters to anyone and everyone he thought might be able to help him. By the end of May his letters had reached the U.S. Senator for Wisconsin, Gaylord Nelson, the director of the 8(a) program for the SBA in Chicago, Edward Goodbout, and the director of the Milwaukee Field Office for the Department of Commerce, David Howe, among others. The letters all had the same purpose, to plead for help in finding the opportunities he'd already been promised.

In his letters, Mack gave his readers the history of Peoples Brewing Company, a chronicle of the terrible struggle they went through to purchase it, and an explanation about how he became the company's president. He made special note of the fact that after their purchase of Peoples, the company became "the first minority-controlled brewery in the United States." Mack also expounded on their accomplishments to date, describing, almost like a proud father, the success they'd had at growing their sales and gaining entry into new cities and towns throughout Wisconsin, Indiana, and even Illinois. After he'd finished making clear to the readers that Peoples was succeeding despite the many obstacles they were facing, he then got to the point.

> When the group, headed by Mr. Mack, was negotiating for the company, many government agencies informed them that since this would be the first minority controlled brewery in the United States, that the federal government and related agencies would be able to purchase all the beer that the Peoples Brewing Company would be able to produce. The group did not wish that the federal government and related agencies would have the responsibility of buying all their products, however, we are appalled of the fact that we have been unable to receive any contracts from federal government or any related agencies. We are writing you, hoping that you will be able to help us in this endeavor.[4]

The letters had their desired effect. They motivated people to action, and by early June, federal employees in Washington, D.C., and elsewhere were trying to figure out how they could help Peoples Brewing Company get the opportunities they'd been promised. Senator Nelson's office contacted the Congressional Research Service of the Library of Congress to find out about training grants available to Peoples. They replied by sending a list of grants the Office of Economic Opportunity could provide as well as the phone numbers for different directors who might be able to help.

The U.S. Department of Labor similarly responded to a request from Nelson and suggested one of their officials would be happy to meet directly with Peoples leadership in Washington to discuss training they might provide funds for. Neither one of these responses was really very helpful to a cash-strapped company that was just barely holding on. Though Mack had requested them, he really didn't need grants to help train them, at least not right now. What the increasingly anxious brewery president needed was sales.

The bottom line was that he needed to move his product, and the best way to do that was through the different contracts that the 8(a) program highlighted as its central benefit. But what government agencies or departments would be interested in purchasing the one product that Peoples Brewing Company sold? Both Theodore Mack and Edward Goodbout, the 8(a) program director out of Chicago, came to the same answer—the military.

When Ted Mack served in the U.S. Army as a youth, he most likely

11. Government Contracts

took away a valuable lesson—soldiers drank beer. A lot of beer. Not only soldiers though, but also sailors, airmen and marines. The military as a whole had been kept lubricated with lagers and ales sold across the country (and world) in officer and enlisted clubs, and in post (or base) exchanges (the military's version of department stores) since the end of the prohibition on beer in 1933. In that year, the sale and consumption of beer with 3.2 percent alcohol by volume (or lower) was approved for all military branches, and it proved to be a very popular policy judging from the income generated from sales of beer on Army, Air Force, Navy and Marine bases. In the 1973 fiscal year alone, the combined domestic sales of alcohol from the military's 476 post exchanges in the continental U.S. amounted to over $386 million dollars.[5]

"Alcohol" sales included both beer and spirits, but of the two, beer was definitely more popular. So much so in fact, that in late 1970, in an attempt to increase recruitment to the soon to be volunteer Army, U.S. Army Chief of Staff General William Westmoreland issued Defense Directive Number 1330.15, changing the drinking policies of domestic Army bases.[6] These new policies allowed soldiers to drink beer in their barracks and in the mess hall with meals (prior to that, military personnel could only drink in off-base housing). This, subsequently, increased beer sales even more. If Peoples was going to sell its product to the U.S. Government, it would have to be to military bases.

In mid–July, Goodbout penned letters on behalf of Peoples to the directors of the exchange services divisions for the U.S. Army, the U.S. Air Force, and the U.S. Marines. In each, Goodbout introduced the reader to the SBA's 8(a) program, saying that it is a "vehicle" to "open the doors of the government contracting opportunities to those Americans, who because of their ethnic origin, are unlikely or unable to participate in the Federal Government's multi-billion dollar a year procurement program."[7] He then discussed Peoples Brewing Company, saying they were being considered for the program because of "the owner's ethnic origin" which caused the company to be denied "access to the avenues which would provide for the realization of its potential." Goodbout then vouched for Peoples' "managerial and technical abilities" as well as their "expertise" as a "most capable brewer." Finally, he stated that "it would be greatly appreciated by this office if you would conduct a requirement search in your Agency to determine if there exist any opportunities which would lend themselves to The People's Brewing Company."

The appeals were significant—Ted Mack had the director of one of the most important civil rights-based programs in the Small Business Administration directly vouching for his company's ability and asking for opportunities on his behalf. The letters were sincere and heartfelt, and

Goodbout's tone is one of genuine concern for Peoples' and its future. They were also, unfortunately, completely pointless.

Mack had already heard the bad news a month earlier. One of the letters he wrote was sent to David Howe, director of the Milwaukee Field Office for the Department of Commerce. Howe, in turn, sent a memo to John Jenkins, the director of the Office of Minority Business Enterprise (OMBE) for the Department of Commerce, concerning the fact that Peoples had not been invited to bid for "the sale of beer in cans or bottle to the various Post Exchanges or Ship Stores." Following receipt of the memo, Jenkins directed his office to investigate this troubling problem. Unfortunately, "investigate" was about all they could do.

The OMBE was created as part of Nixon's black capitalism agenda. The mission outlined for the new agency was to directly help minority-owned businesses and potential minority business owners, but since its inception it ran up against one obstacle after another. For starters it was perceived by those in the SBA as competition. After all, the goals of the Section 8(a) and other programs were very similar, and so they felt the OMBE was a threat for resources, and besides, the OMBE overlapped their own authority. Also, the agency had little to no budget to speak of, and so its "assistance" was limited to education, training programs, and research.[8]

And in their research, Jenkins' staff found out that there were no formal bid mechanisms to sell to military outlets, including post exchanges, ship stores or on-base recreation clubs. In other words, the 8(a) program was completely useless for helping The Peoples Brewing Company, or any brewing company for that matter, especially as it came to the military. To make matters worse—something neither Jenkins, Goodbout or Ted knew—was that the 8(a) program (or any set aside) was particularly unpopular among military procurement officers. Such programs were deemed inefficient because they were thought to end up costing more, thus depleting their budgets, and were more complicated to carry out, thus taking more time and effort.[9] There was little chance that procurement officers would feel sympathy for Peoples' cause and lend their assistance.

Still, after delivering this devastating news in their letter, the OMBE encouraged Mack to "personally contact several of the large military installations in your present market area (preferably those installations which are located in areas where your product sales are strong)."[10] They also suggested he personally contact the base procurement officers to find out about perhaps getting his product on the PX shelves on a trial basis to demonstrate demand. In other words, the government agencies that had promised him the moon only a few years earlier were admitting they couldn't help him at all, he'd have to do it himself.

More letters, all with similarly crushing news, would later find their way to Goodbout, who then forwarded them on to Mack. A letter from the director of the Army and Air Force Exchange Services (AAFES) told Goodbout that the exchange service on Army and Air Force bases "is not affected by Section 8(a) of the Small Business Act." Beer, he explained, "is bought and sold based on customer preference," and that while each of the five exchange regions in the U.S. is free to purchase any beer they prefer, there are limits to the number of brands they can carry and "consumer demand and brand preference are the primary considerations."[11]

A letter from the director of the Marine Corps Exchange Service likewise relayed the same bad news. While confirming that their exchanges "do buy and sell a significant amount of beer," he also informed Goodbout that they are "self-sustaining retail businesses that restrict procurement to those items which have an acceptable level of customer demand to warrant stocking the item." As in previous letters, the Marine Corps Exchange Service Director recommended that Ted "distribute to the exchanges on the attached list, both domestic and overseas, descriptive literature, prices, discount terms, shipping data, and other pertinent information." He was also quick to tell Goodbout that if contacting the exchanges, it shouldn't be implied his letter was an endorsement. However, he also made sure to write that the opportunity to "assist small and/or minority-owned businesses ... is appreciated."[12]

Through late July and into August, letters with the same news were delivered, each one dropping like a hammer on a bell, tolling its way to the end of Mack's dream. On August 9 the Small Business Administration office in Chicago delivered two letters to him from the military which simply stated that "it appears that the 8(a) program may not be able to help you directly."[13] On August 31 he received one from the SBA in Milwaukee explaining that "beer and other like items which are purchased by these exchanges are purchased with non-appropriated funds and therefore are not subject to regular Armed Services procurement regulations." Again, though, the letter writer (Earl L. Knuth, the Acting Branch Manager) was sure to say that "any reputable firm may offer merchandise or services to the exchange service; however, each of these exchanges must be contacted on an individual basics [sic]."[14]

There was little chance of that happening though, despite the kind encouragement they gave. There would have been at least some hope that Peoples might sell to military bases had it not been for the caveat requiring a "demonstrated demand" for the product. This single rule all but eliminated any regional brewer from competing for distribution to post exchanges or base recreational facilities. The exchanges only wanted beer on the shelves that consumers were already familiar with because these brands would sell; little else mattered.

The few brewers that could hope to compete, like Anheuser-Busch, Schlitz, Pabst and Miller, were those that were also large enough to make people familiar with their product throughout the country. These companies spent millions upon millions every year on advertising and marketing, inundating customers with an endless stream of radio spots and television commercials, billboards, sponsorships, and magazine and newspapers ads. For a brewery like Peoples, it was simply too expensive to try to compete with them. If it came down to brand recognition, The Peoples Brewing Company would never make it to the shelves.

But still another problem that kept most regional brewers out of the exchanges was the amount of corruption rampant in beer sales on military bases in those years. This was pointed out by the SEC agent, August Bequai, who began investigating that corruption in 1972. He never said why it occurred so frequently on military bases, perhaps it was because the large brewers knew the potential for sales that military bases represented, but he did say during Congressional testimony that they were particularly wracked with payoffs, bribes and unfair pricing. According to his testimony, it wasn't just those brands that were familiar to consumers that made it to taps and shelves in post exchanges, it was those willing to grease the palms of the post exchange managers.

Some, if not most, of the government officials who contacted Mack must have known this. In 1971 the U.S. Senate had completed an investigation into the "fraud and corruption in management of military club systems."[15] While focusing on military clubs run in Vietnam, the report indicated widespread corruption in the form of kickbacks and price fixing—all of those things SEC agent Bequai had exposed in the beer industry. Uncovered was a particular story about a large Canadian brewery called Carling, which supplied its Saigon, Vietnam-based distributor with a "promotional" allowance of $5,000 per month. The money, according to a brewery spokesman who testified to Congressional investigators was supposed to be used for marketing, but instead was used to provide kickbacks to PX managers in return for stocking Carling beer.[16]

If Mack had more time, considering how good of a salesman he was, maybe he could have figured out how to get onto one or two of the bases with Peoples. But time was quickly running out for him and his company, and he certainly didn't have the economic resources (or moral flexibility) of the big brewers to provide the kickbacks required. Months before the disappointing letters about beer procurement on bases started tumbling in, Peoples had run out of the cash netted from the initial sale of stock. By the end of the summer of 1972, they were scraping by, month by month. They were behind on payments and taxes, and they were desperately searching for new ways to quickly earn money. The distributorships they'd

11. Government Contracts

opened around the state, not to mention those in Indiana and Chicago, were also a constant drain on their accounts as the expenses from fuel, auto services, and salaries for salesmen never let up. It might have been cold comfort for Mack to know that he wasn't alone, there were plenty of other breweries in the exact same uncomfortable position as Peoples.

Between 1970 and 1975, 37 other small breweries shuttered.[17] Of those, at least eight closed in 1972 alone. Small companies like Fitger's Brewery, Maier Brewing Company, and Iriquois and Potosi Brewing had been under pressure from the larger breweries for decades before finally folding. But it wasn't just the modest breweries. Larger brewers, too, like Associated, Ballantine and Dubois Brewing, all succumbed to big beer as well. Frankly, when it came to the economics of beer, size really didn't matter that much. Neither, as it turned out, did age, tradition, or even location. Fitger's Brewing Company, for example, opened in Duluth, Minnesota, in 1881, while the Maier Brewing Company started brewing German lagers in Los Angeles in 1874. These breweries, while never growing past the crowded regions they were founded in, were still steeped in tradition and had loyal followings in their respective hometowns. But that mattered little to the realities of the cut-throat beer business, and, ultimately, they were both memories by the end of 1972.

The surprising closures, though, were the larger ones, especially that of Ballantine. The P. Ballantine and Sons Brewing Company was founded in Newark, New Jersey, in 1840, making it one of the oldest breweries in the nation in 1972. It was also, at one time, one of the biggest breweries, becoming the third largest in the U.S by the mid–1950s. Those were the halcyon days for Ballantine, when they were a powerful company that churned out some of the best and most sought-after beer in America. For a moment they were even a nationwide icon, a result of being the first television sponsor for the New York Yankees. But even they couldn't compete with the distribution, the production capacity, and the marketing budgets of their even bigger rivals.

And neither could Peoples. Mack knew it. He must have seen the writing on the wall by the beginning of that autumn. He probably knew that it was only a matter of time before the brewery he'd put so much of his life into would also fold. The maddening thing is that it shouldn't. There was no reason why his venture should fail. They were so careful. They were so measured. If only they'd been able to get the Army contracts, things would have worked out differently. If only they'd been able to get what they were promised.

And to Ted Mack, that was the sticking point. They were promised something by the Small Business Administration that day back in 1970 when they went in to talk about a loan. They were promised that the federal government would help them, that they needn't worry about finding customers. "The Government would buy all the beer you can make," they were assured. And now, after they'd sacrificed and put their financial futures on the line, they were told "sorry, we can't help." This was the final injustice for Mack, Crosby, Alexander and the rest. They'd had enough.

They'd sat quietly on their hands while the Blatz brewery was taken from them, and now they were expected to again watch silently as The Peoples Brewing Company was slowly falling apart, lurching toward failure like Fitger's, Maiers and Ballantine? Considering the alternative, which was bankruptcy, it really didn't take much to move them to the only action they could think of taking. And after the arrival of just one more piece of bad news, they made up their minds pretty quickly. They were going to sue.

12

Grasping at Straws

It was in early October when the IRS informed Peoples that they owed the government $35,809 and that they had filed a tax lien against them. According to the Treasury Department, Peoples hadn't paid excise taxes on their beer, or Social Security taxes on employee wages, since the beginning of the year.[1] To Mack and the others, getting this news wasn't just disappointing, it must have been downright insulting. After spending much of the year begging the Small Business Administration for help, they were now being accused of not paying their fair share. The punishment was an audit, a tax lien, and worse if they couldn't come up with the funds that were owed. But what punishment was there for the men in Washington who promised them help with contracts?

After trusting the U.S. Government, with all their stated commitments about helping minority businesses, Mack must have come to the conclusion they were completely useless when it actually came to helping those businesses. What made it worse was that they invested their money based on what the sharply dressed men at the SBA had promised. Mack himself had spent tens of thousands of dollars on stock in Peoples, plus tens of thousands in an initial loan, and then there were the personal sacrifices he and his family had gone through to leave their home and jobs to move to a town known for its hostility towards people like them.

But more than their sacrifices of money, time, and labor, there was also the sad fact that they got others to invest their savings as well. People who'd never invested in anything before, who had little money to invest in the first place, put their trust in Mack and the dream of a black-owned brewery that had been sold to them. Ted Mack, Henry Crosby, Ray Alexander, the stockholders: they were owed more than a "sorry" and a tax bill, they were owed what they were promised, and a lawsuit looked like the only way they could collect.

After receiving the notice, Mack and the directors made the painful choice to shut down production at the brewery. After 60 years of use, the brew kettle at the People Brewing Company sat cold and empty. No wort was boiling and no batch of brew was waiting to be hopped. They continued bottling, distributing and selling existing beer (of which they had a lot), but according to Mack there would be nothing new produced by Peoples until the government started making good on the promises it had made them.[2] It could be argued that by halting any new brewing they were merely saving on supplies and labor. But at the same time, they were also making a statement: they would rather end an Oshkosh legacy than comply with a system they now saw as corrupt.

Shortly after ending production, they gathered for a hastily called meeting to talk about their future and make some important decisions about their path going forward. On October 22, Henry Crosby sketched out the details of the discussion between Mack, the directors of Peoples Brewing Company, and representatives from the law office of Edward S. Levin. In a hand-written note, with "Peoples Vs. U.S." penned across the top of the half-torn sheet of paper, Crosby made of list of the points they would be using in their lawsuit:

1. Segregation
2. Discrimination
3. Aiding + abetting lessening of competition
4. Breach of contracts[3]

Not only was this a glimpse into their strategy going into the impending legal battle with the Small Business Administration, but it was also a glimpse into what they saw as the causes behind their own failure. The list suggested the government had not only let them down, but they had discriminated against them and had been an active agent in the whole fiasco.

Based off the company's prospectus and stated mission, to Mack and the directors, the purchase of the brewery had always been about something more. It had been about demonstrating to the black community that they too could own American industry. It was about showing black people that they were every bit as good as white people when it came to conducting business. Black people *could* enter the treasured "corporate structure" of America. The purchase of Peoples was all about giving hope to an oppressed people. But now, with the realization that their own government had driven them to ruin, the entire enterprise took on a new dimension.

Now it was about fighting for their basic right to conduct business, any business, in America. The directors of Peoples Brewing Company, including Theodore Mack, had been of the older, more mature guard of civil rights activists. Unlike the younger crowd that followed them, they believed in fighting oppression through legal action in the courts, not by physical action in the streets. Thus, this response, a lawsuit against their own government, must have seemed the natural one to be pursued by the Peoples' leadership.

The attorneys they chose to represent them in their lawsuit included Edward S. Levin himself, Heiner Giese, and Lloyd A. Barbee. Choosing this group was especially significant because of Lloyd Barbee's participation. Barbee was one of the organizers of Milwaukee Public School bussing boycotts of the early 1960s. These were participated in by activists from different civil rights–based organizations, including CORE, of which Theodore Mack was an active member. Barbee had plenty of experience in civil rights litigation too, especially where it concerned governmental organizations. In 1965 he filed a federal lawsuit against the City of Milwaukee and the Milwaukee Public Schools. That case would be won in 1977, but by late 1972 he was still in the midst of the long, grinding battle to end de facto segregation in Milwaukee schools. The addition of Barbee meant that they viewed the primary issue in the lawsuit as civil rights.

On November 10, a newspaper article revealed that Peoples had stopped production and that they'd had the tax lien levied against them. The reporter tried to talk to Mack about the state of the brewery, but he refused to comment. A secretary, though, told the reporter that he would be giving a press conference the following week at a tavern next door to the brewery. Aside from the tax lien and the news about the halt in production, the article also revealed that Peoples Brewing Company had filed a $100 million dollar lawsuit against the Small Business Administration and the Department of Defense, claiming they'd been denied the fair chance of selling to the armed forces.[4]

The press conference held on November 14 didn't reveal much more. Mack confirmed that production at the brewery had been shut down, but that they were still delivering existing stock. Before production halted, Peoples had 30 regular and part-time employees, but they'd all been laid off except for five delivery drivers. The brewery also had no plans of opening back up anytime soon. The company would remain shut down, Mack said, with a stubborn resolution, "until the Federal Government and the Small Business Administration makes good on its promises to give us a fair proportion of government contracts."[5] He likewise confirmed the lawsuit and said it was intended to force the government into honoring their promises. As to the tax lien of over $35,000? Here, Mack, simply shrugged, telling reporters, "I guess they won't get it until we get ours."[6]

His response isn't at all surprising. In truth, after fighting an uphill battle for the last two years against racism, big beer, regional apathy, the Small Business Administration, and the Department of Defense, Ted Mack was understandably bitter. As a 40-year-old black man from the Jim Crow South, he'd achieved an almost unimaginable dream by becoming the president, and major shareholder, of a long-standing, regional corporation in Wisconsin. But now, at 42, he was about to lose it all. It'd be hard to blame him for his bitterness, or even for downright anger. And on occasion, as he demonstrated in the press conference back on 14th, 1970, those feelings could flare up and reveal themselves, just as they had at other times.

When bigots in Oshkosh got the local residents and taverns to boycott Peoples Brewing Company after he and the others bought it, he challenged them to support the brewery, saying that if they didn't, it would be a black eye on Oshkosh and the entire region, not on him. Likewise, when he felt the black community in Milwaukee wasn't doing its part, wasn't buying their beer, he called them out too, telling reporters that "you have over 100,000 Black people saying we want to do our thing, and when you give them this opportunity, they don't respond."[7] His bitterness, disappointment, and anger were on full display in these episodes. But now it was Milwaukee's turn.

In late November one of Mack's childhood friends named Fred D. Gray was passing through the Milwaukee area on a business trip when he decided to stop to see the embattled president of Peoples. Gray was an accomplished attorney and civil rights activist, and one of the first black lawmakers elected to the state legislature in their home state of Alabama. He had defended Rosa Parks and Martin Luther King, Jr. (among many others), and was at that time leading the lawsuit against the U.S. Public Health Service for their Tuskegee experiments on black men during the Great Depression (the case would define how government-sponsored research, indeed all clinical research in the U.S., was conducted from that point on).

Needless to say, Gray was very accomplished. And so Mack took no time in organizing a quick press conference to put him in front of reporters, telling them that his friend was "a fellow Alabaman coming to Wisconsin asking me to come home."[8] He then told reporters he'd be visiting Alabama in the next ten days, and added "I don't run around the country unless I mean business."

Gray told reporters he'd introduced a bill into the state legislature that would allow brewing in Alabama and that he was interested in his friend's brewery. He also told them that "if things don't go here as well as [Ted] would like, we would be interested in getting his brewery there." At this Mack suddenly acted coy, demurring and saying that the lawsuit against the government came first, so they'd be staying at least until that had been settled. But he left hanging what might happen after the lawsuit had concluded.

The entire episode—from calling the press conference to trotting

12. Grasping at Straws

Gray out in front of the cameras—was simply Mack's way of calling out the entire region for what he must have perceived as their failure to support his brewery. After all, it was implied that Peoples Brewing Company could just as easily make beer in Alabama as it could in Oshkosh. And in Alabama, as he was smugly attempting to demonstrate to the reporters, he had important friends. His threat was clear: support us or we'll leave. What wasn't clear was the kind of support he was expecting. What did he hope to gain by the press conference? A reporter even suggested that his financial situation, which he told them was the federal government's fault because they refused to award Peoples any contracts, wouldn't really be improved by moving. To this point Mack really didn't have an answer. In the end, his threat really didn't seem all that alarming. It was made even less so when Gray actually admitted he didn't come through town on official business, but was instead only there because he wanted to see his friend. It must have been a bit embarrassing to witness.

But frankly, Mack had sad few options left and he knew it. Moving to Alabama really wasn't even a viable strategy (after all, the Peoples' Board of Directors and all of its investors lived in Wisconsin), but he was desperate to find a way to keep the corporate structure he fought so hard to gain. And as he was looking for a solution, a man named Darwin W. Bolden stepped in and gave him the briefest moment of hope.

Bolden was a Yale Law School graduate and former director of the Interracial Council for Business Opportunity, which provided technical and managerial advice and information to minority-owned businesses around the United States. Before that position he had worked for three years in the international business sector in East Africa. Now he was the director of the Pan African Business Information Center (or PanAf), which had just opened as a "capital resource agency for minority owned companies interested in export/import operations or engaging in joint ventures with the African, Caribbean, or Central American countries."[9] To fulfill these duties, PanAf provided four different types of services to minority-owned businesses in the U.S., including counseling services, information services, brokerage services and capital assistance.

Ray Alexander, one of the directors of the Peoples Brewing Company, a close friend of Mack, and the executive director of the Afro Urban Institute in Milwaukee, had received a letter from PanAf attempting to solicit help from the institute. Bolden hoped that Alexander could spread the word about PanAf to local, minority-owned businesses in and around the Milwaukee area. He was especially interested, he wrote, in "entrepreneurs … who may be interested in off-shore operations."[10] Alexander most likely forwarded the letter to Mack and the other directors. Short of opportunities, Mack reached out to Bolden, and within no time he was on his way to Nigeria in the hopes of forming the Peoples Brewing Company in Africa.

For much of its modern history the beer industry in Nigeria was dominated by a single corporate conglomerate called Nigerian Breweries, which was formed by six of the largest import companies on the African continent in 1945 (most of them importing beer). With Heineken as its brewing advisor, Nigerian Breweries began producing a light lager in Lagos, the country's largest city, in 1949. It expanded with breweries at two more cities by 1963 and was one of the largest corporations in the country by 1971. In 1962 it was joined in Lagos by the Guinness Brewery, and together the two companies supplied most of the domestically made beer to a very thirsty Nigeria for decades. In 1971 the beer production of the country was over 24 million gallons,[11] produced by only the two major breweries.

Further, according to the World Health Organization (WHO) Global Alcohol Database, beer consumption in Africa was generally on the rise during the 1960s.[12] Both of these, a limited number of competitors and a rising trend in consumption, were pretty clear reasons for native entrepreneurs to begin looking into opening their own brewing companies. For Mack and the Peoples Brewing Company, the entrepreneurs in question were located in Ogbomosho, a small, rural city in south-western Nigeria.

A weary Ted Mack landed in Lagos, Nigeria, on January 10, 1973, two days after he left the U.S. Meeting him at the airport was a police commander who escorted him 81 miles to the city of Ibadin. There they met Prince Oladunni Oyewumi, who accompanied them another 67 miles further until they arrived in Ogbomosho on January 12.[13] The trip could not have been an easy one to make. Aside from the extended travel time it took to get to Lagos by plane in 1973, travel in the country itself would have been pretty difficult too. Most of the roads were unpaved and dangerous, there was little of the modern infrastructure Mack was used to, and the area was quite rural. Ogbomosho did have a local water plant and electricity, but they were available to only select locations in the region, and most homes in the city had neither luxury.

Prince Oladunni Oyewumi was a local leader born into a traditional royal family. Though Nigeria had (and has) a democratically elected government, they recognized local influencers and leadership systems in small towns and villages throughout the country (a custom still carried on today). These people don't rule, per se, but were and are instead local notables who help lead the populations in the regions in which they reside. The positions and roles are taken very seriously, and they are looked up to as powerful people in the areas they influence. Oyewumi was a businessman who owned an import/export business, local hotels, and stores. He was also part of a group called the Ogbomosho Investment Club, which was populated by fellow local, wealthy (by Nigerian standards) entrepreneurs looking for regional economic opportunities. Another member of the group with whom Mack met was Chief Ayantayo Ayandele. The meetings were held at Ayandele's house between Ted Mack, Oyewumi, and the other members of the club. In no time at all they had agreed on a grand plan to create The Peoples Brewery of Nigeria, Limited, a brewing company co-owned by the Nigerian investors and the owners of the Peoples Brewing Company in Oshkosh.

The operation was going to be substantial for the region, but not by the standards of Mack's competitors back home. Instead of what would be a modern brewery in the U.S., capable of well over a million barrels per year, they planned for a 200,000 barrel per year brewery at a cost of approximately $8 million dollars (U.S.). The money would be raised through the sale of stock and investment by notable residents of the region and beyond. Ted Mack personally inspected the available infrastructure, from the water to the power supply, and signed off on their quality and availability (in only a matter of a few short days). The whirlwind tour ended with a memo of understanding between the Peoples Brewing Company and the Ogbomosho Investment Club, signed by both Mack and Ayandele. The Ogbomosho businessmen would primarily take responsibility for investigating the legal requirements and investment strategies. Mack, meanwhile, would await correspondence from them to start necessary planning from his end in the U.S.

That's what he told them anyway. In truth, nothing real would ever come from any of this. Mack was back in Milwaukee by the end of January, writing a letter to the stockholders to fill them in on the latest developments from the failing brewery. In the letter he mentioned the Nigeria trip, telling readers that "at this time The Peoples Brewing Company is not in a position to reveal what transpired there."[14] Probably because it all amounted to nothing. When he'd left in early January, he certainly had hope that something would eventually come from the trip and the connections he was going to make, but those hopes must have quickly faded once he saw the state of the country he was supposed to do business with. It was rural, dusty, and lacking basic infrastructure. Most of all, it seemed, absolutely lawless. Nigeria had ended a thirty-month civil war only the year before, and that had left well over a million people dead, while millions more were mired in desperate poverty. To add to this, Idi Amin and the army of Uganda overthrew the democratically elected president of that country and established Amin himself as leader. The region itself was, it seemed, in a constant state of turmoil.

All of this must have worried the already worried Ted Mack, and while he was frantic to find a way to save his flailing company, he probably wasn't ready to uproot his family again (this time to internationally displace them), and go to an unstable and poverty-stricken land thousands of miles away. Eventually the plan was dropped and never mentioned again. Mack was back where he started, in Oshkosh with a cold brew kettle, a failing company, and a lot of debt.

13

Last Ditch Efforts

The reason Mack wrote the January letter to the company's stockholders was to provide the latest news about Peoples, and the news was all bad. The brewery had stopped production, the company was in the midst of a lawsuit with the federal government, and the loan they had secured from the Marshall & Ilsley Bank had just reverted to the Small Business Administration due to lack of payment. Mack placed the fault for these calamities on the government. The letter told stockholders it was because the Department of Defense refused to provide contracts and opportunities to Peoples; no other reason.

The year before, the letter to stockholders had briefly discussed a loss in business but it had blamed it on the cost of expansion, the purchase of new equipment, and the small, racist boycott in Oshkosh. There was no mention at all of government contracts or any pursuit to gain them. This letter suggested there had been a two-year ordeal that led to the mess they were in. If that was true it must have come as a surprise to those reading the letter.

The letter also called for the annual stockholder's meeting for February 20 at Jabber's Bar next to the brewery. They couldn't meet at the brewery itself because the power was off in all of its buildings and Oshkosh was bone-chillingly cold in February. Only 20 stockholders of the hundreds who actually owned stock bothered to show up. Once there they heard Mack repeat much of what he'd already told them in the letter because he really had few other updates to give them. He spoke at length about the lawsuit and about why they felt forced to sue the government back in November. He also talked about the need for getting the contracts they had filed the lawsuit over in the first place. Interestingly, he also told them that should prospects change, should they get a contract or the suit be settled or won, they would be able to resume operations within two days, because he "and a group of friends" were holding supplies and equipment "at an adequate level."[1] He didn't elaborate so there's no way of knowing who these friends were, what they must have been storing to enable the entire brewery (capable of 5,000 barrels per month) to start operations almost immediately, or where they were storing all these supplies.

The most important development of the meeting, though, was the vote against bankruptcy by the stockholders in attendance.[2] This kept the Peoples Brewing Company technically in business, and perhaps most importantly, it kept hope alive for Ted Mack and the directors. The only question was whether they could actually restore operations somehow, and even with the slow process of the lawsuit trudging along, they had come up with some ideas to get the old brew kettle boiling again. The first of those ideas came once more from Mack's old friend, Ray Alexander.

As the director of the Afro Urban Institute, Alexander had a vested interest in seeing Peoples Brewing Company prove successful. The Institute's goal, after all, was to help the black community by creating or finding opportunities for them. Never mind that Mack was his friend, or that Alexander had his own money invested in the venture, Peoples meant so much more. The brewery was something Alexander could point to as an example of what was possible for those from the Inner Core of Milwaukee. It was a symbol of hope. And hope was something the black community could desperately use in the early 1970s.

To this end, Alexander put together a proposal for a study conducted by the Afro Urban Institute in partnership with the University of Wisconsin–Milwaukee.[3] The study would focus on the market acceptance of a minority-owned business by the general public. The proposal began by introducing the Peoples Brewing Company and its history leading up to the state it was in at that time. It also pointed out what Mack had found out the hard way: that many of the assumptions made about the market of the product were wrong, especially the assumption that because it was owned and managed by black people, Peoples would sell well in black areas. "It is the purpose of this proposal," Alexander wrote, "to try to identify the reasons for this unusual reception of a minority-produced beverage product...." The "unusual reception" he spoke of was the apathy from the black customers and the embrace from the white ones (they had expected the opposite).

To help them understand why things turned out this way, the Afro Urban Institute was requesting at least $35,000 from the Department of Commerce's Office of Minority Business Enterprise. If accepted, the proposal pointed out that the experiment should start before spring, 1973, to capitalize on the prime beer drinking season. It also explained that as part of its investigation, it would be exploring "potential market acceptance of such a product [Peoples Beer] in other large minority areas as Milwaukee, Kansas City, Gary, Indiana, Washington D.C. and California," all areas that Peoples was once in or had planned on expanding to.

13. Last Ditch Efforts

The "study" that Alexander was proposing was probably no more than a ruse intended to imbue Peoples with an aura of importance, to gain a partnership with the UW–Milwaukee, and to gain even a small amount of capital for the brewery. Whether Alexander ever really thought they would conduct the study or not didn't really matter, nothing really came of it and he had taken the only shot he had at helping Mack and the brewery. The next proposal, though, would not be nearly so modest.

Like Alexander, Mack also wrote a proposal with the goal of getting Peoples Brewing Company actually brewing again. His pitch to the Small Business Administration, titled, "A Proposal for the Resumption of Operations,"[4] was explicitly about saving the brewery. Where Alexander's proposal was dryly academic and provided rationale for the study and details about the resulting benefits, Mack's was much more a statement about Peoples and what it meant to the black community. After introducing the current state of the brewery and how it got to that point, he turned to many of the themes he recorded in the past. Much of those themes were about black America and what owning the brewery meant to it. He quoted extensively from the position paper released by the United Black Enterprises group back in 1969 (despite having sworn two years earlier that Peoples was not UBE). He also reminded readers that the Peoples Brewing Company was the only black-owned brewery in the U.S., and that the black community, in general, owns few, if any, corporations.

Lastly, he compared Peoples to its competitors to demonstrate just what an uphill battle they'd been waging since they bought the company. He pointed out the amount of money that companies like Anheuser-Busch spent on marketing the previous year (over $69 million) versus Peoples (a little over $23 thousand). This disparity, according to the proposal was the primary cause of the brewery's downfall. If they could expand their marketing, it argued, Peoples could compete. The proposal ended with a request for almost $2.5 million (over $14 million today), which, it stated, would support the firm's advertising (as well as operational costs) for three years.

Perhaps to deliver this proposal in person, on March 23, Ted Mack, along with Peoples Brewing Board Officers Ray Alexander, Henry Crosby and Samuel Ross, and Oshkosh City Council President Byron Murken, traveled to Madison to meet with a group of SBA officers, including Wisconsin SBA Director, Richard D. Murray. If they were meeting about either of the proposals, they must have known the conversations would be tense (especially considering that Peoples was in the midst of suing the SBA at the time) and that the proposals themselves would be longshots, but that's all they had left.

In the end, neither of their plans were accepted, and the group could only hang their heads and hope that something would come out of their lawsuit. But that hope too was dashed. In late January, federal judge Myron Gordon had denied a preliminary injunction against the government, stating that Peoples had not convinced him that their lawsuit would be successful.[5] Once that occurred, the government filed a motion to dismiss the case outright, and in early June, Gordon made his decision. The government's request was granted, because, according to Gordon, the issuance of contracts was not a sure thing. Rather, he wrote in his judgment, contracts are either given or not based on a multitude of reasons. Since that was the case, there was no assurance that Peoples would have received any contracts at all, and therefore there was no merit to the charge of discrimination. Had Peoples been promised specific contracts but then were denied those contracts, the lawsuit would have been successful. Peoples, however, was only promised the prospect of contracts.[6]

And so, on June 3, 1973, Myron Gordon put an end to any hope that Mack, the directors, the stockholders, and any others had that Peoples might reopen. With Gordon's dismissal of the case, the ebbing optimism some of them might have felt finally vanished for good. Accepting the end of their venture into the corporate structure of America, the directors went back to what they were already doing before the venture started, and Mack went back to doing what he seemed to do best by once more joining the ranks of New York Life Insurance and selling policies in Oshkosh.

But the episode hadn't really ended. There was, after all, the matter of the $400,000 loan they'd taken out, not to mention the $35,000 in back taxes the company owed. As far as Mack and the others were concerned, the matter was over, but the government disagreed. They wanted to get paid, and they intended to get at least some of their money back. The brewery might have been sitting cold and empty for the first time in 60 years, but it was still worth something after all. And if the SBA and IRS couldn't get their money out of the company's leadership, they could still get something out of the buildings and equipment owned by them.

In October, Henry Crosby, corporate secretary and a director of Peoples, received a letter from the Small Business Administration notifying him that they were seizing the property of the brewery. The letter stated that it was being seized because it was being vandalized and the corporation was not keeping insurance on it. The government was taking it, therefore, "to prevent a wasteing [sic] away of assets securing this loan."[7] By this time, Mack had gone back to work for New York Life, and the Peoples Brewing Company was just a sad, bitter memory. So, with no plans to reopen Peoples anytime soon, he and the others had nothing to offer in response, and the SBA quickly chained the doors of the brewery building and claimed it as their own.

13. Last Ditch Efforts

The next year, on April 14, a small, 3-inch by 4-inch advertisement appeared exclusively in the *Milwaukee Journal* seeking bids for "all personal property formerly owned by Peoples Brewery," which included "vehicles, furniture and fixtures (including all brewing and bottling equipment), bottles and cooperage."[8] The bids were due no later than April 25, 1974, only 11 days later, and payment would be expected when awarded. This was the SBA's initial method of recovering at least some of the money owed to it by Mack and the company's Directors. The men were personally liable for the $390,000 loan, but considering they paid $435,000 for the brewery, and then made additional updates and improvements, the SBA's sale should have gone a long way towards paying down their debt. At least that's what you'd think.

But then, in early May, the SBA announced it had accepted a bid from the Klein Industrial Corporation of Milwaukee in the amount of $24,250 (or just over $126,000 in 2022). This was an absurdly low price for all the equipment, supplies, property, buildings and vehicles, especially considering how much was paid for all of it only a few years earlier. As soon as the accepted bid was announced, reporters began asking why the SBA would settle for such a low price. "It was a fair offer,"[9] was the answer given by their Public Information Officer, Robert Miller. But to the local journalists, something seemed odd. Despite Miller's insistence that the agency did more than put the single ad into the paper, reporters couldn't find anyone who'd been notified by phone, mail or other means. And when asked why the SBA didn't hold a public auction as they'd done in the past instead of requesting sealed bids for the company's estate as a package, Miller didn't have any answers.

Almost six weeks later, on June 18, the Klein Industrial Corporation had its own auction, and according to the tally from reporters in attendance, made out very well on their less than $25,000 investment. A company from Tampa, Florida, for example, paid over $40,000 for some of the equipment, including 859 beer kegs. Pabst and Leinenkugel breweries also spent at least $20,000 to buy almost 13,000 cases of beer bottles they would eventually use themselves.[10] Other bidders walked away with the labeling and bottling machines, boilers and delivery trucks, and even the brew kettle, which was fabricated in Germany from copper and weighed 5,000 pounds.[11]

When the kettle sold, crews had to use a wrecking ball on the old brewery to get it out. While the bottle house and office buildings remained standing, the 63-year-old brew house was demolished. All told, the Klein Industrial Corporation made between $114,000–$125,000[12] from the auction. The money could have gone to pay down the debt that Peoples owed, but instead it was pocketed by a private company, and Mack and the others were still on the hook for the rest of the loan. The whole episode left reporters stunned[13].[14] Why would the SBA do that? What could possibly motivate them to take the loss and continue to leave the Peoples leadership liable for the rest of the money?

The SBA never had any answers for these questions, instead insisting they followed routine procedures. It's worth remembering, though, that Mack had not only been vocal, but loudly vocal about the extent to which the SBA failed his company. His lawsuit was specifically about those failures, and at every press conference and meeting, and in any letter to stockholders or others, he made sure to point a finger at the SBA and put the blame on them. Whether they deserved the blame or not was beside the point to Mack, the SBA was at fault for his ruin, and he was going to let everyone know about it, including Congress. In June 1974, the Congressional Subcommittee on Banking held hearings in Milwaukee for an investigation into potential misconduct within the Office of Minority Business Enterprise and the SBA, and Ted Mack was invited to tell his story.

Mack may have been right in his suspicions about the SBA. Although the problems of the agency became magnified during the Nixon administration, it had been riddled with embarrassing scandals for years. Since its inception there had been a torrent of accusations of favoritism, payback, and grift, perhaps not unnatural at all considering it was an agency responsible for doling out loans and grants, large amounts of money that was sometimes hard to track. In the early 1960s it was revealed that the SBA had made loans to organized crime figures, and in the late 1960s it was discovered that loans meant for minority-owned businesses, intended to solve the problems of poverty in the ghetto, had instead gone to businesses owned by wealthy African Americans, including Jackie Robinson.[15]

Nixon's pick for directing the SBA was a Hispanic businessman from El Paso, Texas, named Hilary Sandoval. Sandoval had little experience in administration, and was by all accounts completely and unabashedly inept at his job (his short appointment was reportedly Nixon's repayment to his political allies in Texas).[16] Sandoval, in turn, selected one of his friends, Albert Fuentes to serve as one of his four special assistants. In 1969 it was revealed that Fuentes was involved in shaking down an El Paso firm owned by Emanuel Salaiz for company stocks in return for a $10,000 SBA loan.[17] Fuentes was subsequently fired and indicted by a grand jury on fraud and bribery charges.[18] The whole scene added to the pall that had been draped over the SBA since it was reported they had lent money to the mafia. In the coming years, even more revelations would be uncovered.

The investigation that put Mack in front of Congress focused on loans which appeared to be made as political favors. The loans were risky, and borrowers often lacked the proper collateral for them. Perhaps more

13. Last Ditch Efforts

telling, an audit report from that investigation specifically named the Milwaukee SBA office as one of the offices making such loans. In fact, the reports suggested that over 60 percent of their loans were either made to people who were considered "credit risks," or had generally violated policy in some other way. According to author Jonathan Bean, Milwaukee had in fact been officially reprimanded for throwing wild parties, acting unprofessionally and lacking self-discipline or work quality.[19]

This was the agency that enthusiastically helped Mack and the others attain the brewery. And such an environment wasn't limited to Milwaukee, the corruption was systemic. Twenty-two other offices were also investigated, turning up a number of violations, and many of them criminal. Interestingly, the Philadelphia SBA office was additionally one of those that was examined, and the director there, Russell Hamilton, Jr., the man who would have been responsible for approving the loan guarantee for the fraudster A. Bart Starr in his purchase of the Sunshine Brewery, was convicted of accepting kickbacks for loan approvals.[20]

On June 25, 1974, it was Mack's turn to tell his story to Congress at the subcommittee hearing held in Milwaukee. He gave them a history of his journey from UBE and the failed campaign to purchase Blatz to the successful purchase of Peoples and then its eventual failure. Much of his testimony was spent on the promises made at the SBA office in Milwaukee, one of the offices accused of corruption and under investigation. Many of the questions directed by the Congressmen were about this office, about what Mack was promised, and about the procedures the office followed. Mack reported that they were promised technical assistance and contracts when they were signing the paperwork for the loan, and that the loan officer was enthusiastic about getting them approved. He also reiterated the point many times that none of these promises ever materialized, the promises all turned out to be lies.

When asked if the information, the promises, were put in writing, Mack told them no because he trusted the government. Besides, he rationed that it was "written down" in the news and laws that Congress passed, and that the 8(a) program was common knowledge, so why should he have it written down in person? That seemed to make sense to the legislators and investigators of the sub-committee, who moved on to different questions.

One of those questions involved the guarantees that the board of directors had to give in order to get the SBA loan in the first place. Mack was asked by Congressional Chief Investigator Curtis Prins if they personally signed the loan guarantee. Mack replied that all five members of the board, plus their wives, had to personally sign for it. This made the men (and their wives) all personally liable for the money that was being loaned to them for the business. Wisconsin Representative Henry Reuss then asked how many shares of the company the men who signed for the loan owned combined, to which Mack answered that the five owned 37 percent of the company.

"I ask," Representative Ruess then said to him, "because the SBA apparently made no effort whatever to get personal guarantees from two of the wealthiest men in Wisconsin who between them owned 25% of the stock of another company that got a loan. So I think your complaint is well taken and SBA has much on its conscience."[21] Mack simply nodded and answered, "Yes sir, I heard about that." The implication was clear, the SBA's rules applied to some, but not to others, and especially not black businessmen from the Inner Core of Milwaukee.

In truth it seemed the SBA's loan officers really didn't care that much about Nixon's black capitalism agenda. As it turned out, they had quotas to meet, and the more minority loans they made, the better. Mack had wondered about the loan officer's enthusiasm when he talked to him three years earlier, but it seems it was only because of the color of Mack's skin, and not the value of his enterprise. The SBA was eager to demonstrate to both Congress and the media that it was obligated to helping African Americans, but in demonstrating that eagerness the outcomes devolved into simple, raw, quantitative proof: the more loans they gave to black people the better. The quality of those ventures, whether they were profitable and thrived, or failed and vanished, was not really a consideration (indeed, neither was the quality or potential for success of the applicants themselves).

Though the goals were noble, the facilitation of them were astounding failures of the SBA, its programs, and its staff. And to get Mack to agree to that loan the SBA's representative became little more than a salesman, reciting stories about mythical Section 8(a) programs and set-aside loans—mechanisms that would be sure to help Ted's business (with little thought about how practical such promises might actually be). If only those myths turned out to be true.

It would be cold comfort to Mack and the others, but the investigations did lead to an overhaul of Wisconsin's SBA. Questionable loans were revoked and new mechanisms were put into place to better guard against fraud. Wisconsin's former SBA director, Richard D. Murray, the same one Mack had met with the previous March, and who was suspected of giving loans to friends, lost his job as bank president, and had his name forever tied to incompetence and corruption. But, the damage to the men who gambled on the small brewery in Oshkosh was already complete. They had lost thousands of dollars—tens of thousands in Mack's case—and endured three years of defeat at the hands of racist locals who boycotted them, corrupt competitors who massively outspent them, black consumers who wouldn't support them, and an inept and dishonest government that misled them.

Their attempt to enter the corporate structure, in other words, had ended in ruin and defeat, and Ted Mack's foray into the beer industry was over. He'd lost his money, lost his job, and uprooted his family, and all for naught. Personally, he was crushed, not even able to visit the part of town where his brewery used to proudly stand.[22] By the end of 1974, heavy equipment was moved onto the brewery grounds and demolition of its buildings had started. By the end of January 1975, the buildings had been leveled and the evidence that the Peoples Brewing Company had at one time been making beer in the city of Oshkosh, Wisconsin, had almost completely vanished.

14

Ted Mack's Legacy

Ted Mack's legacy in brewing is small, but it's definitely there. In fact, Oak Park Brewing Company in Sacramento, CA, a small, black-owned brewery, makes a "Peoples Beer" tribute beer in honor of his legacy (using a matching recipe and logo). Further, if you search his name on the internet, you'll find a dozen articles about "the only black brewery owner in America's history." That's what he's known for. The stories are fairly similar. They almost all talk about the black man from Alabama who moved to Milwaukee, worked for Pabst in the mid-1960s, and who, through grit and hard work, bought a small brewery in nearby Oshkosh. Most of the articles also talk at least a bit about the racism he encountered after purchasing Peoples, and they all highlight his eventual failure. But none of them really discuss the more important points of the story, especially the groundbreaking civil rights battle the entire venture represented. That's what the whole pursuit was about, after all, civil rights. Mack never set out to just make and sell beer, he intended something much bigger than that. But of all the tragedies in his story, the true tragedy was that nobody recognized what he was trying to do.

In 1995, writer Jack Dougherty was in Milwaukee conducting research for his book, *More Than One Struggle: The Evolution of Black School Reform in Milwaukee*, when he sat down with area civil rights leader Reuben Harpole, Jr. The latter had been an important part of the civil rights movement in Milwaukee during the 1960s, and especially in the school desegregation efforts. He had been at the center of much of these noble activities because he was the marketing and circulation manager of the *Milwaukee Star*, the black-themed newspaper that covered so much of the activism, including the protests and boycotts of the schools. Harpole and his wife also helped organize and run the "Freedom Schools," which were held in the basements of local churches and community organizations throughout Milwaukee to give black school children someplace to go and learn while they were boycotting the school district. In short, he was and is considered an important figure in the fight for civil rights in Wisconsin's biggest city.

14. Ted Mack's Legacy

The conversation he had with Dougherty was far-reaching, but concerned the events and people that featured into the activism of the 1960s. In their discussion, names closely tied with the protests and struggles were raised and highlighted. They talked about Father Groppi, the white, often caustic but charismatic Catholic priest who was so closely associated with the NAACP Youth Council and the marches for fair housing. They also talked about Vel Phillips, the first black alderperson in the city of Milwaukee, who was an outspoken advocate of the protests and marches. Harpole also had fond memories of Calvin Sherard, Dick Gregory, and many others. Then at one point, as he was remembering the leaders of the school boycotts, he ran through a list of names, mentioning almost as an aside the name of Ted Mack, who he said was trying to start a business. Dougherty interjected with "That brewery?" but Harpole mentioned another business Ted may have been starting, and then moved on. They never came back to talk about him again.

In truth, the name Theodore Mack is really absent from any of the written history about the civil rights movement in Milwaukee. And at first glance, this might make sense. After all, unlike Mack, people like Father Groppi, Vel Phillips, and Lloyd Barbee made civil rights activism their life's work. Father Groppi risked his personal safety to lead the NAACP Youth Council on street marches all the way into the late 1960s, and continued being active in the community well after the street marches waned. Vel Phillips, who introduced legislation to help the black community throughout her public life as an alderwoman, stayed close to the Inner Core of North Milwaukee that she represented. And Lloyd Barbee fought against the de facto segregation of the Milwaukee Public School in the courts until he finally won the case in 1976, a full ten years after he started his fight.

Ted Mack, on the other hand, dropped out of the daily skirmishes on the streets of the Inner Core to take a job at Pabst. Though he used to be a public servant, helping the poor and marginalized as a social worker for the county, he gave that up to work at a corporation and wear a suit. Maybe that's the reason he's so overlooked as a civil rights icon while so many others are praised.

But from another perspective, perhaps Theodore Mack also deserves to be recognized for his activism. Sure, he left behind the daily civil rights battles waged on the streets or sidewalks of Milwaukee, but he never really stopped fighting. Instead, he entered the larger war for civil rights in America with the hope of gaining full equality for black people. He was still engaged in battles, but they were fought in boardrooms, beer distributors, newspapers, and strategy meetings. This was a space that afforded him no comfort, no safety, and nowhere to retreat to. If he failed it would be a total failure. He would have no job, no savings account, and no welcoming neighborhood to shelter him. Leaving the "Inner Core behind and moving to an almost completely white city without any connections was a move only the most courageous could make.

Activism, after all, takes many forms. Sure, when we hear the word, we might immediately picture a crowd of marchers, holding hands and singing in one voice, "We shall overcome." But activism can manifest itself in a multitude of different ways and can be called a number of different things. Judicial activism, political activism, consumer activism, shareholder activism, environmental activism—these are all different terms for movements bound together by a common characteristic. They all depend on ideology-led action (rather than idle consideration) and a guiding belief that an institution can be improved by said action. Theodore Mack's ideology was the belief that the black community needed to enter the corporate structure, that they needed to be producers, not just consumers. His action was to purchase an existing corporation and use it to empower the black community by hiring them and by placing them in management positions. There's no telling exactly when he came to the conclusion that this should be his activism, but he began engaging in it the moment he assembled the team of United Black Enterprises with the aim of buying Blatz in 1968. He pursued it right up until the federal government took away and sold Peoples Brewing Company in 1974. Ultimately, then, Ted Mack never stopped pushing for civil rights, for equality, for justice for the black community, he just did it in a different way, his own way.

Mack was undoubtedly a pioneer in many respects. His unshakeable belief that black people must become part of the corporate structure in America is one that many people today are still pursuing. And, due to indefatigable people like Ted Mack, the atmosphere of business is changing, and black professionals have started making inroads into corporate America. But, as always, there is still much work to do. In 1971, Mack pointed out that "there are 500 major corporations in this country and not even one of them is under the control or even the management of blacks."[1]

As of May 2022, there were six black CEOs of Fortune 500 companies in the U.S.[2] That's arguably better than the alternative of Mack's time, but that's still only 1 percent out of a population that makes up over 13 percent of the country. However, there have been some very positive changes, like more assistance programs today for minority entrepreneurs than ever before. And, many large public and private companies have recently committed to social justice within their own ranks, pledging to move minority members into the upper echelons of management. Mack would have appreciated that.

Surprisingly, though, after all he went through, there's really scant mention about Mack in the records of U.S. beer history either. While there have been the occasional article or blog post, none of the celebrated books

14. Ted Mack's Legacy

about the history of beer in America even give him a mention. But, though he is undoubtedly a pioneer in the history of brewing in the United States, Peoples Brewing, and for that matter Blatz Brewing, were never about beer but about civil rights. Brewing was simply the one industry he thought he knew well enough to conduct business in, but it could have been any other industry under the sun he chose instead. Had he been hired within a completely different industry than brewing, perhaps an automobile company, or maybe a shoe manufacturer, he would probably have bought a corporation in one of those sectors instead, because that would have been the industry he knew.

Ironically though, out of all the industries he could have chosen, brewing was probably the one he was least likely to be successful in. When Mack purchased the Oshkosh-based brewery in 1970, there were 137 other breweries in the United States. Within ten years, that number had fallen to 101. The biggest brewers continued taking over the smallest breweries, and thirty years later, the top three firms, Anheuser-Busch, Miller and Coors, accounted for 81 percent of the beer brewed and sold in the country. From one perspective it seems that little has changed. Those top breweries still had (and have) enormous marketing campaigns and sponsorships. But while the beer barons felt safe in controlling the majority of beer sales in the U.S., little did they know that the next few decades would offer a different type of competition that would completely change the landscape for brewing in America.

According to U.S. District Judge Stanley Weigel, who oversaw a 1966 court case that pitted the Federal Trade Commission against Joseph Schlitz Brewing Company for violating the Clayton Act when they tried to buy controlling interest in two different breweries (similar to what Pabst had tried to do with Blatz), it was "extremely difficult for a new firm to enter the United States brewing industry due to the great expense of buying or building a plant and acquiring sufficient business to support it."[3] According to the Court's opinion, it cost between $30 and $35 million to build a new, one-million-barrel brewery in the U.S. that would be able to compete with the others, and that only a single brewery in the twenty years before the court case had successfully entered the American brewing market. Judging by these numbers, Ted Mack, who spent only $460,000 on his brewery and had a fraction of that for marketing, had no chance at all. And further, these numbers looked even worse in the climate of the 1970s and 1980s as the industry continued its race to concentrate.

However, Weigel's opinion was framed by a number of assumptions. First it assumed that any other companies starting breweries actually intended to compete with the biggest breweries in the county—especially Anheuser-Busch, Coors, Miller, Schlitz and Pabst. If that was the case, then yes, they would certainly need deep pockets to do so, and even the almost ludicrously high number he quotes ($270 to $315 million today) might be too little. If, on the other hand, a brewery was organized that was intentionally regional, that is, they didn't really want to sell outside of their city or maybe even neighborhood, then Weigel's point was moot. Such a brewery would require far less capital to start up and run.

Another assumption the opinion made was that any new brewery would try to replicate the success of the large breweries by replicating their products too. By the time the brewing industry became the most concentrated in the U.S. in the 1970s and 1980s (but also by the time Weigel wrote his opinion in 1966), the major brands sold beer that was pretty much all alike. American lager beer (the most consumed and brewed by all of the large breweries) was quite uniform in appearance and taste. The large breweries "deemphasized hoppiness and malt flavors"[4] in their beer. In other words, the most produced and sold beer in the country was sort of bland.

But what if an organization didn't want to make the same type of product as the larger breweries did, what if an organization instead wanted to make something different, something much more like pre-prohibition beers, with more intense flavors and *pronounced* hoppiness and malt flavors? If a company might come along and leave these two assumptions behind, perhaps it might have a chance. And that's exactly what happened.

In 1969, Fritz Maytag (of the Maytag Appliance Company) took an interest in brewing and bought a small San Francisco brewery that was on the verge of failure. After purchase and some thought, he immediately proved that Weigel's assumptions were only that—assumptions and not facts—by opening the Anchor Brewing Company. Knowing he could never compete with Coors, Pabst or the others, he instead decided to make the highest quality of beer he could. He also decided to make his beer completely unique. Instead of trying to compete with the big brewers for distributorships or television ads, he spent his money on quality ingredients from Europe, and within a short time was known throughout the Bay Area.[5]

One Bay Area resident, Jack McAuliffe, seeing the success of Anchor Brewing, and being interested in brewing himself, also decided to get into the beer business. Again, bucking the assumptions of Weigel's opinion, McAuliffe didn't want to create an enormous brewery making light, pale yellow, bland lagers. He wanted bigger, bolder flavors in his beers, like the ones he'd sampled while serving in Europe in the U.S. Navy. After saving money and moving to Sonoma, California, where the real estate was less expensive than San Francisco, and after taking on two friends as business partners, he opened New Albion Brewing Company in 1976.[6] This would later be recognized as the first microbrewery in the U.S., and would create a template for hundreds, if not thousands of others in the years to come. Commonly recognized brands on the shelves today, like Sierra Nevada or Mendocino Brewing, would credit McAuliffe's vision and model as their inspiration.[7]

Another important turning point for the U.S. brewing industry occurred in 1978 when President Jimmy Carter signed House Resolution 1337, permitting people to make beer in their own households. When the 21st Amendment to the U.S. Constitution (eliminating prohibition) was passed in 1933, it specifically made legal only the commercial manufacturing and sale of alcohol, leaving out the personal or household manufacture of it. House Resolution 1337 finally made home brewing federally legal for the first time since 1918 (though 13 states had already made it legal themselves; it would take until 2013 for the rest to join).

According to researchers,[8] the legalization of home brewing led to a boom in the founding of small breweries around the nation, most likely led by people like Jack McAuliffe: entrepreneurs who loved beer and brewed out of their passion for the craft. This only makes sense, because, after all, dropping the prohibition on home brewing provided an opportunity for novelty, invention, and exploration, and further allowed people who might have been in other professions to explore brewing and to eventually become experts themselves.

And the market responded favorably to these new pursuits. From a low of only 49 brewers in 1983, the U.S. Tax and Trade Bureau reported 13,380 total brewing permits by the year 2021.[9] This number includes both a limited number of very large brewers, and the smallest of the microbrewers producing beer for their small restaurant or pub. Although this seems to bode well for an industry previously so concentrated that regional breweries were inevitably either bought or forced out of business, there really has been little change to the greater market. As of 2020, two companies—Anheuser-Busch InBev SA/NV and Molson Coors Beverage Company—still controlled 65 percent of the beer market in the United States.[10] In fact, despite all of the efforts the federal government has gone to in ensuring the beer industry stays competitive, it admits that in the past two decades the most prolific brewers have become even more concentrated. While the strategy of dropping off big sums of cash to retailers (i.e., black-bagging) might be considered a relic of the past (though to be fair there's no evidence big brewers either stopped or continued the practice), big brewers do still remain committed to a ruthless pursuit of profit and market dominance.

According to a report by the U.S Treasury, the mergers of the biggest brewing companies in the U.S. with international brewing concerns, specifically Anheuser-Busch with InBev (itself the product of a merger between Belgium and Brazilian brewing companies) in 2008 creating AB InBev, and with Molson (a Canadian brewing company) and Coors in 2005, created many concerns for the government. To justify these mergers, the companies generally had argued that the new resulting businesses would decrease prices for consumers by more efficiently integrating supplies and resources, but instead they proved to create widespread price increases for the most popular products, which were now all under the control of a few monopolies.[11]

The report goes on to detail two mergers attempted by AB InBev, one in 2013 where it attempted to buy out Grupo Modelo, the third-largest brewer of beer sold in the U.S., and then another in 2015 of SAB Miller, the second largest brewer in the world. In both cases, as in the cases in the mid–20th century, the U.S. Government sued AB InBev and forced it to divest itself or end the mergers or buyout attempts. But, of course, there are other ways for big breweries to meddle.

The Treasury Department, in the same 2022 report, also argues that the largest few brewers may be "capable of tacit coordination … with respect to prices." In other words, through more sophisticated actions they are still able, and indeed may be actively engaging in, price fixing. Next, through pressure on the beer distribution industry, an industry which itself has seen massive concentration so that only a few large distributors control beer distribution in the country, the large brewers are able to stifle competition by ensuring distributors don't carry the products of competitors, guaranteeing that those smaller brewers remain small brewers.

Lastly, the report details concerns about big beer buying into the craft beer scene. Through hard work, risk, and innovation, the craft beer industry is thriving in the U.S. However, recently, companies like AB InBev have started investing into some of the more popular craft breweries, and own stakes, some minor and some larger, in many of them throughout the country. At issue is the access these particular breweries will have to distribution networks not available to others because they will use the same networks available to the big breweries that own a stake in them. This will inevitably create unfair reach and threaten the markets of regional brewers with only small distributors available to them. One might hope there won't be a repeat of the concentration in the industry like the kind that ultimately helped put Ted Mack out of business, but even so, it's clear from the U.S. Treasury's report that the big brewers have lost none of their cunning or quest for absolute dominance.

Another trend that was beginning to hit its stride while Mack was struggling to make Peoples Brewery successful was the popularity of malt liquor in the black community. This product became even more closely tied to African American culture in the decades that followed Peoples' closing. Thanks to targeted advertising that started in the 1970s, and which grew even more targeted (and exploitative) in the 1980s, malt liquor tied specifically to the rap and street cultures that dominated and influenced the popular perception of black adolescence. Brands Old English or St. Ide's were particularly popular in the rap community, appearing in multiple music videos and even advertised by rap artists (Ice Cube claimed in one commercial that St. Ides will "get your girl in the mood quicker" and "get your Jimmy thicker").[12]

Through a proliferation of advertising, the total output of malt liquor production hit its zenith in the mid–1990s. In 1974 the leading producers brewed 3.4 million barrels of malt liquor, but in 1996 that total reached 8.9 million.[13] Put another way, it increased from a total market share of 2.3 percent in 1974 to 4.6 percent in 1996, and African Americans accounted for more than 30 percent of sales.[14] The volume and market shares have dropped off since those highs, but there's little doubt about the adverse effects the commercially-wrought malt liquor popularity had on the black community at the time.

But in terms of those continuing trends that stretch back to Ted Mack's tenure, perhaps most worrying is the visible absence of African Americans at every level of the beer industry. In 1951, black workers in breweries made up one-half of one percent of the total number of workers nationwide. In that year, out of 10,000 brewery workers in New York City alone, only 50 were black[15] (presumably this calculation is limited to the production staff). This low representation might be understood, of course, after considering factors like the prohibitions on the hiring of African Americans that were common to the brewers' unions in those years. But staggeringly little progress has been made in the decades following that statistic. In 2018, black people accounted for a paltry 1.8 percent of all craft brewery positions, and only .4 percent of production staff.[16] In a word, it seems the trend is actually going backwards. And the news is not much better with regards to brewery ownership. Of over 8,000 craft breweries surveyed in a 2018 study, only one percent of them were owned by African Americans.[17]

Again, there's really no good reason for this, or rather, no good apparent reason. The trade unions that kept out black workers in the early to mid–20th century no longer exist, and the brew rooms and bottling lines were long ago integrated—though this shouldn't at all be taken to mean there's no discrimination in brewing (it's not even close, actually). A 2019 racial discrimination lawsuit brought into sharp focus just how bigoted the industry could be. A former black employee of Michigan's Founders Brewing Company alleged the organization's environment was inherently racist, with open animosity towards himself and others like him. After an immense amount of damage to its reputation and character (owing, for starters, to a manager stating in court that he didn't know the employee was black, nor did he know the same of Barack Obama or Michael Jordan[18]), the company settled, but it threw into stark relief the lingering racial strife in the beer business.

And this was far from the only such court case involving craft breweries and racial discrimination against African Americans. But not only have craft breweries been guilty of such biases, big beer too had taken part in similar behaviors. Anheuser-Busch was found guilty of discrimination in 1983 and ordered to pay a substantial fine ($3 million, which was then appealed down to $300,000), followed by three separate suits against Miller Brewing in 1993 (which were all settled out of court), and then again in 1994 when they were sued by 97 former black employees (in that case they were ordered to pay $2.7 million in damages).[19] So, certainly it could be said that the environment of the brewing industry itself discourages diversity through its own history of really terrible actions against African Americans.

Then again, others point to major cultural issues as impediments to diversity in the beer business. Of these issues, the foremost might be financial. One of the reasons the Johnson administration authorized the use of the SBA as a resource for black business enterprise was that he recognized the disparity that African Americans faced when trying to access finances for business pursuits. The Nixon administration likewise understood this, and so accelerated lending to minority (especially black) entrepreneurs (granted, the SBA was almost fatally corrupt and inept in these and subsequent administrations, but *some* assistance was given). But not only financial assistance is needed, financial literacy education and business training are also required.

Only too late did Ted Mack petition the SBA for these types of assistance via the SBA's organization, SCORE (created precisely to provide such help to small businesses). By the time Mack had filled out his application (June 6, 1972[20]), Peoples Brewery was already out of money and owed the IRS in back taxes. It was too little too late. Mack and his associates, like many other budding African American entrepreneurs, simply did not have the resources needed—be it financial or informational—to successfully start and run a business, especially not a brewery. The same could be true for many others, which could help to explain why so few breweries have black owners.

Another factor could be as simple as an address. Some theorists believe that the urban setting in which many African Americans live—typically through historic segregation as in the inner core of

Milwaukee—also keeps them from participating in the craft beer culture in America and could be a reason we don't see many black people in production roles (or any role, really) in breweries.[21] And it makes sense. Craft breweries are located in much more trendy areas, perhaps in a warehouse in a gentrified area of a small town or city, or maybe in a suburban strip mall somewhere. In any case, one most likely wouldn't find them in a densely packed inner-city neighborhood with high crime rates and intense poverty.

Finally, there is the culture of beer itself. When some residents of Oshkosh found out that Ted Mack and his all–black group of associates bought Peoples Brewing Company, they were outraged, staged boycotts, and generally threatened to derail the whole enterprise before it even got started. Now some of this was certainly due to the racially skewed treatment given them by the *Milwaukee Sentinel* newspaper reports. But some of it could also be the perception that Mack and the others were threatening something seen as an important cultural artifact to the descendants of Bavarian immigrants. To them, beer was more than simply a beverage, it was a regional identifier (after all, dating back to the Middle Ages, many small German towns had their own style of lager brewed exclusively there), an excuse for social bonding (for hundreds of years, German families spent Sundays after church at beer gardens), and even a token of their identity (as much as bratwurst, sauerkraut, and gingerbread).

Their resentment could have been born from people who they perceived as outsiders appropriating their legacy. Such claims of ownership from white beer makers could manifest in ways that keep black people out of the industry. From another perspective, researchers also suggest there is an innate "whiteness" in the current craft beer movement, and that historically the story of beer and African Americans has centered on the negative, specifically that of malt liquor and the inner-city gang/rap cultures.[22] Peering at the industry through this lens makes one quickly realize that perhaps beer is not a positive cultural marker, but is instead anathema to a generation of exploited, inner-city kids.

In response to these many issues, the beer industry is trying to make changes to address some of the problems. In 2018 the Brewers Association (BA), a not-for-profit organization representing American craft and independent brewing companies, appointed Professor J. Nikol Jackson-Beckham as its first ever "Diversity Ambassador." Charged with discussing diversity challenges and ideas leading to more minority-involvement with the organization's state-level chapters and members, Dr. Jackson-Beckham represents the BA's growing commitment to diversity in craft brewing.[23] While hiring Jackson-Beckham and creating her position could be dismissed by the pessimist as virtue signaling or even pandering, it might mean something more. After all, it was the BA itself that actually commissioned the study indicating such a low presence by minorities in the craft beer industry in the first place.

Creating a space for, and then choosing a diversity ambassador after discovering how woefully left behind minorities are in the brewing industry, is actually rather refreshing—they really are doing something about the problem. The BA is also providing grants to support "inclusivity programming," which it says helps to "foster a diverse and inclusive craft beer industry."[24] Many other private organizations and companies are taking similar steps to enable a more diverse brewing culture, like an initiative called "8 Trills Pils" launched by Crown & Hops—a black-owned Inglewood, CA, brewery, and BrewDog, a Scottish craft brewery. The initiative will go to support and highlight black craft brewers in order to achieve equity in the industry.[25]

Other initiatives are slowly but steadily emerging to help achieve more diversity in brewing, such as Pittsburgh's Barrel & Flow Fest, a street beer festival that highlights black craft brewers, and the nonprofit Beer Kulture, formed specifically to advance the cause and presence of African Americans in brewing through grants, recognition, internships, and outreach. Each of these initiatives forces one to wonder how successful Mack would have been had he started his venture fifty years later. In a modern environment, he might have found more celebration for his small, regional brewery than he found in 1970. He also might have found a more welcoming environment in which a group of black business people buying a brewery weren't seen as an oddity (which was clearly the case at the time, judging from all of the racialized headlines attached to the stories about them). Instead, they may have been recognized and buoyed by the media, by the government, and by others in the industry. For certain, Ted Mack was ahead of his time, which unfortunately was one of his problems.

Mack had the benefit of none of what is currently available to black brewers (or any black business people), and so Peoples Brewing Company eventually went the way of hundreds of others of breweries at the time, crushed under the weight of competition and corruption. Sadly, after the failure of the Peoples Brewing Company, he was a changed man. He never again attempted anything so lofty, though he continued building his own businesses as an entrepreneur. At first, he went back to selling insurance once more for New York Life. Then, by the late 1970s, he opened a chain of state-approved halfway houses for incarcerated juveniles in the Milwaukee area called Crispus Attucks. The name is drawn from the first person reportedly killed in the Boston Massacre, a man from African and Native American descent. It was meant to symbolize the courage of those who passed through the doors of the halfway houses, and maybe for the owner of the halfway houses too. After successfully running these businesses through the 1970s, he left Milwaukee for good in the early 1980s and relocated to Atlanta.

But the experience with Peoples left its mark. Later, Ted admitted to a reporter that the loss of the brewery left him utterly depressed. But then he started thinking of lessons learned so many years ago from Woody Hayes at Ohio State. "One day," Ted said,

> I was sitting there feeling sorry for myself and I thought "When was the last time I've felt this bad?" It was when we lost to [Ohio State rival] Michigan. I laughed, got off my butt and got going again. When I was flying high as president of Peoples Brewery and speaking everywhere and being very successful, it was like playing for a winning program. When I lost everything, I was able to handle that: it didn't destroy me. It was like losing a game to Michigan. If you have an affirmative attitude you can bounce back, and I've got things going for me again.[26]

Ted Mack was a lot of things. He was the impoverished son of a single sharecropper mother. He was a high school graduate, and a U.S. Army war veteran. He was a scholarship football player for Ohio State University, and a college graduate from Marquette University. He was a social worker in the Inner Core of North Milwaukee, and a civil rights leader. And he was the first black president of a brewing company in the history of the United States. He was a lot of things, and all of them noteworthy and deserving a place in the annals of civil rights, business history, beer history, and black entrepreneurship. And although after his experience with Peoples he chose to be a humble, doting father instead of celebrated businessman again, the chapters of that story and the lessons they provide should serve history for ages to come. Theodore A. Mack, Sr., passed away on February 4, 2019, in Atlanta, surrounded by the family he loved.

Chapter Notes

Preface

1. An early draft of the Introduction and Chapters 1 and 2 were published in the *Brewery History Journal*, issue 188. Used here with permission.

Introduction

1. Russell, J. (February 21, 1973). "Beer Stockholders Back Mack." *Daily Northwestern*, 4.
2. Theodore Mack, Sr., Past President and Chairman of the Board of People's Brewing Co., Milwaukee, Wis., Accompanied by Ray Alexander, Member of the Board of Directors (June 1974). *Hearings Before the Subcommittee on Small Business of the Committee on Banking and Currency, House of Representatives, 1974*. U.S. Government Printing Office.
3. Mack, T. (February 5, 1973). *Letter to Stockholders*. Crosby Papers, University of Wisconsin-Milwaukee.
4. Alexander, R.A., Crosby, H.S., Ouley, W., Ross, S. (February 2, 1922). "Letter to Ted Mack, Sr., President of Peoples Brewing Company." *Crosby Papers, University of Wisconsin-Milwaukee*.
5. Aid Given to Brewery (March 8, 1973). *Oshkosh Advance-Titan*, 24.
6. Brewing Equipment Auctioned (June 19, 1974). *Daily Northwestern*, 4.
7. Auction to Be Held Tuesday at Former Peoples Brewery (June 15, 1974). *Daily Northwestern*, 18.
8. Auction of People's Brewery Still Making Noise (June 20, 1974). *Daily Northwestern*, 2.
9. Auction of People's Brewery Still Making Noise (June 20, 1974). *Daily Northwestern*, 2.
10. Gordon, M. (June 13, 1973). *United States District Court Eastern District of Wisconsin Decision and Order*. Crosby Papers, University of Wisconsin-Milwaukee.
11. Greene, B. (May 11, 1971). "Blacks Buy Oshkosh Brewery." *Freeport Journal-Standard*, 17.
12. Chapman, N.G., and Brunsma, D.L. (2020). *Beer and Racism: How Beer Became White, Why It Matters, and Movements to Change it*, 178. Policy Press.
13. Akin, R., Reiherzer, L. (2012). *The Breweries of Oshkosh: Their Rise and Fall*. Akin & Reiherzer.
14. Personal interview, Vernon Wiedenhaft, 15th January 2019.
15. Theodore Mack, Sr., Past President and Chairman of the Board of People's Brewing Co., Milwaukee, Wis., Accompanied by Ray Alexander, Member of the Board of Directors (June 1974). *Hearings Before the Subcommittee on Small Business of the Committee on Banking and Currency, House of Representatives, 1974*. U.S. Government Printing Office.

Chapter 1

1. Twelfth Census of the United States: Population Schedule, Sheet 17–18 (1900). *Department of Commerce—Bureau of the Census*. Government Accounting Office.
2. Thirteenth Census of the United States: Population Schedule, Sheet 19-B (1910). *Department of Commerce—Bureau of the Census*. Government Printing Office.

Notes—Chapter 1

3. Fourteenth Census of the United States, State Compendium: Wisconsin (1925). *Department of Commerce, Bureau of the Census*. Government Printing Office.

4. Foner, E. (2014). *Reconstruction: America's Unfinished Revolution, 1863–1877*. Harper Collins.

5. Embree, E.R. (1936, March). "Southern Farm Tenancy." *Survey Graphic*, 25(3), 149.

6. Carson, Scott A. (March 2006). "African-American and White Living Standards in the 19th Century American South: A Biological Comparison." *CESifo Working Paper Series No. 1696*.

7. Brown, S.A. (1950). "Negro Folk Expression." *Phylon*, 11(4), 318–325.

8. The General Condition of the Alabama Negro (March 1965). *Student Nonviolent Coordinating Committee*.

9. Embree, E.R. (1936, March). "Southern farm tenancy." *Survey Graphic*, 25(3), 149.

10. Fifteenth Census of the United States: 1903—Population, Volume III, Part 2, Montana-Wyoming. U.S. (1932). *Department of Commerce, Bureau of the Census*. Government Printing Office.

11. Sixteenth Census of the United States: Population Schedule, Sheet 9-B. (1940). *Department of Commerce-Bureau of the Census*. Government Printing Office.

12. Mack, T.A., Sr. (June 12, 1972). *Letter from Theodore A. Mack Sr., to Edward Goodbout, Chief of 8-A Program, Small Business Administration*. Crosby Papers, University of Wisconsin-Milwaukee.

13. Sixteenth Census of the United States: Population Schedule, Sheet 9-B (1940). *Department of Commerce-Bureau of the Census*. Government Printing Office.

14. Peoples Brewery Saluted (October 11, 1970). *Post Crescent*, D2.

15. Redcay, E.E. (1935). *County Training Schools and Public Secondary Education for Negroes in the South*. The John F. Slater Fund.

16. Lynching in America: Confronting the Legacy of Racial Terror, County Data Supplement (January 2022). *Equal Justice Initiative*.

17. Negro Brute: Pays the Penalty of His Atrocious Crime—Unwritten Law Executed—Hanged to a Pine Limb and Riddled with Shot (May 6, 1904). *The Prattville Progress*, 1.

18. Sheriff M'Williams Writes Gov. Cunningham (September 2, 1904). *The Prattville Progress*, 2.

19. No Court in Autauga: Judge T.S. Sayre Writes the Governor, Will Not Now Investigate Gaines Hall Crime (May 20, 1904). *The Prattville Progress*, 3.

20. Redcay, E. (1935). *County Training Schools and Public Secondary Education in the South*. The John F. Slater Fund.

21. Lottman, M. S. (July 27–28, 1968). "Federal Judges Block Negro School Addition." *The Southern Courier*, 10

22. Moorer, H.C., Falk, G. (October 3–4, 1965). "Negroes Boycott Training School." *The Southern Courier*, 4.

23. Strasser, M. (November 4, 1978). "Mack Treasures Knowing Woody." *The Oshkosh Northwestern*, B1.

24. (March 1965). *The General Condition of the Alabama Negro*. Student Nonviolent Coordinating Committee.

25. Mack, T.A., Sr. (June 12, 1972). *Letter from Theodore A. Mack Sr., to Edward Goodbout, Chief of 8-A Program, Small Business Administration*, Crosby Papers, University of Wisconsin-Milwaukee.

26. Napier, W. (July 1, 2021), "A Short History of Integration in the U.S. Armed Forces." *U.S. Air Force*. Retrieved from https://www.af.mil/News/Commentaries/Display/Article/2676311/a-short-history-of-integration-in-the-us-armed-forces/.

27. Wakesfeld, W.E. (1997). *Playing to Win: Sports and the American Military 1898–1945*. State University of New York Press.

28. Mack, T.A., Sr. (June 12, 1972). *Letter from Theodore A. Mack Sr., to Edward Goodbout, Chief of 8-A Program, Small Business Administration*, Crosby Papers, University of Wisconsin-Milwaukee.

29. Lombardo, J. (2005). *A Fire to Win: The Life and Times of Woody Hayes*. Thomas Dunne Books.

30. Schechter, B. (November 24, 1953). "Brubaker, Borton Named Co-Captains." *Ohio State Lantern*, 4–7.

31. Strasser, M. (November 4, 1978). "Mack Treasures Knowing Woody." *The Oshkosh Northwestern*, B1.

32. Strasser, M. (November 4, 1978). "Mack Treasures Knowing Woody." *The Oshkosh Northwestern*, B1.
33. People's Beer Coming to City... Black Capitalism Brewing (May 22, 1971). *Sheboygan Press*, 2.
34. Middletonian Dies in Fall from 100-Foot Scaffold (June 5, 1954). *The Middletown Ohio Journal*, 2.
35. Obituary for Thomas J. Mack (June 7, 1954). *Journal Herald, Dayton, Ohio*, 2.
36. Fall Victim's Widow Treated by Aid Squad (June 6, 1954). *The Middletown, Ohio, Sunday News-Journal*, 5.
37. Foltman, L., and Jones, M. (February 28, 2019). "How Redlining Continues to Shape Racial Segregation in Milwaukee." *WisCONTEXT*. Retrieved from https://www.wiscontext.org/how-red-lining-continues-shape-racial-segregation-milwaukee.

Chapter 2

1. Dornbusch, Horst D. (1997). *Prost!: The Story of German Beer*. Siris Books.
2. Akin, R., Reiherzer, L. (2012). *The Breweries of Oshkosh: Their Rise and Fall*. Akin & Reiherzer.
3. Tremblay, V.J., Tremblay, C.H. (2005). *The U.S. Brewing Industry: Data Analysis and Economic Analysis*. The MIT Press.
4. Cochran, T.C. (1948). *The Pabst Brewing Company: The History of an American Business*. New York University Press.
5. Tremblay, V.J., Tremblay, C.H. (2005). *The U.S. Brewing Industry: Data Analysis and Economic Analysis*. The MIT Press.
6. Akin, R., Reiherzer, L. (2012). *The Breweries of Oshkosh: Their Rise and Fall*. Akin & Reiherzer.
7. Lorence, J. J. (1983). "'Dynamite for the Brain': The Growth and Decline of Socialism in Central and Lakeshore Wisconsin, 1910–1920." *Wisconsin Magazine of History*, 66(4), 251–273.
8. Guyton, G. P. (1999). "A Brief History of Workers' Compensation." *The Iowa Orthopaedic Journal*, 19, 106–110.
9. Schlüter, H. (1910). *The Brewing Industry and the Brewery Workers' Movement in America*. International Union of United Brewery Workmen of America.
10. Stack, M. (2000). "Local and Regional Breweries in America's Brewing Industry, 1865 to 1920." *Business History Review*, 74(3), 435–463.
11. In his book, Schlüter only discusses the large cities of a region, but suggests that the surrounding and smaller towns and cities would have also followed suit in organizing. Thus, it should be intuited that as Milwaukee was organizing, so too would Madison, Oshkosh, and other, smaller cities.
12. Schlüter, H. (1910). *The Brewing Industry and the Brewery Workers' Movement in America*. *International Union of United Brewery Workmen of America*, 141.
13. Breweries did anything they could to survive, most all switched to making soft drinks, since their brewing equipment could easily be modified for it. None of it was ever that popular, though, and most breweries simply went under. Still other diversified even more (Coors, famously, tried its hand at making ceramics). For a comprehensive history of America's brewing industry, see Ogle, M. (2019). *Ambitious Brew: A History of American Beer*. Blue Willow Books.
14. Tremblay, V.J., Tremblay, C.H. (2005). *The U.S. Brewing Industry: Data Analysis and Economic Analysis*. The MIT Press.
15. Tremblay, V.J., Tremblay, C.H. (2005). *The U.S. Brewing Industry: Data Analysis and Economic Analysis*. The MIT Press.
16. Tremblay, V.J., Tremblay, C.H. (2005). *The U.S. Brewing Industry: Data Analysis and Economic Analysis*. The MIT Press.

Chapter 3

1. Slesinger, D.P., Grigsby, E. H., Taeuber, K. (2006). *African Americans in Wisconsin: A Statistical Overview* (2nd ed). University of Wisconsin.
2. Trotter, J.W. (2007). *Black Milwaukee: The Making of an Industrial Proletariat, 1915–1945*. University of Illinois Press.

3. Trotter, J.W. (2007). *Black Milwaukee: The Making of an Industrial Proletariat, 1915–1945*. University of Illinois Press.

4. Tolnay, S.E. (2003). "The African American 'Great Migration' and Beyond." *Annual Review of Sociology*, 29, 209–232.

5. Grossman, J.R. (1989). *Land of Hope: Chicago, Black Southerners, and the Great Migration*. University of Chicago Press.

6. Connell, T. (2016). "1950s Milwaukee: Race, Class, and a City Divided." *Labor Studies Journal*, 42(1), 27–51.

7. Trotter, J.W. (2007). *Black Milwaukee: The Making of an Industrial Proletariat, 1915–1945*. University of Illinois Press.

8. Strickland, A.E. (1966). *History of the Urban League of Chicago (Volume 1)*. University of Chicago Press.

9. Parris, G, Brooks, L. (1971). *Black in the City: A History of the National Urban League*. Little, Brown and Company.

10. Parris, G, Brooks, L. (1971). *Black in the City: A History of the National Urban League*, 29. Little, Brown and Company.

11. Reynolds Told to Pick Negro or Lose Votes (March 4, 1964). *The Eau Claire Leader*, 1.

12. Ask Negro Judge for Milwaukee (March 4, 1964). *The Capital Times*, 3.

13. Hanley, D.P., Jr. (March 4, 1964). "Governor Told: Negro Judge or No Votes." *Wisconsin State Journal*, 1.

14. Wrong Way to Go at It (March 5, 1964). *Racine Journal-Times*, 7.

15. Jenson, H. (March 11, 1964). "No Governor Should Be Subjected to Threats." *Wisconsin State Journal*, 12.

16. Jones P.D. (2010). "'Get Up Off of Your Knees!': Competing Visions of Black Empowerment in Milwaukee during the Early Civil Rights Era." In: Joseph P.E. (eds). *Neighborhood Rebels. Contemporary Black History*. Palgrave Macmillan.

17. The struggle for civil rights in Milwaukee has a complex and dynamic history (though it is in no way concluded). Important resources for this chapter and further reading can be found in Jack Dougherty's *More Than One Struggle: The Evolution of Black School Reform in Milwaukee*, Patrick D. Jones' *The Selma of the North: Civil Rights Insurgency in Milwaukee*, and Joe William Trotter, Jr.'s, *Black Milwaukee: The Making of an Industrial Proletariat, 1915–1945*.

18. Jones, P. D. (2009). *Selma of the North: Civil Rights Insurgency in Milwaukee*. Harvard University Press.

19. Second Program in Human Rights Series Sunday (April 10, 1964). *The Sheboygan Press*, 4.

20. Euchner, C. (2010). *Nobody Turn Me Around: A People's History of the March on Washington D.C.* Beacon Press.

21. Kenoshans Will Join in March (August 26, 1963). *Kenosha News*, 14.

22. Last Minute Funds Aid State Group (August 27, 1963). *The Capital Times*, 2.

23. Marchers Return to Milwaukee (August 30, 1963). *Kenosha News*, 2.

24. For Jobs and Freedom: 50 Years and Counting (August 26, 2013). *Milwaukee PBS*.

25. Jones, W.P. (2014). *The March on Washington: Jobs, Freedom, and the Forgotten History of Civil Rights*. W, W. Norton & Company.

26. Bell, D. (2005). *Silent Covenants: Brown v. Board of Education and the Unfulfilled Hopes for Racial Reform*. Oxford University Press.

27. Milwaukee School Bus Issue Hot (October 13, 1965). *Kenosha News*, 3.

28. Bonds, M., Farmer-Hinton, R. L., Epps, E. G. (2009). "African Americans' Continuing Struggle for Quality Education in Milwaukee, Wisconsin." *The Journal of Negro Education*, 78(1), 55–69.

29. School Attendance Light in Milwaukee Boycott (May 18, 1964). *The Racine Journal-Times*, 1.

30. Harris, I. M (1983). "Criteria for Evaluating School Desegregation in Milwaukee." *Journal of Negro Education*, 52(4), 423–435.

31. Madison "Rights" Unit to Back State Boycott (May 17, 1964). *Racine Sunday Bulletin*, 3A.

32. For Jobs and Freedom: 50 Years and Counting (August 26, 2013). *Milwaukee PBS*.

33. Jones, P. D. (2009). *Selma of the North: Civil Rights Insurgency in Milwaukee*. Harvard University Press.

34. Trotter, J.W. (2007). *Black Milwaukee: The Making of an Industrial Proletariat, 1915–1945*. University of Illinois Press.

35. Racial Membership Rule Protested Here: NAACP Youth Unit Pickets Eagles (May 25, 1966). *The Capital Times*, 4.

36. Aukofer, F. A. (2007). *City with a Chance: A Case History of Civil Rights Revolution*. Marquette University Press.

37. Jones, P. D. (2009). *Selma of the North: Civil Rights Insurgency in Milwaukee*. Harvard University Press.

38. Jones, P. D. (2009). *Selma of the North: Civil Rights Insurgency in Milwaukee*. Harvard University Press.

Chapter 4

1. Cullen, K. M. (2011). "Rediscovering Milwaukee's Historic Breweries Part I: Milwaukee's Downtown Breweries." *Brewery History*, 140, 71–86.

2. Magee, B. (2014). *Brewing in Milwaukee*. Arcadia.

3. Pabst Acquires Blatz Brewery for $161/2 Million (July 31, 1958). *Appleton Post-Crescent*, 2.

4. Keeping Things Small (October 24, 1959). *Monroe Morning World*, 5.

5. Stevens, W. H. (1915). "The Clayton Act." *The American Economic Review*. 5(1), 38–54.

6. *United States v. Pabst Brewing Co.*, 384 U.S. 546 (1966). Retrieved from https://www.loc.gov/item/usrep384546/.

7. Tremblay, V.J., Tremblay, C.H. (2005). *The U.S. Brewing Industry: Data Analysis and Economic Analysis*. The MIT Press.

8. United States of America, *Plaintiff vs. Jos. Schlitz Brewing Company and General Brewing Company, Defendants: Final Judgement and Decree* (March 28, 1966). The United States District Court for the Northern District of California Southern Division.

9. James C. Windham, 63, Chairman and Top Executive Officer of Pabst (May 13, 1977). *The New York Times*, 24.

10. Breweries Lift 50-Yr. Ban (July 29, 1950). *The New Tribune*, 3.

11. Biondi, M. (2006). *To Stand and Fight: The Struggle for Civil Rights in Postwar New York City*. Harvard Press.

12. Hill, H. (1961). "Racism Within Organized Labor: A Report of Five Years of the AFL-CIO, 1955–1960." *The Journal of Negro Education*, 30(2), 109–118.

13. Marshal, R. (January 1964). "Unions and the Negro Community." *Industrial and Labor Relations Review*, 17(2), 179–202.

14. Trotter, J.W. (2007). *Black Milwaukee: The Making of an Industrial Proletariat, 1915–1945*. University of Illinois Press.

15. Jones, P. D. (2009). *Selma of the North: Civil Rights Insurgency in Milwaukee*. Harvard University Press.

16. Biondi, M. (2006). *To Stand and Fight: The Struggle for Civil Rights in Postwar New York City*. Harvard Press.

17. Marshal, R. (January 1964). "Unions and the Negro Community." *Industrial and Labor Relations Review*, 17(2), 179–202.

18. Breweries Lift 50-Yr. Ban (July 29, 1950). *The New Tribune*, 3.

19. What Kind of Man Is Your New York Life Agent? (October 1965). *Ebony*, 8.

20. Peoples Brewery Saluted (October 11, 1970). *Post Crescent*, D2.

21. Blatz Sale Pondered in Trust Suit (March 26, 1969). *Charleston Daily Mail*, 7.

22. Opinion of Chief Judge Tehan on *United States v. Pabst Brewing* (August 6, 1969). The United States District Court for the Eastern District of Wisconsin.

23. Grain Belt Withdraws Offer to Acquire Blatz from Pabst (July 9, 1969). *Milwaukee Journal Business News*, 3.

24. Black Group Reveals Support in Blatz Bid (July 9, 1969). *Milwaukee Journal Business News*, 3.

25. Prospectus of the United People's Brewing Ltd. (July 25, 1970). *United People's Brewing, Ltd.* Crosby Papers, University of Wisconsin-Milwaukee.

26. Radio Broadcasting Pioneer Harold "Hal" B. Jackson Remembered, Passes at 96 (June 7, 2012). *Milwaukee Courier*. Retrieved from https://milwaukeecourieronline.com/index.php/2012/06/07/radio-broadcasting-pioneer-harold-hal-b-jackson-remembered-passes-at-96/.

27. Obituary for Honorable Harold B. Jackson, Jr. (February 2016). *Schramka Funeral Home*. Retrieved from https://www.schramkafuneralhome.com/memorials/Jackson-Honorable Harold/2380067/obituary.php

28. Black Group Reveals Support in Blatz Bid (July 9, 1969). *Milwaukee Journal Business News*, 3.
29. Black Group Reveals Support in Blatz Bid (July 9, 1969). *Milwaukee Journal Business News*, 3.
30. History of Paradise Valley Distributing Company (September 6, 1941). *The Detroit Tribune*, 6.
31. Black Enterprises, 2 Others Submit Bid to Buy Blatz (July 14, 1969). *The Milwaukee Journal*, 5.
32. Negro Business Group Raising Funds to Bid for Blatz Brewery (July 10, 1969). *The Wall Street Journal*, 10.
33. Malone, C., Novick, D. (July 12, 1969). "The Blacker the Beer." *The Milwaukee Courier*, 2.
34. Blacks Bid for Milwaukee Brewery (July 12, 1969). *The Greater Milwaukee Star*, 10.
35. United Black Enterprises: All Media Release (July 9, 1969). *United Black Enterprises*. Crosby Papers, University of Wisconsin-Milwaukee.
36. Black Enterprises, 2 Others Submit Bid to Buy Blatz (July 14, 1969). *The Milwaukee Journal*, 5.
37. Blatz Plan Reiterated by Black Enterprises (July 22, 1969). *The Milwaukee Journal*, 4.
38. Blatz Delay Is Deferred (July 17, 1969). *Milwaukee Sentinel*, 3.
39. Blatz Delay Is Deferred (July 17, 1969). *Milwaukee Sentinel*, 3.
40. United Black Enterprises: All Media Release (July 9, 1969). *United Black Enterprises*. Crosby Papers, University of Wisconsin-Milwaukee.
41. Judge Rejects UBE Request (July 23, 1969). *Milwaukee Sentinel*, 8.
42. UBE Will Fight Tehan Decision (July 26, 1969). *The Greater Milwaukee Star*, 12.
43. Beer Fight Goes On (July 26, 1969). *The Milwaukee Courier*, 3.
44. UBE Will Fight Tehan Decision (July 26, 1969). *The Greater Milwaukee Star*, 12.
45. Beer Fight Goes On (July 26, 1969). *The Milwaukee Courier*, 3.
46. Blatz Brand Is Shifted to Heilman (September 3, 1969). *Milwaukee Sentinel*, 5.
47. Beer Fight Goes On (July 26, 1969). *The Milwaukee Courier*, 3.
48. Beer Fight Goes On (July 26, 1969). *The Milwaukee Courier*, 3.

Chapter 5

1. Cesur, R., Kelly, I.R. (2014). "Who Pay the Bar Tab? Beer Consumption and Economic Growth in the United States." *Economic Inquiry*, 52(1), 477–494.
2. Greene, B. (May 11, 1971). "Blacks Buy Oshkosh Brewery." *Freeport Journal-Standard*, 17.
3. Negro Firm Contracts Area Brewery (November 8, 1969). *Fond Du Lac Commonwealth Reporter*, 11.
4. Pecor, J. (April 14, 1970). "Black Group Bidding for Brewery." *Milwaukee Sentinel*, 3.
5. Black Group May Buy Out Peoples (April 14, 1970). *Daily Northwestern*, 3.
6. Black Firm Is Now Seeking Oshkosh Unit (April 14, 1970). *Kenosha News*, 14.
7. Blacks Buy Oshkosh Brewery (April 18, 1970). *The Milwaukee Courier*, 6.
8. Black Brewery to Open Within Two Months (April 18, 1970). *The Greater Milwaukee Star*, 9.
9. Eifert, C.A. (April 15, 1970). "Peoples Brewery Sold to Milwaukee Group." *The Paper for Central Wisconsin*, 13.
10. Black Brewery to Open Within Two Months (April 18, 1970). *The Greater Milwaukee Star*, 9.
11. Blacks Buy Oshkosh Brewery (April 18, 1970). *The Milwaukee Courier*, 6.
12. Prospectus of the United People's Brewing Ltd. (July 25, 1970). *United People's Brewing, Ltd*. Crosby Papers, University of Wisconsin-Milwaukee.
13. Bates, T. (1989). "The Changing Nature of Minority Business: A Comparative Analysis of Asian, Non-Minority, and Black-Owned Businesses." *Review of Black Political Economy*, 18, 25–42.
14. Fairlie R.W., Robb, A.M. (2007). "Why Are Black-Owned Businesses Less Successful Than White-Owned Businesses? The Role of Families, Inheritances, and Business Human Capital." *Journal of Labor Economics*, 25(2), 289–323.
15. Walker, J.E.K. (2009). The History of Black Business in America: Capitalism,

Race, Entrepreneurship. The University of North Carolina Press.

16. Oshkosh Brewery Sale Approved (April 15, 1970). *Stevens Point Daily Journal*, 11.

17. Prospectus of the United People's Brewing Ltd. (July 25, 1970). *United People's Brewing, Ltd.* Crosby Papers, University of Wisconsin-Milwaukee.

18. Prospectus of the United People's Brewing Ltd. (July 25, 1970). *United People's Brewing, Ltd.* Crosby Papers, University of Wisconsin-Milwaukee.

19. Black Businessmen Buy Peoples Brewery (April 15, 1970). *Daily Northwestern*, 4.

20. Theodore Mack, Sr., Past President and Chairman of the Board of People's Brewing Co., Milwaukee, Wis., Accompanied by Ray Alexander, Member of the Board of Directors (June 1974). *Hearings Before the Subcommittee on Small Business of the Committee on Banking and Currency, House of Representatives, 1974.* U.S. Government Printing Office.

21. Bean, J. (2014). *Big Government and Affirmative Action: The Scandalous History of the Small Business Administration.* University Press of Kentucky.

22. Bean, J. (2014). *Big Government and Affirmative Action: The Scandalous History of the Small Business Administration.* University Press of Kentucky.

23. Kotlowski, D. (1998). "Black Power —Nixon Style: the Nixon Administration and Minority Business Enterprise." *Business History Review,* 72(3), 409–445.

24. Stans, M.H. (1996). "Richard Nixon and His Bridges to Human Dignity." *Presidential Studies Quarterly,* 26(1), 179–183.

25. SBA's "8(a) Program": Overview, History, and Current Issues (November 2021). *Congressional Research Service.*

26. Black Beer Group Sets Sale of Stock (July 25, 1970). *The Milwaukee Journal,* 5.

27. Brewery Has New Owner in Oshkosh (April 24, 1970). *Daily Northwestern,* 5.

28. Kenney, R. (August 1, 1970). "People's Offer Piques Interest." *Milwaukee Sentinel,* 7.

29. Black Beer Group Sets Sale of Stock (July 25, 1970). *The Milwaukee Journal,* 5.

30. Kenney, R. (August 1, 1970). "People's Offer Piques Interest." *Milwaukee Sentinel,* 7.

31. Prospectus of the United People's Brewing Ltd. (July 25, 1970). *United People's Brewing, Ltd.* Crosby Papers, University of Wisconsin-Milwaukee.

32. Prospectus of the United People's Brewing Ltd. (July 25, 1970). *United People's Brewing, Ltd.* Crosby Papers, University of Wisconsin-Milwaukee.

33. Prospectus of the United People's Brewing Ltd. (July 25, 1970). *United People's Brewing, Ltd.* Crosby Papers, University of Wisconsin-Milwaukee.

34. Prospectus of the United People's Brewing Ltd. (July 25, 1970). *United People's Brewing, Ltd.* Crosby Papers, University of Wisconsin-Milwaukee.

35. Prospectus of the United People's Brewing Ltd. (July 25, 1970). *United People's Brewing, Ltd.* Crosby Papers, University of Wisconsin-Milwaukee.

36. Prospectus of the United People's Brewing Ltd. (July 25, 1970). *United People's Brewing, Ltd.* Crosby Papers, University of Wisconsin-Milwaukee.

37. Prospectus of the United People's Brewing Ltd. (July 25, 1970). *United People's Brewing, Ltd.* Crosby Papers, University of Wisconsin-Milwaukee.

38. Prospectus of the United People's Brewing Ltd. (July 25, 1970). *United People's Brewing, Ltd.* Crosby Papers, University of Wisconsin-Milwaukee.

39. Prospectus of the United People's Brewing Ltd. (July 25, 1970). *United People's Brewing, Ltd.* Crosby Papers, University of Wisconsin-Milwaukee.

40. Prospectus of the United People's Brewing Ltd. (July 25, 1970). *United People's Brewing, Ltd.* Crosby Papers, University of Wisconsin-Milwaukee.

41. Prospectus of the United People's Brewing Ltd. (July 25, 1970). *United People's Brewing, Ltd.* Crosby Papers, University of Wisconsin-Milwaukee.

42. Blacks Buy Oshkosh Brewery (April 18, 1970). *The Milwaukee Courier,* 6.

43. Seek Brewery Financing (August 9, 1970). *Racine Sunday Bulletin,* 8D.

44. Black Beer Group Sets Sale of Stock (July 25, 1970). *The Milwaukee Journal,* 5.

45. Brewing Firm Offers Public Sale of

Stock (July 30, 1970). *Appleton Post Crescent*, B3.

46. Blackwell, E.H. (October 11, 1970). "Black Managed Brewery Opens Doors." *The Milwaukee Journal Business News*, 14.

47. Good Stuff (October 15, 1970). *Oshkosh Advance-Titan*, 2.

48. Wigs Worth $700 Stolen at Hotel (October 12, 1970). *Daily Northwestern*, 4.

49. Visitors Flock to Oshkosh Home of People's Beer (October 11, 1970). *The Milwaukee Courier*, 3.

50. Blackwell, E.H. (October 11, 1970). "Black Managed Brewery Opens Doors." *The Milwaukee Journal Business News*, 14.

51. Peoples Brewery Saluted (October 11, 1970). *Post Crescent*, D2.

52. Prospectus of the United People's Brewing Ltd. (July 25, 1970). *United People's Brewing, Ltd.* Crosby Papers, University of Wisconsin-Milwaukee.

53. Peoples Brewery Saluted (October 11, 1970). *Post Crescent*, D2.

Chapter 6

1. Thirteenth Census of the United States Taken in the Year 1910, Statistic for Wisconsin (1918). *Department of Commerce, Bureau of the Census.* Government Printing Office.

Fourteenth Census of the United States, State Compendium: Wisconsin (1925). *Department of Commerce, Bureau of the Census.* Government Printing Office.

Fifteenth Census of the United States: 1903—Population, Volume III, Part 2, Montana-Wyoming. U.S. (1932). *Department of Commerce, Bureau of the Census.* Government Printing Office.

2. Akin, R., Reiherzer, L. (2012). *The Breweries of Oshkosh: Their Rise and Fall.* Akin & Reiherzer.

3. Trotter, J.W. (2007). *Black Milwaukee: The Making of an Industrial Proletariat, 1915–1945.* University of Illinois Press.

4. Trotter, J.W. (2007). *Black Milwaukee: The Making of an Industrial Proletariat, 1915–1945.* University of Illinois Press.

5. Hill, H. (1961). Racism Within Organized Labor: A Report of Five Years of the AFL-CIO, 1955–1960. The Journal of Negro Education, 30(2). 109–11.

6. Revived Ku Klux Klan Grows Rapidly (December 24, 1920). *The Daily Northwestern*, 13.

7. Goldberg, R. A. (1974). "The Ku Klux Klan in Madison, 1922–1927." *The Wisconsin Magazine of History*, 31–44.

8. Lee, G.H. (August 1968). *The Ku Klux Klan in Wisconsin in the 1920s* [unpublished thesis paper]. Wisconsin State University—La Crosse.

9. Goldberg, R. A. (1974). "The Ku Klux Klan in Madison, 1922–1927." *The Wisconsin Magazine of History*, 31–44.

10. Lee, G.H. (August 1968). *The Ku Klux Klan in Wisconsin in the 1920s* [unpublished thesis paper]. Wisconsin State University—La Crosse.

11. Expect Thousands at Gathering of the Ku Klux Klan (July 29, 1927). *Daily Northwestern*, 4.

12. Correspondence: Up-to-date (May 27, 1921). *The Baltimore Afro-American*, 1.

13. Wallace Called Advocate of Evil (March 25, 1964). *The New York Times*, 25.

14. Gov. Wallace Reaffirms Intent to Keep Segregation (February 10, 1963). *Southern School News*, 2.

15. Prigge, M.J. (December 22, 2015). "Dixie North: George Wallace and the 1964 Wisconsin Presidential Primary." *Shepherd Express*. Retrieved from https://shepherdexpress.com/culture/milwaukee-history/dixie-north-george-wallace-1964-wisconsin-presidential-primary/.

16. How Winnebago County Voted (April 8, 1964). *Oshkosh Daily Northwestern*, 34.

17. Prigge, M.J. (December 22, 2015). "Dixie North: George Wallace and the 1964 Wisconsin Presidential Primary." *Shepherd Express*. Retrieved from https://shepherdexpress.com/culture/milwaukee-history/dixie-north-george-wallace-1964-wisconsin-presidential-primary/.

18. Wallace in Wisconsin (March 31, 1964). *The Afro-American*, 4.

19. U.S. Census of Population: 1960. Vol. I, Characteristics of Population. Part 51, Wisconsin, U.S. (1963). *Department of Commerce, Bureau of the Census.* Government Printing Office.

20. Loewan. J.W. (2005). *Sundown Towns: A Hidden Dimension of American Racism.* Touchstone.

21. Finner, R.E. (November 1968). "Black Discontent." *Oshkosh Advance-Titan*, 2.
22. McCreary, S. (October 3, 1968). "Black Students Face City, Campus Prejudice." *Oshkosh Advance Titan*, 5.
23. McCreary, S. (October 3, 1968). "Black Students Face City, Campus Prejudice." *Oshkosh Advance Titan*, 5.
24. Finner, R.E. (November 21, 1968). "Black Discontent." *Oshkosh Advance Titan*, 2.
25. Campus Mayhem (November 22, 1968). *Daily Northwestern*, 10.
26. Pecor, J. (April 14, 1970). "Black Group Bidding for Brewery." *Milwaukee Sentinel*, 3.
27. Russell, J. (April 27, 1970). "'Falsehoods' Rapped by Brewery President." *Daily Northwestern*, 8.
28. Black Brewery to Open Within Two Months (April 18, 1970). *The Greater Milwaukee Star*, 9.
29. People's Sale: Hits the Spot? (April 26, 1970). *Sunday Post-Crescent*, B1.
30. Luebke, M.H. (May 16, 1970). "Man Not System at Fault Today." *The Daily Northwestern*, 8.
31. Schmid, D. (May 18, 1970). "Good News Cannot Be Delayed Longer." *The Daily Northwestern*, 2.
32. Black Group Reveals Support in Blatz Bid (July 9, 1969). *Milwaukee Journal Business News*, 3.
33. Negro Business Group Raising Funds to Bid for Blatz Brewery (July 10, 1969). *The Wall Street Journal*, 10.
34. Blacks Bid for Milwaukee Brewery (July 12, 1969). *The Greater Milwaukee Star*, 10.
35. Black Group May Buy Out Peoples (April 14, 1970). *Daily Northwestern*, 3.
36. Black Firm Is Now Seeking Oshkosh Unit (April 14, 1970). *Kenosha News*, 14.
37. Blacks Purchase Upstate Brewery. (April 16, 1970). *The Capital Times*, 4.
38. Blacks Buy Oshkosh Brewery (April 18, 1970). *The Milwaukee Courier*, 6.
39. Black Brewery to Open Within Two Months (April 18, 1970). *The Greater Milwaukee Star*, 9.
40. Grossman, R. (September 25, 2015). "Chicago's Lager Beer Riot Proved Immigrants' Power." *Chicago Tribune*. Retrieved from https://www.chicagotribune.com/history/ct-know-nothing-party-lager-beer-riot-per-flashback-jm-20150925-story.html.
41. Alberts, B., Holston, C. (July 15, 2020). "'Streets as Stages'—The Munich Beer Riots of 1844." *Good Beer Hunting*. Retrieved from: https://www.goodbeerhunting.com/blog/2020/7/13/streets-as-stages-the-munich-beer-riots-of-1844.
42. Black Brewery to Begin Sales (February 17, 1971). *Eau Claire Leader-Telegram*, 1.

Chapter 7

1. Blacks Buy Oshkosh Brewery (April 18, 1970). *The Milwaukee Courier*, 6.
2. Group to Acquire Oshkosh Brewery (April 14, 1970). *Milwaukee Journal*, 3.
3. Eifert, C.A. (April 15, 1970). "Peoples Brewery Sold to Milwaukee Group." *The Paper for Central Wisconsin*, 13.
4. Russell, J. (April 27, 1970). "'Falsehoods' Rapped by Brewery President." *Daily Northwestern*, 8.
5. Prospectus of the United People's Brewing Ltd. (July 25, 1970). *United People's Brewing, Ltd.* Crosby Papers, University of Wisconsin-Milwaukee.
6. Milwaukee Group Buys Peoples Beer (April 15, 1970). *The Paper for Central Wisconsin*, 3.
7. Some Don't Drink Peoples Anymore (April 26, 1970). *Sunday Post-Crescent*, B2.
8. Russell, J. (April 27, 1970). "'Falsehood' Rapped by Brewery President." *Daily Northwestern*, 8.
9. Peoples Beer Sales Ahead of Last Year (September 17, 1971). *Daily Northwestern*, 4.
10. New Members Introduced (January 23, 1971). *Daily Northwestern*, 9.
11. Youth Council Swells United Fund (January 28, 1971). *Daily Northwestern*, 2.
12. Russert, E. (March 17, 1971). "He's Clever." *Daily Northwestern*, 14.
13. Paine Employes [sic] Express Interest (November 19, 1971). *Daily Northwestern*, 3.
14. Russert, E. (March 17, 1971). "He's Clever." *Daily Northwestern*, 14.
15. Sayrs, J.H. (July 3, 1971). "Mack Sees

Conspiracy Against Peoples Beer." *Daily Northwestern*, 4.

16. Tenny, R.I., Dakin, P.E. (1984). "History of the American Society of Brewing Chemists." *Journal of the American Society of Brewing Chemists: The Science of Beer*, 42(3).

17. Letter from J.E. Siebel Sons' Company, Inc. and Certificate of Analysis (April 5, 1971). *J.E. Siebel Sons' Company, Inc.* Crosby Papers, University of Wisconsin-Milwaukee.

18. Mack, T., Sr. (April 21, 1971). *Letter to Peoples Beer Customers*. Crosby Paper, University of Wisconsin-Milwaukee.

19. Prospectus of the United People's Brewing Ltd. (July 25, 1970). *United People's Brewing, Ltd.* Crosby Papers, University of Wisconsin-Milwaukee.

20. 'Peoples Beer' Going on Sale Here (March 18, 1971). *The Capital Times*, 31.

21. Mack, T., Sr. (March 24, 1972). *Letter to Stockholders*. Crosby Papers, University of Wisconsin-Milwaukee.

22. Blackwell, E.H. (September 17, 1971). "Beer Business Different, Mack Finds." *Milwaukee Journal Business News*, 16.

23. Black Brewery May Leave Milwaukee (September 11, 1971). *Milwaukee Star*, 18.

24. Peoples Brewery Saluted (October 11, 1970). *Post Crescent*, D2.

25. Good Stuff (October 15, 1970). *Oshkosh Advance-Titan*, 2.

26. Russell, J. (April 27, 1970). "'Falsehoods' Rapped by Brewery President." *Daily Northwestern*, 8.

27. Greene, B. (May 10, 1971). "Black-Owned Brewery Welcomes the 'Thirsty' Months." *The Capital Times*, 11.

Chapter 8

1. Greene, B. (May 10, 1971). "Black-Owned Brewery at Oshkosh." *Stevens Point Daily Journal*, 8.

2. Peoples Beer Sales Ahead of Last Year (September 17, 1971). *Daily Northwestern*, 4.

3. Peoples Beer Sales Ahead of Last Year (September 17, 1971). *Daily Northwestern*, 4.

4. Brewery Will Expand; Add to Its Payroll (September 3, 1970). *Daily Northwestern*, 5.

5. Planning Peoples Beer Distribution in Area (September 28, 1970). *Racine Journal-Times*, 5B.

6. Expansion Planned by Peoples Brewery (June 18, 1971). *The Milwaukee Journal*, 3.

7. Peoples Beer Sales Ahead of Last Year (September 17, 1971). *Daily Northwestern*, 4.

8. 'Peoples Beer' Going on Sale Here (March 18, 1971). *The Capital Times*, 31.

9. Black Firm to Sell Beer at Stadium (February 16, 1971). *The Milwaukee Journal*, 7.

10. NOW! Pop-top Cans (November 20, 1970). *Daily Northwestern*, 15.

11. Peoples Brewing "Set to Compete": Mack (January 12, 1972). *Daily Northwestern*, 3.

12. Brewery Buys Old Tews Site (November 18, 1970). *The Milwaukee Journal*, 11.

13. Peoples Puts Out New Holiday Brew (December 5, 1970). *Greater Milwaukee Star*, 3.

14. Prospectus of the United People's Brewing Ltd. (July 25, 1970). *United People's Brewing, Ltd.* Crosby Papers, University of Wisconsin-Milwaukee.

15. Akin, R., and Reiherzer, L. (2012). *The Breweries of Oshkosh: Their Rise and Fall.* Akin & Reiherzer.

16. Brewing Company Future Is Subject to Speculation (October 20, 1971). *Oshkosh Daily Northwestern*, 4.

17. Black Brewery to Begin Sales (February 17, 1971). *Eau Claire Leader-Telegram*, 1.

18. Sayrs, J.H. (July 3, 1971). "Mack Sees Conspiracy Against Peoples Beer." *Daily Northwestern*, 4.

19. Brewery Venture Snarled in Indiana (July 3, 1971). *The Milwaukee Journal*, 9.

20. Brewery Venture Snarled in Indiana (July 3, 1971). *The Milwaukee Journal*, 9.

21. Sayrs, J.H. (July 3, 1971). "Mack Sees Conspiracy Against Peoples Beer." *Daily Northwestern*, 4.

22. Brewery Venture Snarled in Indiana

Notes—Chapter 8

(July 3, 1971). *The Milwaukee Journal*, 9.

23. Negro Beer Confiscated (July 2, 1971). *Ironwood, Daily Globe*, 12.

24. Indiana Authorities Impound Peoples Beer (July 3, 1971). *Wisconsin State Journal*, 2-2.

25. Indiana Impounds Beer from Oshkosh (July 2, 1971). *Fond du Lac Commonwealth Reporter*, 2-3.

26. Peoples Beer Charges Indiana Harassment (July 6, 1971). *Wisconsin State Journal*, 2-2.

27. Indiana Impounds Beer from Oshkosh (July 2, 1971). *Fond du Lac Commonwealth Reporter*, 2-3.

28. Brewery Venture Snarled in Indiana (July 3, 1971). *The Milwaukee Journal*, 9.

29. Sayrs, J.H. (July 3, 1971). "Mack Sees Conspiracy Against Peoples Beer." *Daily Northwestern*, 4.

30. Sayrs, J.H. (July 3, 1971). "Mack Sees Conspiracy Against Peoples Beer." *Daily Northwestern*, 4.

31. Peoples Brewing "Set to Compete": Mack (January 12, 1972). *Daily Northwestern*, 3.

32. Black Brewery Set $Million Goal This Year (June 17, 1971). *Jet*, 16.

33. Fleming, G.J. (February 13, 1971). "Now and Then: Traveling in Wisconsin." *Baltimore Afro-American*, 4.

34. Black-Owned Concern Is Brewing Success (March 15, 1971). *New York Times*, 28.

35. Peoples Brewing "Set to Compete": Mack (January 12, 1972). *Daily Northwestern*, 3.

36. Mack Is Speaker for Optimist Club (August 27, 1970). *Daily Northwestern*, 2.

37. Green Lake Hosts Area Lions Club (November 4, 1971). *Daily Northwestern*, 21.

38. Egan, J. (February 20, 1971). "Deep Meaning in Doing to Others." *Daily Northwestern*, 9.

39. Akin, R., Reiherzer, L. (2012). *The Breweries of Oshkosh: Their Rise and Fall*. Akin & Reiherzer.

40. Black Capitalism a Myth, Black Businessman Says (March 7, 1971). *Appleton Post Crescent*, B1.

41. Brimmer, A.F., Terrell, H.S. (1969). "The Economic Potential of Black Capitalism." *82nd Annual Meeting of the American Economic Association*, New York, 1.

42. Guest Speakers Outline Role of Black Americans (February 10, 1972). *Oshkosh Advance-Titan*, 28.

43. Guest Speakers Outline Role of Black Americans (February 10, 1972). *Oshkosh Advance-Titan*, 28.

44. 'Priorities Change Needed' Retired Persons Are Told (June 16, 1971). *Daily Northwestern*, A2.

45. Plans Completed for Annual WRTA Event (October 7, 1971). *Daily Northwestern*, 5.

46. Green Lake Hosts Area Lions Club (November 4, 1971). *Daily Northwestern*, 21.

47. "Priorities Change Needed" Retired Persons Are Told (June 16, 1971). *Daily Northwestern*, A2.

48. Brewery Venture Snarled in Indiana (July 3, 1971). *The Milwaukee Journal*, 9.

49. Lucey Endorses Business Plan (September 10, 1971). *The Milwaukee Journal*, 4.

50. S.C. Johnson on Lucey's Blue-ribbon Business Panel (January 20, 1971). *Racine Journal-Times*, 5.

51. 25 Business Leaders to Advise Governor (January 19, 1971). *Appleton Post Crescent*, 4A.

52. Black Capitalism a Myth, Black Businessman Says (March 7, 1971). *Appleton Post Crescent*, B1.

53. Negro Businessmen Tired of Being Studied (March 1, 1971). *Ironwood Daily Globe*, 5.

54. Peoples Brewing 1st Year Loss $100,000 (January 4, 1972). *Racine Journal-Times*, 11A.

55. Philip J. Siegel & Co. (January 14, 1972). *Report of Independent Certified Accountants The Peoples Brewing Company*. Crosby Papers, University of Wisconsin-Milwaukee.

56. (March 24, 1972). *The Peoples Brewing Company: Annual Report Year Ended September 30, 1971*. Crosby Papers, University of Wisconsin-Milwaukee.

57. The Peoples Brewing Company: Annual Report Year Ended September 30, 1971 (March 24, 1972). Peoples Brewing

Company. Crosby Papers, University of Wisconsin-Milwaukee.

Chapter 9

1. Peoples Brewery Saluted (October 11, 1970). *Post Crescent*, D2.
2. Peter Hemmings (N.D.). *Monticello*. Retrieved from https://www.monticello.org/site/research-and-collections/peter-hemings#footnote5_rip2u79
3. Negro Pioneers in Brewery Firm: First Negro Owned Brewery (November 26, 1955). *The Roanoke Tribune*, 1.
4. Sunshine Brewery Has Record Year (November 1970). *Brewers Digest*, 38.
5. Wagner, R. (2019). "Post Prohibition Brewing in Reading, PA." *Museum of Beer and Brewing*, 40.
6. Jaspin, E. (September 20, 1977). "The Region's Vanishing Breweries." *Pottsville Republican*, 1.
7. Barlett, D.L., Steele, J.B. (April 18, 1974). "Affluent Bloom Owes Big Tax: But IRS Doesn't Press for $729,833." *The Philadelphia Inquirer*, 290(108), 11-B.
8. (July 25, 1970). *Prospectus: United People's Brewing Ltd.*, Crosby Papers, University of Wisconsin-Milwaukee.
9. Sayrs, J.H. (July 3, 1971). "Mack Sees Conspiracy Against Peoples Beer." *Daily Northwestern*, 4,
10. Negro Firm Contracts Area Brewery (November 8, 1969). *Fond Du Lac Commonwealth Reporter*, 11.
11. For a Brighter Future…BLACK PRIDE (November 24, 1969). *Brewers Digest*, 35.
12. For a Brighter Future…BLACK PRIDE (November 24, 1969). *Brewers Digest*, 35.
13. Sayrs, J.H. (July 3, 1971). "Mack Sees Conspiracy Against Peoples Beer." *Daily Northwestern*, 4.
14. Winship, K. (April 29, 2012). "Malt Liquor: A History." *Faithful Readers*. Retrieved from https://faithfulreaders.com/2012/04/29/malt-liquor-a-history/
15. Kelly, I.R. (2014). Who Pays the Bar Tab? Beer Consumption and Economic Growth in the United States. Economic Inquiry 52(1), 477–494.
16. Winship, K. (April 29, 2012). "Malt Liquor: A History." *Faithful Readers*. Retrieved from https://faithfulreaders.com/2012/04/29/malt-liquor-a-history/
17. Winship, K. (April 29, 2012). "Malt Liquor: A History." *Faithful Readers*. Retrieved from https://faithfulreaders.com/2012/04/29/malt-liquor-a-history/
18. Brewers Diversify to Malt Liquor (March 9, 1964). *Broadcasting*, 38.
19. Winship, K. (April 29, 2012). "Malt Liquor: A History." *Faithful Readers*. Retrieved from https://faithfulreaders.com/2012/04/29/malt-liquor-a-history/
20. Kurlander, D. (N.D.). Capture the Rapture: "'Take in a Bottle, 40, Quart or Can': 1985–2017." David Kurlander: Popular History, Criticism, and Archival Exploration. Retrieved from https://kurlanderblog.wordpress.com/capture-the-rapture/.
21. Brenkert, G. C. (1998). "Marketing to Inner-City Blacks: Powermaster and Moral Responsibility." *Business Ethics Quarterly*, 8(1), 1–18.
22. Lowe, B. (1972). "Black Brewer Prospers in Oshkosh." *Oshkosh Advance-Titan*, 8.
23. Blackwell, E.H. (September 17, 1971). "Beer Business Different, Mack Finds." *Milwaukee Journal Business News*, 16.
24. Blackwell, E.H. (September 17, 1971). "Beer Business Different, Mack Finds." *Milwaukee Journal Business News*, 16.
25. Blackwell, E.H. (September 17, 1971). "Beer Business Different, Mack Finds." *Milwaukee Journal Business News*, 16.
26. Black Brewery May Leave Milwaukee (September 11, 1971). *Milwaukee Star*, 18.
27. Peoples Beer Sales Ahead of Last Year (September 17, 1971). *Daily Northwestern*, 4.
28. Black Brewery May Leave Milwaukee (September 11, 1971). *Milwaukee Star*, 18.
29. Philip J. Siegel & Co. (January 14, 1972). *Report of Independent Certified Accountants The Peoples Brewing Company*. Crosby Papers, University of Wisconsin-Milwaukee.
30. Blackwell, E.H. (September 17, 1971).

"Beer Business Different, Mack Finds." *Milwaukee Journal Business News,* 16.

31. Blackwell, E.H. (September 17, 1971). "Beer Business Different, Mack Finds." *Milwaukee Journal Business News,* 16.

32. Black Brewery May Leave Milwaukee (September 11, 1971). *Milwaukee Star,* 18.

33. Blackwell, E.H. (September 17, 1971). "Beer Business Different, Mack Finds." *Milwaukee Journal Business News,* 16.

34. Blackwell, E.H. (September 17, 1971). "Beer Business Different, Mack Finds." *Milwaukee Journal Business News,* 16.

35. Black Brewery May Leave Milwaukee (September 11, 1971). *Milwaukee Star,* 18.

36. Ray's Beverage Advertisement (December 15, 1971). *Daily Northwestern,* 10.

37. The Beverage Mart Advertisement (March 12, 1971). *Daily Northwestern,* 12.

38. Town 'N' Country Liquors Advertisement (January 21, 1972). *Kenosha News,* 8–9.

39. Town 'N' Country Liquors Advertisement (June 1, 1973). *Kenosha News,* 4–5.

40. Peoples Brewing "Set to Compete": Mack (January 12, 1972). *Daily Northwestern,* 3.

41. Peoples Brewing Advertisements (N.D.). *Peoples Brewing Company.*

Chapter 10

1. Greene, B. (May 11, 1971). "Blacks Buy Oshkosh Brewery." *Freeport Journal-Standard,* 17.

2. Keithahn, C.F. (December 1978). "The Brewing Industry. Staff Report of the Bureau of Economics." *Federal Trade Commission.*

3. Philip J. Siegel & Co. (January 14, 1972). *Report of Independent Certified Accountants The Peoples Brewing Company.* Crosby Papers, University of Wisconsin-Milwaukee.

4. Tremblay, V.J., Tremblay, C.H. (2005). *The U.S. Brewing Industry: Data Analysis and Economic Analysis.* The MIT Press.

5. Theodore Mack, Sr., Past President and Chairman of the Board of People's Brewing Co., Milwaukee, Wis., Accompanied by Ray Alexander, Member of the Board of Directors (June 1974). *Hearings Before the Subcommittee on Small Business of the Committee on Banking and Currency, House of Representatives, 1974.* U.S. Government Printing Office.

6. Theodore Mack, Sr., Past President and Chairman of the Board of People's Brewing Co., Milwaukee, Wis., Accompanied by Ray Alexander, Member of the Board of Directors (June 1974). *Hearings Before the Subcommittee on Small Business of the Committee on Banking and Currency, House of Representatives, 1974.* U.S. Government Printing Office.

7. Suit Names Big Brewers (November 8, 1972). *The Milwaukee Journal,* 15.

8. 3 Milwaukee Brewers Are Accused of Payoffs (April 10, 1976). *The Milwaukee Journal,* 7.

9. Brandon, M.M., Jr. (February 1961). "Fee Enterprise—Price Discrimination Under the Clayton Act." *Louisiana Law Review,* 21(2), 507–514.

10. Kenyon, R. (April 18, 1976). "Insider Affirms Beer Payoffs." *The Milwaukee Journal,* 9.

11. 3 Milwaukee Brewers Are Accused of Payoffs (April 10, 1976). *The Milwaukee Journal,* 7.

12. Peoples Beer Sales Ahead of Last Year (September 17, 1971). *Daily Northwestern,* 4.

13. Beal, D.L. (April 11, 1976). "Refused Price Deal, Beer Dealer Claims." *The Milwaukee Journal,* 19.

14. Kenyon, R. (April 18, 1976). "Insider Affirms Beer Payoffs." *The Milwaukee Journal,* 9.

Chapter 11

1. Theodore Mack, Sr., Past President and Chairman of the Board of People's Brewing Co., Milwaukee, Wis., Accompanied by Ray Alexander, Member of the Board of Directors (June 1974). *Hearings Before the Subcommittee on Small Business of the Committee on Banking and Currency, House of Representatives, 1974.* U.S. Government Printing Office.

2. SBA's "8(a) Program": Overview, History, and Current Issues (November 2021). *Congressional Research Service.*
3. SBA's "8(a) Program": Overview, History, and Current Issues (November 2021). *Congressional Research Service.*
4. Mack, T., Sr. (June 12, 1972). *Letter to Mr. Edward Goodbout. The Peoples Brewing Company.* Crosby Papers, University of Wisconsin-Milwaukee.
5. State Taxation of Military Income and Store Sales (July 1976). *Advisory Commission on Intergovernmental Relations.*
6. Department of Defense Appropriation for 1972 (1971). *Hearings Before a Subcommittee of the Committee on Appropriations House of Representatives.* Government Printing Office: Washington, D.C.
7. Goodbout, E.A. (July 18, 1972). *Letter to Marine Corps Exchange Service Headquarters.* Crosby Papers, University of Wisconsin-Milwaukee.
8. Bean, J. (2014). *Big Government and Affirmative Action: The Scandalous History of the Small Business Administration.* University Press of Kentucky.
9. Bean, J. (2014). *Big Government and Affirmative Action: The Scandalous History of the Small Business Administration.* University Press of Kentucky.
10. Rubin, I. (June 22, 1972). *Letter to Theodore Mack.* Crosby Papers, University of Wisconsin-Milwaukee.
11. Powers, N.D. (August 10, 1972). *Letter to E. A. Goodbout.* Crosby Papers, University of Wisconsin-Milwaukee.
12. Beal, D. (August 7, 1972). *Letter to E.A. Goodbout.* Crosby Papers, University of Wisconsin-Milwaukee.
13. Gordon, R.W. (August 9, 1972). *Letter to Theodore Mack, Sr.* Crosby Papers, University of Wisconsin-Milwaukee.
14. Knuth, E.L. (August 31, 1972). *Letter to Theodore Mack.* Crosby Papers, University of Wisconsin-Milwaukee.
15. Fraud and Corruption in Management of Military Club Systems: Illegal Currency Manipulations Affecting South Vietnam (1971). *Report of the Committee on Government Operations United States Senate Made by Its Permanent Subcommittee on Investigations.* Government Printing Office.
16. Fraud and Corruption in Management of Military Club Systems: Illegal Currency Manipulations Affecting South Vietnam (1971). *Report of the Committee on Government Operations United States Senate made by its Permanent Subcommittee on Investigations.* Government Printing Office.
17. Tremblay, V.J., Tremblay, C.H. (2005). *The U.S. Brewing Industry: Data Analysis and Economic Analysis.* The MIT Press.

Chapter 12

1. People Brewing Company Stops Production (November 10, 1972). *The Journal Times,* 5C.
2. Peoples Lays Off Workers (November 14, 1972). *Milwaukee Journal Business News,* 16.
3. Crosby, H. (October 22, 1972). *People vs. U.S.,* Handwritten Note. Crosby Papers, University of Wisconsin-Milwaukee.
4. People Brewing Company Stops Production (November 10, 1972). *The Journal Times,* 5C.
5. Peoples Lays Off Workers (November 14, 1972). *Milwaukee Journal Business News,* 16.
6. Larger Contracts Key to Brewery's Future (November 15, 1972). *The Journal Times,* 9A.
7. Black Brewery May Leave Milwaukee (September 11, 1971). *Milwaukee Star,* 18.
8. Powell, E. A. (December 2, 1972). "Black Brewery Might Go to Alabama." *The Milwaukee Journal,* 3.
9. PanAf Informational Brochure (N.D.). *PanAf.* Crosby Papers, University of Wisconsin-Milwaukee.
10. Bolden, D.W (January 31, 1973). *Letter to Ray A. Alexander.* Crosby Papers, University of Wisconsin-Milwaukee.
11. Heap, S. (November 2010). "Marketing Modernity: Star Lager Beer in Late Colonial and Early Independent Nigeria." Paper presented at *Elite Formation, Consumption and Urban Spaces—Cultural Perspectives on African Decolonization,* International Research Centre, Humboldt–Universität zu Berlin, Berlin, Germany.
12. Jernigan, D.H., Obot, I.S. (2006).

"Thirsting for the African Market." *African Journal of Drug & Alcohol Studies,* 5(1), 57–70.

13. Memorandum of Understanding Peoples Brewing Company and Ogbomosho Investment Club (January 16, 1973). *Ogbomosho Investment Club.* Crosby Paper, University of Wisconsin-Milwaukee.

14. Mack, T., Sr. (February 5, 1973). *Letter to Stockholders.* Crosby Papers, University of Wisconsin-Milwaukee.

Chapter 13

1. Aid Given to Brewery (March 8, 1973). *Oshkosh Advance-Titan,* 24.

2. Aid Given to Brewery (March 8, 1973). *Oshkosh Advance-Titan,* 24.

3. Research Proposal Between the Afro-Urban Institute and the University of Wisconsin (N.D.). *Afro-Urban Institute.* Crosby Papers, University of Wisconsin-Milwaukee.

4. A Proposal for the Resumption of Operations (N.D.). *Peoples Brewing Company.* Crosby Papers, University of Wisconsin-Milwaukee.

5. Beer Exports Denied (February 8, 1973). *Oshkosh Advance-Titan,* 7.

6. Gordon, M. (June 13, 1973). *United States District Court Eastern District of Wisconsin: Decision and Order.* Crosby Papers, University of Wisconsin-Milwaukee.

7. Ford, H. (October 10, 1973). *Letter to Mr. and Mrs. Henry S. Crosby.* Crosby Papers, University of Wisconsin-Milwaukee.

8. Small Business Administration Invites Bids for the Purchase of Personal Property at Peoples Brewery—Oshkosh, WI (April 14, 1974). *Small Business Administration.* Crosby Paper, University of Wisconsin-Milwaukee.

9. Seig, D.J. (June 20, 1974). "People Pay in Auction of Brewery." *The Milwaukee Journal,* 6.

10. Peoples Brewing Equipment Auctioned (June 19, 1974). *Daily Northwestern,* 4.

11. Auction to Be Held Tuesday at Former Peoples Brewery (June 15, 1974). *Daily Northwestern,* 18.

12. Peoples Brewing Co. Ends with Auction (June 20, 1974). *Wisconsin State Journal,* 2–6.

13. Brewery Auction Defended (June 20, 1974). *The Milwaukee Journal,* 5.

14. Auction of People's Brewery Still Making Noise (June 20, 1974). *Daily Northwestern,* 2.

15. Bean, J. (2014). *Big Government and Affirmative Action: The Scandalous History of the Small Business Administration.* University Press of Kentucky.

16. Bean, J. (2014). *Big Government and Affirmative Action: The Scandalous History of the Small Business Administration.* University Press of Kentucky.

17. Johnson, E. (July 11, 1969). "Sandoval Has the One Duty He Wants in the Capital." *Amarillo Globe-Times,* 15.

18. *United States of America v. Albert Fuentes, Jr., and Edward J. Montez* (October 5, 1970). *U.S. Court of Appeals for the Fifth Circuit.* Retrieved from https://law.justia.com/cases/federal/appellate-courts/F2/432/405/17901/.

United States v. Pabst Brewing Co., 384 U.S. 546 (1966). Retrieved from https://www.loc.gov/item/usrep384546/.

19. Bean, J. (2014). *Big Government and Affirmative Action: The Scandalous History of the Small Business Administration.* University Press of Kentucky.

20. Jaspin, E. (September 20, 1977). "The Region's Vanishing Breweries." *Pottsville Republican,* 1.

21. Theodore Mack, Sr., Past President and Chairman of the Board of People's Brewing Co., Milwaukee, Wis., Accompanied by Ray Alexander, Member of Board of Directors (June 1974). *Hearings Before the Subcommittee on Small Business of the Committee on Banking and Currency, House of Representatives, 1974.* U.S. Government Printing Office.

22. Theodore Mack, Sr., Past President and Chairman of the Board of People's Brewing Co., Milwaukee, Wis., Accompanied by Ray Alexander, Member of the Board of Directors (June 1974). *Hearings Before the Subcommittee on Small Business of the Committee on Banking and Currency, House of Representatives, 1974.* U.S. Government Printing Office.

Chapter 14

1. Menzel, M. (March 7, 1971). "Black Capitalism a Myth, Black Businessman Says." *Sunday Post-Crescent*, B1.

2. McGlauflin, P. (May 2022). "The Number of Black Fortune 500 CEOs Returns to Record High—Meet the 6 Chief Executive." *Fortune*. Retrieved from https://fortune.com/2022/05/23/meet-6-black-ceos-fortune-500-first-black-founder-to-ever-make-list/.

3. United States of America, *Plaintiff vs. Jos. Schlitz Brewing Company and General Brewing Company*, Defendants: Final Judgement and Decree (March 28, 1966). The United States District Court for the Northern District of California Southern Division.

4. Warner, A.G. (2010). "The Evolution of the American Brewing Industry." *Journal of Business Case Studies*, 6(6), 31–46.

5. Warner, A.G. (2010). "The Evolution of the American Brewing Industry." *Journal of Business Case Studies*, 6(6), 31–46.

6. Acitelli, T. (2013). *The Audacity of Hops: The History of America's Craft Beer Revolution*. Chicago Review Press.

7. Warner, A.G. (2010). "The Evolution of the American Brewing Industry." *Journal of Business Case Studies*, 6(6), 31–46.

8. McCullough, M., Berning, J., Hanson, J.L. (2019). "Learning by Brewing: Homebrewing Legalization and the Brewing Industry." *Contemporary Economic Policy*, 37(1).

9. The U.S. Beer Industry 2021. (N.D.). *National Beer Wholesalers Association*. Retrieved from https://www.nbwa.org/resources/industry-fast-facts.

10. Competition in the Markets for Beer, Wine, and Spirits (February 2022). *U.S. Treasury Department*.

11. Competition in the Markets for Beer, Wine, and Spirits (February 2022). *U.S. Treasury Department*.

12. Herd, D.A. (1996). "The Politics of Representation: Marketing Alcohol through Rap Music." In Sulkunen, P., Holmwood, J., Radner, H., Schulze, G. (eds.) *Constructing the New Consumer Society*, 134–151. St. Martin's Press.

13. Tremblay, V.J., Tremblay, C.H. (2005). *The U.S. Brewing Industry: Data Analysis and Economic Analysis*. The MIT Press.

14. Lusane, C. (2004). "Rap, Race, and Politics." In Foreman, M., Neal, M. A. (eds.). *That's the Joint! The Hip-Hop Studies Reader*, Routledge.

15. Biondi, M. (2006). *To Stand and Fight: The Struggle for Civil Rights in Postwar New York City*. Harvard Press.

16. Cleveland, W., Snider, M. (August 8, 2020). "Brewing in America: The Nation's Craft Beer Industry Has a Diversity Problem but It's Trying to Fix It." *Evening Sun*. Retrieved from https://www.usatoday.com/story/money/food/2020/08/08/brew-diversity-efforts-cultivate-black-owned-breweries/3326121001/.

17. Wilson, E. R. (2022). "'It Could Never Be Just About Beer': Race, Gender, and Marked Professional Identity in the U.S. Craft Beer Industry." *Journal of Professions and Organizations*, 1–17.

18. Noel, J. (October 25, 2019). "Founders Brewing Faces Fallout in Chicago and Elsewhere Following Racial Discrimination Lawsuit Details." *Chicago Tribune*. Retrieved from https://www.chicagotribune.com/dining/drink/ct-dining-founders-lawsuit-racism-20191024-6hx2szcoarfcllrrh6uktoeif4-story.html.

19. Kapur, A., Kleiner, B.H. (September 2000). "Discrimination in the Workplace of the Beer Industry." *Equal Opportunities International*, 19(6/7), 83–87.

20. Small Business Administration Request for Counseling (June 22, 1972). *Small Business Administration*. Crosby Papers, University of Wisconsin-Milwaukee.

21. Cleveland, W., Snider, M. (August 8, 2020). "Brewing in America: The Nation's Craft Beer Industry Has a Diversity Problem but It's Trying to Fix It." *Evening Sun*. Retrieved from https://www.usatoday.com/story/money/food/2020/08/08/brew-diversity-efforts-cultivate-black-owned-breweries/3326121001/.

22. Cleveland, W., Snider, M. (August 8, 2020). "Brewing in America: The Nation's Craft Beer Industry Has a Diversity Problem but It's Trying to Fix It." *Evening Sun*. Retrieved from https://www.usatoday.com/story/money/food/2020/08/08/brew-diversity-efforts-cultivate-black-owned-breweries/3326121001/.

23. J. Nikol Jackson-Beckham Named

First Diversity Ambassador at the Brewers Association (April 24, 2018). *Brewers Association*. Retrieved from https://www.brewersassociation.org/press-releases/j-nikol-jackson-beckham-named-first-diversity-ambassador-at-the-brewers-association/.

24. Brewers Association Announces Recipients of Inaugural Diversity and Inclusion Event Grants (May 7, 2019). *Brewers Association*. Retrieved from https://www.brewersassociation.org/press-releases/brewers-association-announces-recipients-of-inaugural-diversity-and-inclusion-event-grants/.

25. Crown & Hops Launches $100,000 Grant to Support Black-Owned Breweries (August 5, 2020). *Hop Culture*. Retrieved from https://www.hopculture.com/crowns-hops-launches-100000-grant-to-support-black-owned-breweries/.

26. Strasser, M. (November 1978). "Mack Treasures Knowing Woody." *The Northwestern*, B1.

Works Cited

Acitelli, T. (2013). *The Audacity of Hops: The History of America's Craft Beer Revolution.* Chicago Review Press.
Aid Given to Brewery (March 8, 1973). *Oshkosh Advance-Titan,* 24.
Akin, R., Reiherzer, L. (2012). *The Breweries of Oshkosh: Their Rise and Fall.* Akin & Reiherzer.
Alberts, B., Holston, C. (July 15, 2020). "'Streets as Stages'—The Munich Beer Riots of 1844." *Good Beer Hunting.* Retrieved from: https://www.goodbeerhunting.com/blog/2020/7/13/streets-as-stages-the-munich-beer-riots-of-1844.
Alexander, R.A., Crosby, H.S., Ouley, W., Ross, S. (February 2, 1922). "Letter to Ted Mack, Sr., President of Peoples Brewing Company." *Crosby Papers, University of Wisconsin–Milwaukee.*
Ask Negro Judge for Milwaukee (March 4, 1964). *The Capital Times,* 3.
Auction of People's Brewery Still Making Noise (June 20, 1974). *Daily Northwestern,* 2.
Auction to Be Held Tuesday at Former Peoples Brewery (June 15, 1974). *Daily Northwestern,* 18.
Aukofer, F. A. (2007). *City with a Chance: A Case History of Civil Rights Revolution.* Marquette University Press.
Barlett, D.L., Steele, J.B. (April 18, 1974). "Affluent Bloom Owes Big Tax: But IRS Doesn't Press for $729,833." *The Philadelphia Inquirer,* 290(108), 11-B.
Bates, T. (1989). "The Changing Nature of Minority Business: A Comparative Analysis of Asian, Non-Minority, and Black-Owned Businesses." *Review of Black Political Economy,* 18, 25–42.
Beal, D. (August 7, 1972). *Letter to E.A. Goodbout.* Crosby Papers, University of Wisconsin–Milwaukee.
Beal, D.L. (April 11, 1976). "Refused Price Deal, Beer Dealer Claims." *The Milwaukee Journal,* 1, 19.
Bean, J. (2014). *Big Government and Affirmative Action: The Scandalous History of the Small Business Administration.* University Press of Kentucky.
Beer Exports Denied (February 8, 1973). *Oshkosh Advance-Titan,* 7.
Beer Fight Goes On (July 26, 1969). *The Milwaukee Courier,* 3.
Bell, D. (2005). *Silent Covenants: Brown v. Board of Education and the Unfulfilled Hopes for Racial Reform.* Oxford University Press.
The Beverage Mart Advertisement (March 12, 1971). *Daily Northwestern,* 12.
Biondi, M. (2006). *To Stand and Fight: The Struggle for Civil Rights in Postwar New York City.* Harvard Press.
Black Beer Group Sets Sale of Stock (July 25, 1970). *The Milwaukee Journal,* 5.
Black Brewery May Leave Milwaukee (September 11, 1971). *Milwaukee Star,* 18.
Black Brewery Set $Million Goal This Year (June 17, 1971). *Jet,* 16.
Black Brewery to Begin Sales (February 17, 1971). *Eau Claire Leader-Telegram,* 1.
Black Brewery to Open Within Two Months (April 18, 1970). *The Greater Milwaukee Star,* 9.
Black Businessmen Buy Peoples Brewery (April 15, 1970). *Daily Northwestern,* 4.

Works Cited

Black Enterprises, 2 Others Submit Bid to Buy Blatz (July 14, 1969). *The Milwaukee Journal*, 5.
Black Firm Is Now Seeking Oshkosh Unit (April 14, 1970). *Kenosha News*, 14.
Black Firm to Sell Beer at Stadium (February 16, 1971). *The Milwaukee Journal*, 7.
Black Group May Buy Out Peoples (April 14, 1970). *Daily Northwestern*, 3.
Black Group Reveals Support in Blatz Bid (July 9, 1969). *Milwaukee Journal Business News*, 3.
Black-Owned Concern Is Brewing Success (March 15, 1971). *New York Times*, 28.
Blacks Bid for Milwaukee Brewery (July 12, 1969). *The Greater Milwaukee Star*, 10.
Blacks Buy Oshkosh Brewery (April 18, 1970). *The Milwaukee Courier*, 6.
Blacks Purchase Upstate Brewery (April 16, 1970). *The Capital Times*, 4.
Blackwell, E.H. (October 11, 1970). "Black Managed Brewery Opens Doors." *The Milwaukee Journal Business News*, 14.
Blackwell, E.H. (September 17, 1971). "Beer Business Different, Mack Finds." *Milwaukee Journal Business News*, 16.
Blatz Brand Is Shifted to Heilman (September 3, 1969). *Milwaukee Sentinel*, 5.
Blatz Delay Is Deferred (July 17, 1969). *Milwaukee Sentinel*, 3.
Blatz Plan Reiterated by Black Enterprises (July 22, 1969). *The Milwaukee Journal*, 4.
Blatz Sale Pondered in Trust Suit (March, 26, 1969). *Charleston Daily Mail*, 7.
Bolden, D.W. (January 31, 1973). *Letter to Ray A. Alexander*. Crosby Papers, University of Wisconsin–Milwaukee.
Bonds, M., Farmer-Hinton, R. L., Epps, E. G. (2009). "African Americans' Continuing Struggle for Quality Education in Milwaukee, Wisconsin." *The Journal of Negro Education*, 78(1), 55–69.
Brandon, M.M., Jr. (February, 1961). "Fee Enterprise—Price Discrimination Under the Clayton Act." *Louisiana Law Review*, 21(2), 507–514.
Brenkert, G. C. (1998). "Marketing to Inner-City Blacks: Powermaster and Moral Responsibility." *Business Ethics Quarterly*, 8(1), 1–18.
Breweries Lift 50-Yr. Ban (July 29, 1950). *The New Tribune*, 3.
Brewers Association Announces Recipients of Inaugural Diversity and Inclusion Event Grants (May 7, 2019). *Brewers Association*. Retrieved from https://www.brewersassociation.org/press-releases/brewers-association-announces-recipients-of-inaugural-diversity-and-inclusion-event-grants/.
Brewers Diversify to Malt Liquor (March 9, 1964). *Broadcasting*, 38.
Brewery Auction Defended (June 20, 1974). *The Milwaukee Journal*, 5.
Brewery Buys Old Tews Site (November 18, 1970). *The Milwaukee Journal*, 11.
Brewery Has New Owner in Oshkosh (April 24, 1970). *Daily Northwestern*, 5.
Brewery Venture Snarled in Indiana (July 3, 1971). *The Milwaukee Journal*, 9.
Brewery Will Expand; Add to Its Payroll (September 3, 1970). *Daily Northwestern*, 5.
Brewing Company Future Is Subject to Speculation (October 20, 1971). *Oshkosh Daily Northwestern*, 4.
Brewing Equipment Auctioned (June 19, 1974). *Daily Northwestern*, 4.
Brewing Firm Offers Public Sale of Stock (July 30, 1970). *Appleton Post Crescent*, B3.
Brimmer, A.F., Terrell, H.S. (1969). "The Economic Potential of Black Capitalism." *82nd Annual Meeting of the American Economic Association*, 1.
Brown, S.A. (1950) "Negro Folk Expression." *Phylon*, 11(4), 318–325.
Campus Mayhem (November 22, 1968). *Daily Northwestern*, 10.
Carson, Scott A. (March, 2006). "African-American and White Living Standards in the 19th Century American South: A Biological Comparison." *CESifo Working Paper Series No. 1696*.
Cesur, R., Kelly, I.R. (2014). "Who Pay the Bar Tab? Beer Consumption and Economic Growth in the United States." *Economic Inquiry*, 52(1), 477–494.
Chapman, N.G., and Brunsma, D.L. (2020) *Beer and Racism: How Beer Became White, Why it Matters, and Movements to Change It.* Policy Press.
Cleveland, W., and Snider, M. (August 8, 2020). "Brewing in America: The Nation's Craft Beer Industry Has a Diversity Problem but It's Trying to Fix It." *Evening Sun*. Retrieved

from https://www.usatoday.com/story/money/food/2020/08/08/brew-diversity-efforts-cultivate-black-owned-breweries/3326121001/.

Cochran, T.C. (1948). *The Pabst Brewing Company: The History of an American Business.* New York University Press.

Competition in the Markets for Beer, Wine, and Spirits (February, 2022). *U.S. Treasury Department.*

Connell, T. (2016). "1950s Milwaukee: Race, Class, and a City Divided." *Labor Studies Journal,* 42(1), 27–51.

Correspondence: Up-to-date (May 27, 1921). *The Baltimore Afro-American,* 1.

Crosby, H. (October 22, 1972). *People vs. U.S.,* Handwritten Note. Crosby Papers, University of Wisconsin–Milwaukee.

Crown & Hops Launches $100,000 Grant to Support Black-Owned Breweries (August 5, 2020). *Hop Culture.* Retrieved from https://www.hopculture.com/crowns-hops-launches-100000-grant-to-support-black-owned-breweries/.

Cullen, K. M. (2011). "Rediscovering Milwaukee's Historic Breweries Part I: Milwaukee's Downtown Breweries." *Brewery History,* 140, 71–86.

Department of Defense Appropriation for 1972 (1971). *Hearings Before a Subcommittee of the Committee on Appropriations House of Representatives.* Government Printing Office: Washington, D.C.

Dornbusch, Horst D. (1997). *Prost!: The Story of German Beer.* Siris Books.

Egan, J. (February 20, 1971). "Deep Meaning In Doing to Others." *Daily Northwestern,* 9.

Eifert, C.A. (April 15, 1970). "Peoples Brewery Sold to Milwaukee Group." *The Paper for Central Wisconsin,* 13.

Embree, E.R. (1936, March). "Southern Farm Tenancy." *Survey Graphic,* 25(3), 149.

Euchner, C. (2010). *Nobody Turn Me Around: A People's History of the March on Washington, D.C.* Beacon Press.

Expansion Planned by Peoples Brewery (June 18, 1971). *The Milwaukee Journal,* 3.

Expect Thousands at Gathering of the Ku Klux Klan (July 29, 1927). *Daily Northwestern,* 4.

Fairlie R.W., Robb, A.M. (2007). "Why are Black-Owned Businesses Less Successful than White-Owned Businesses? The Role of Families, Inheritances, and Business Human Capital" *Journal of Labor Economics,* 25(2), 289–323.

Fall Victim's Widow Treated by Aid Squad (June 6, 1954). *The Middletown, Ohio, Sunday News-Journal,* 5.

Fifteenth Census of the United States: 1903—Population, Volume III, Part 2, Montana-Wyoming. U.S. (1932). *Department of Commerce, Bureau of the Census.* Government Printing Office.

Fifteenth Census of the United States: Population Schedule, Sheet 15-B (1930). *Department of Commerce—Bureau of the Census.* Government Printing Office.

Finner, R.E. (November 21, 1968). "Black Discontent." *Oshkosh Advance-Titan,* 2.

Fleming, G.J. (February 13, 1971). "Now and Then: Traveling in Wisconsin." *Baltimore Afro-American,* 4.

Foltman, L., and Jones, M. (February 28, 2019). "How Redlining Continues to Shape Racial Segregation in Milwaukee." *WisCONTEXT.* Retrieved from https://www.wiscontext.org/how-redlining-continues-shape-racial-segregation-milwaukee.

Foner, E. (2014). *Reconstruction: America's unfinished revolution, 1863–1877.* HarperCollins.

For a Brighter Future…BLACK PRIDE (November 24, 1969). *Brewers Digest,* 35.

For Jobs and Freedom: 50 Years and Counting (August 26, 2013). *Milwaukee PBS.*

Ford, H. (October 10, 1973). *Letter to Mr. And Mrs. Henry S. Crosby.* Crosby Papers, University of Wisconsin–Milwaukee.

Fourteenth Census of the United States: Population Schedule, Sheet 15-B (1920). *Department of Commerce—Bureau of the Census.* Government Printing Office.

Fourteenth Census of the United States, State Compendium: Wisconsin (1925). *Department of Commerce, Bureau of the Census.* Government Printing Office.

Fraud and Corruption in Management of Military Club Systems: Illegal Currency Manipulations Affecting South Vietnam (1971). *Report of the Committee on Government*

Operations United States Senate made by its Permanent Subcommittee on Investigations. Government Printing Office.
The General Condition of the Alabama Negro (March 1965). *Student Nonviolent Coordinating Committee*.
Goldberg, R. A. (1974). "The Ku Klux Klan in Madison, 1922–1927." *The Wisconsin Magazine of History*, 31–44.
Good Stuff (October 15, 1970). *Oshkosh Advance-Titan*, 2.
Goodbout, E.A. (July 18, 1972). *Letter to Marine Corps Exchange Service Headquarters*. Crosby Papers, University of Wisconsin–Milwaukee.
Gordon, M. (June 13, 1973). *United States District Court Eastern District of Wisconsin Decision and Order*. Crosby Papers, University of Wisconsin–Milwaukee.
Gordon, R.W. (August 9, 1972). *Letter to Theodore Mack, Sr*. Crosby Papers, University of Wisconsin–Milwaukee.
Gov. Wallace Reaffirms Intent to Keep Segregation (February 10, 1963). *Southern School News*, 2.
Grain Belt Withdraws Offer to Acquire Blatz from Pabst (July 9, 1969). *Milwaukee Journal Business News*, 3.
Green Lake Hosts Area Lions Club (November 4, 1971). *Daily Northwestern*, 21.
Greene, B. (May 10, 1971). "Black-Owned Brewery at Oshkosh." *Stevens Point Daily Journal*, 8.
Greene, B. (May 10, 1971). "Black-Owned Brewery Welcomes the 'Thirsty' Months." *The Capital Times*, 11.
Greene, B. (May 11, 1971). "Blacks Buy Oshkosh Brewery." *Freeport Journal-Standard*, 17.
Grossman, J.R. (1989). *Land of Hope: Chicago, Black Southerners, and the Great Migration*. University of Chicago Press.
Grossman, R. (September 25, 2015). "Chicago's Lager Beer Riot Proved Immigrants' Power." *Chicago Tribune*. Retrieved from https://www.chicagotribune.com/history/ct-know-nothing-party-lager-beer-riot-per-flashback-jm-20150925-story.html.
Group to Acquire Oshkosh Brewery (April 14, 1970). *Milwaukee Journal*, 3.
Guest Speakers Outline Role of Black Americans (February 10, 1972). *Oshkosh Advance-Titan*, 28.
Guyton, G. P. (1999). "A Brief History of Workers' Compensation." *The Iowa Orthopaedic Journal*, 19, 106–110.
Hanley, D.P., Jr. (March 4, 1964). "Governor Told: Negro Judge or No Votes." *Wisconsin State Journal*, 201(156), 1.
Harris, I. M (1983). "Criteria for Evaluating School Desegregation in Milwaukee." *Journal of Negro Education*, 52(4), 423–435.
Heap, S. (November, 2010). "Marketing Modernity: Star Lager Beer in Late Colonial and Early Independent Nigeria." Paper presented at *Elite Formation, Consumption and Urban Spaces—Cultural Perspectives on African Decolonization*, International Research Centre, Humboldt–Universität zu Berlin, Berlin, Germany.
Herd, D.A. (1996). "The Politics of Representation: Marketing Alcohol Through Rap Music." In Sulkunen, P.,
Hill, H. (1961). "Racism within Organized Labor: A Report of Five Years of the AFL-CIO, 1955–1960." *The Journal of Negro Education*, 30(2), 109–118.
History of Paradise Valley Distributing Company (September 6, 1941). *The Detroit Tribune*, 6.
Holmwood, J., Radner, H., Schulze, G. (eds.) *Constructing the New Consumer Society*, St. Martin's Press: New York, 134–151.
How Winnebago County Voted (April 8, 1964). *Oshkosh Daily Northwestern*, 34.
Indiana Authorities Impound Peoples Beer (July 3, 1971). *Wisconsin State Journal*, 2–2.
Indiana Impounds Beer from Oshkosh (July 2, 1971). *Fond du Lac Commonwealth Reporter*, 2–3.
J. Nikol Jackson-Beckham Named First Diversity Ambassador at the Brewers Association (April 24, 2018). *Brewers Association*. Retrieved from https://www.brewersassociation.org/press-releases/j-nikol-jackson-beckham-named-first-diversity-ambassador-at-the-brewers-association/.

Works Cited

James C. Windham, 63, Chairman and Top Executive Officer of Pabst (May 13, 1977). *The New York Times*, 24.
Jaspin, E. (September 20, 1977). "The Region's Vanishing Breweries." *Pottsville Republican*, 1.
Jenson, H. (March, 11, 1964). "No Governor Should Be Subjected to Threats." *Wisconsin State Journal*, 12.
Jernigan, D.H., Obot, I.S. (2006). "Thirsting for the African Market." *African Journal of Drug & Alcohol Studies*, 5(1), 57–70.
Johnson, E. (July 11, 1969). "Sandoval Has the One Duty He Wants in the Capital." *Amarillo Globe-Times*, 15.
Jones, P. D. (2009). *Selma of the North: Civil Rights Insurgency in Milwaukee*. Harvard University Press.
Jones, P.D. (2010) "'Get Up Off of Your Knees!': Competing Visions of Black Empowerment in Milwaukee During the Early Civil Rights Era." In: Joseph P.E. (eds) *Neighborhood Rebels. Contemporary Black History*. Palgrave Macmillan.
Jones, W.P. (2014). *The March on Washington: Jobs, Freedom, and the Forgotten History of Civil Rights*. W, W. Norton & Company: NY.
Judge Rejects UBE Request (July 23, 1969). *Milwaukee Sentinel*, 8.
Kapur, A., Kleiner, B.H. (September, 2000). "Discrimination in the Workplace of the Beer Industry." *Equal Opportunities International*, 19(6/7), 83–87.
Keeping Things Small (October 24, 1959). *Monroe Morning World*, 5.
Keithahn, C.F. (December 1978). "The Brewing Industry. Staff Report of the Bureau of Economics." *Federal Trade Commission*.
Kelly, I.R. (2014). Who Pays the Bar Tab? Beer Consumption and Economic Growth in the United States. Economic Inquiry 52(1), 477–494.
Kenney, R. (August 1, 1970) "People's Offer Piques Interest." *Milwaukee Sentinel*, 7.
Kenoshans will join in march (August 26, 1963). *Kenosha News*, 14.
Kenyon, R. (April 18, 1976). "Insider Affirms Beer Payoffs." *The Milwaukee Journal*, 9.
Knuth, E.L. (August 31, 1972). Letter to Theodore Mack. Crosby Papers, University of Wisconsin–Milwaukee.
Kotlowski, D. (1998). "Black Power—Nixon Style: The Nixon Administration and Minority Business Enterprise." *Business History Review*, 72(3), 409–445.
Kurlander, D. (N.D.) Capture the Rapture: "'Take It in a Bottle, 40, Quart or Can': 1985–2017." David Kurlander: Popular History, Criticism, and Archival Exploration. Retrieved from https://kurlanderblog.wordpress.com/capture-the-rapture/.
Lanier, C. (2022). Peoples Beer: brewing and bigotry in America. *Brewery History Journal*, 188, 13–29.
Larger Contracts Key to Brewery's Future (November 15, 1972). *The Journal Times*, 9A.
Last Minute Funds Aid State Group (August 27, 1963). *The Capital Times*, 2.
Lee, G.H. (August, 1968). *The Ku Klux Klan in Wisconsin in the 1920s* [unpublished thesis paper]. Wisconsin State University—La Crosse.
Letter from J.E. Siebel Sons' Company, Inc. and Certificate of Analysis (April 5, 1971). *J.E. Siebel Sons' Company, Inc.* Crosby Papers, University of Wisconsin–Milwaukee.
Loewan. J.W. (2005). Sundown Towns: A Hidden Dimension of American Racism. Touchstone.
Lombardo, J. (2005). *A Fire to Win: The Life and Times of Woody Hayes*. Thomas Dunne Books.
Lorence, J. J. (1983). "'Dynamite for the Brain': The Growth and Decline of Socialism in Central and Lakeshore Wisconsin, 1910–1920." *Wisconsin Magazine of History*, 66(4), 251–273.
Lottman, M. S. (July 28, 1968) "Federal Judges Block Negro School Addition." *The Southern Courier*, 10.
Lowe, B. (1972). "Black Brewer Prospers in Oshkosh." *Oshkosh Advance-Titan*, 8.
Lucey Endorses Business Plan (September 10, 1971). *The Milwaukee Journal*, 4.
Luebke, M.H. (May 16, 1970). "Man Not System at Fault Today." *The Daily Northwestern*, 8.
Lusane, C. (2004). "Rap, Race, and Politics." In Foreman, M., Neal, M. A. (eds.) *That's the Joint! The Hip-Hop Studies Reader*, Routledge.

Works Cited

Lynching in America: Confronting the Legacy of Racial Terror, County Data Supplement (January 2022). *Equal Justice Initiative.*
Mack, T. (February 5, 1973). *Letter to Stockholders. Crosby Papers, University of Wisconsin–Milwaukee.*
Mack, T., Sr. (March 24, 1972) *Letter to Stockholders.* Crosby Papers, University of Wisconsin–Milwaukee.
Mack, T., Sr.(April 21, 1971). *Letter to Peoples Beer Customers.* Crosby Paper, University of Wisconsin–Milwaukee.
Mack, T., Sr. (June 12, 1972) *Letter from Theodore A. Mack Sr., to Edward Goodbout, Chief of 8-A Program, Small Business Administration.* Crosby Papers, University of Wisconsin–Milwaukee.
Mack Is Speaker for Optimist Club (August 27, 1970). *Daily Northwestern,* 2.
Madison 'Rights' Unit to Back State Boycott (May 17, 1964). *Racine Sunday Bulletin,* 3A.
Magee, B. (2014). *Brewing in Milwaukee.* Arcadia.
Malone, C., Novick, D. (July 12, 1969) "The Blacker the Beer." *The Milwaukee Courier,* 2.
Marchers return to Milwaukee (August 30, 1963). *Kenosha News,* 2.
Marshal, R. (January, 1964). "Unions and the Negro Community." *Industrial and Labor Relations Review,* 17(2), 179–202.
McCreary, S. (October 3, 1968). "Black Students Face City, Campus Prejudice." *Oshkosh Advance Titan,* 5.
McCullough, M., Berning, J., Hanson, J.L. (2019). "Learning by Brewing: Homebrewing Legalization and the Brewing Industry." *Contemporary Economic Policy,* 37(1).
McGlauflin, P. (May, 2022). "The Number of Black Fortune 500 CEOs Returns to Record High—Meet the 6 Chief Executive." *Fortune.* Retrieved from https://fortune.com/2022/05/23/meet-6-black-ceos-fortune-500-first-black-founder-to-ever-make-list/.
Memorandum of Understanding Peoples Brewing Company and Ogbomosho Investment Club (January 16, 1973). *Ogbomosho Investment Club.* Crosby Paper, University of Wisconsin–Milwaukee.
Menzel, M. (March 7, 1971). "Black Capitalism a Myth, Black Businessman Says." *Sunday Post-Crescent,* B1.
Middletonian Dies in Fall from 100-Foot Scaffold (June 5, 1954). *The Middletown Ohio Journal,* 2.
Milwaukee Group Buys Peoples Beer (April 15, 1970). *The Paper for Central Wisconsin,* 3.
Milwaukee School Bus Issue Hot (October 13, 1965). *Kenosha News,* 3.
Moorer, H.C., Falk, G. (October 4, 1965) "Negroes Boycott Training School." *The Southern Courier,* 4.
Napier, W. (July 1, 2021), "A Short History of Integration in the U.S. Armed Forces." *U.S. Air Force.* Retrieved from https://www.af.mil/News/Commentaries/Display/Article/2676311/a-short-history-of-integration-in-the-us-armed-forces/.
Negro Beer Confiscated (July 2, 1971). *Ironwood, Daily Globe,* 12.
Negro Brute: Pays the Penalty of HIS Atrocious Crime—Unwritten Law Executed—Hanged to a Pine Limb and Riddled with Shot (May 6, 1904). *The Prattville Progress,* 1.
Negro Business Group Raising Funds to Bid for Blatz Brewery (July 10, 1969). *The Wall Street Journal,* 10.
Negro Businessmen Tired of Being Studied (March 1, 1971). *Ironwood Daily Globe,* 5.
Negro Firm Contracts Area Brewery (November 8, 1969). *Fond Du Lac Commonwealth Reporter,* 11.
Negro Pioneers in Brewery Firm: First Negro Owned Brewery (November 26, 1955). *The Roanoke Tribune,* 1.
New Members Introduced (January 23, 1971). *Daily Northwestern,* 9.
No Court in Autauga: Judge T.S. Sayre Writes the Governor, Will Not Now Investigate Gaines Hall Crime (May 20, 1904). *The Prattville Progress,* 3.
Noel, J. (October 25, 2019). "Founders Brewing Faces Fallout in Chicago and Elsewhere Following Racial Discrimination Lawsuit Details." *Chicago Tribune.* Retrieved from https://www.chicagotribune.com/dining/drink/ct-dining-founders-lawsuit-racism-20191024-6hx2szcoarfcllrrh6uktoeif4-story.html.

Works Cited

NOW! Pop-top Cans (November 20, 1970). *Daily Northwestern*, 15.
Obituary for Honorable Harold B. Jackson, Jr. (February, 2016). *Schramka Funeral Home*. Retrieved from https://www.schramkafuneralhome.com/memorials/Jackson-HonorableHarold/2380067/obituary.php
Obituary for Thomas J. Mack (June 7, 1954). *Journal Herald, Dayton, Ohio*, 2.
Ogle, M. (2019). *Ambitious Brew: A History of American Beer*. Blue Willow Books.
Opinion of Chief Judge Tehan on United States v. Pabst Brewing (August 6, 1969). *The United States District Court for the Eastern District of Wisconsin*.
Oshkosh Brewery Sale Approved (April 15, 1970). *Stevens Point Daily Journal*, 11.
Pabst Acquires Blatz Brewery for $161/2 Million (July 31, 1958). *Appleton Post-Crescent*, 2.
Paine Employes [sic] Express Interest (November 19, 1971). *Daily Northwestern*, 3.
PanAf Informational Brochure (N.D.). *PanAf.* Crosby Papers, University of Wisconsin–Milwaukee.
Parris, G, Brooks, L. (1971). *Black in the City: A History of the National Urban League*. Little, Brown and Company.
Pecor, J. (April 14, 1970). "Black Group Bidding for Brewery." *Milwaukee Sentinel*, 3.
People Brewing Company Stops Production (November 10, 1972). *The Journal Times*, 5C.
Peoples Beer Charges Indiana Harassment (July 6, 1971). *Wisconsin State Journal*, 2-2.
People's Beer Coming to City... Black Capitalism Brewing (May 22, 1971). *Sheboygan Press*, 2.
'Peoples Beer' Going On Sale Here (March 18, 1971). *The Capital Times*, 31.
Peoples Beer Sales Ahead of Last Year (September 17, 1971). *Daily Northwestern*, 4.
Peoples Peoples Brewery Saluted (October 11, 1970). *Post Crescent*, D2.
Peoples Brewing Advertisements (N.D.) *Peoples Brewing Company.*
Peoples Brewing Co. Ends with Auction (June 20, 1974). *Wisconsin State Journal*, 2-6.
The Peoples Brewing Company: Annual Report Year Ended September 30, 1971 (March 24, 1972).
Peoples Brewing Company. Crosby Papers, University of Wisconsin–Milwaukee.
Peoples Brewing 1st Year Loss $100,000 (January 4, 1972). *Racine Journal-Times*, 11A.
Peoples Brewing "Set to Compete": Mack (January 12, 1972). *Daily Northwestern*, 3.
Peoples Lays Off Workers (November 14, 1972). *Milwaukee Journal Business News*, 16.
Peoples Puts Out New Holiday Brew (December 5, 1970). *Greater Milwaukee Star*, 3.
People's Sale: Hits the Spot? (April 26, 1970). *Sunday Post-Crescent*, B1.
Peter Hemmings (N.D.). *Monticello*. Retrieved from https://www.monticello.org/site/research-and-collections/peter-hemings#footnote5_rip2u79
Philip J. Siegel & Co. (January 14, 1972). *Report of Independent Certified Accountants The Peoples Brewing Company*. Crosby Papers, University of Wisconsin–Milwaukee.
Planning Peoples Beer Distribution in Area (September 28, 1970). *Racine Journal-Times*, 5B.
Plans Completed for Annual WRTA Event (October 7, 1971). *Daily Northwestern*, 5.
Powell, E. A. (December 2, 1972). "Black Brewery Might Go to Alabama." *The Milwaukee Journal*, 3.
Powers, N.D. (August 10, 1972). *Letter to E. A. Goodbout*. Crosby Papers, University of Wisconsin–Milwaukee.
Prigge, M.J. (December 22, 2015). "Dixie North: George Wallace and the 1964 Wisconsin Presidential Primary." *Shepherd Express*. Retrieved from https://shepherdexpress.com/culture/milwaukee-history/dixie-north-george-wallace-1964-wisconsin-presidential-primary/.
'Priorities Change Needed' Retired Persons Are Told (June 16, 1971). *Daily Northwestern*, A2.
A Proposal for the Resumption of Operations (N.D.) *Peoples Brewing Company*. Crosby Papers, University of Wisconsin–Milwaukee.
Prospectus of the United People's Brewing Ltd. (July 25, 1970). *United People's Brewing, Ltd.* Crosby Papers, University of Wisconsin–Milwaukee.
Racial Membership Rule Protested Here: NAACP Youth Unit Pickets Eagles (May 25, 1966). *The Capital Times*, 4.
Radio Broadcasting Pioneer Harold 'Hal' B. Jackson Remembered, Passes at 96 (June 7, 2012). *Milwaukee Courier*. Retrieved from https://milwaukeecourieronline.com/index.

Works Cited

php/2012/06/07/radio-broadcasting-pioneer-harold-hal-b-jackson-remembered-passes-at-96/.

Ray's Beverage Advertisement (December 15, 1971). *Daily Northwestern*, 10.

Redcay, E.E. (1935). *County Training Schools and Public Secondary Education for Negroes in the South.* The John F. Slater Fund.

Research Proposal Between the Afro-Urban Institute and the University of Wisconsin (N.D.). *Afro-Urban Institute.* Crosby Papers, University of Wisconsin–Milwaukee.

Revived Ku Klux Klan Grows Rapidly (December 24, 1920). *The Daily Northwestern*, 13.

Reynolds Told to Pick Negro or Lose Votes (March 4, 1964). *The Eau Claire Leader*, 1.

Rubin, I. (June 22. 1972). *Letter to Theodore Mack.* Crosby Papers, University of Wisconsin–Milwaukee.

Russell, J. (April 27, 1970). "'Falsehoods' Rapped by Brewery President." *Daily Northwestern*, 8.

Russell, J. (February 21, 1973). "Beer stockholders back Mack." *Daily Northwestern*, 4.

Russert, E. (March 17, 1971). "He's Clever." *Daily Northwestern*, 14.

Sayrs, J.H. (July 3, 1971). "Mack Sees Conspiracy Against Peoples Beer." *Daily Northwestern*, 4.

SBA's '8(a) Program': Overview, History, and Current Issues (November, 2021). *Congressional Research Service.*

S.C. Johnson on Lucey's Blue-ribbon Business Panel (January 20, 1971). *Racine Journal-Times*, 5.

Schechter, B. (November 24, 1953). "Brubaker, Borton Named Co-Captains." *Ohio State Lantern*, 4–7.

Schlüter, H. (1910). *The Brewing Industry and the Brewery Workers' Movement in America.* International Union of United Brewery Workmen of America.

Schmid, D. (May 18, 1970). "Good News Cannot Be Delayed Longer." *The Daily Northwestern*, 2.

School Attendance Light in Milwaukee Boycott (May 18, 1964). *The Racine Journal-Times*, 1.

Second Program in Human Rights Series Sunday (April 10, 1964) *The Sheboygan Press*, 4.

Seek Brewery Financing (August 9, 1970). *Racine Sunday Bulletin*, 8D.

Seig, D.J. (June 20, 1974). "People Pay in Auction of Brewery." *The Milwaukee Journal*, 6.

Sheriff M'Williams Writes Gov. Cunningham (September 2, 1904). *The Prattville Progress*, 2.

Sixteenth Census of the United States: Population Schedule, Sheet 9-B (1940). *Department of Commerce-Bureau of the Census.* Government Printing Office.

Slesinger, D.P., Grigsby, E. H., Taeuber, K. (2006). *African Americans in Wisconsin: A Statistical Overview* (2nd ed). University of Wisconsin.

Small Business Administration Invites Bids for the Purchase of Personal Property at Peoples Brewery—Oshkosh, WI (April 14, 1974). *Small Business Administration.* Crosby Paper, University of Wisconsin–Milwaukee.

Small Business Administration Request for Counseling (June 22, 1972). *Small Business Administration.* Crosby Papers, University of Wisconsin–Milwaukee.

Some Don't Drink Peoples Anymore (April 26, 1970). *Sunday Post-Crescent*, B2.

Stack, M. (2000). "Local and Regional Breweries in America's Brewing Industry, 1865 to 1920." *Business History Review*, 74(3), 435–463.

Stans, M.H. (1996). "Richard Nixon and His Bridges to Human Dignity." *Presidential Studies Quarterly*, 26(1), 179–183.

State Taxation of Military Income and Store Sales (July, 1976). *Advisory Commission on Intergovernmental Relations.*

Stevens, W. H. (1915). "The Clayton Act." *The American Economic Review.* 5(1), 38–54.

Strasser, M. (November 4, 1978) "Mack Treasures Knowing Woody." *The Oshkosh Northwestern*, B1.

Strickland, A.E. (1966). *History of the Urban League of Chicago (volume 1).* University of Chicago Press.

Suit Names Big Brewers (November 8, 1972). *The Milwaukee Journal*, 15.

Works Cited

Sunshine Brewery has Record Year (November, 1970). *Brewers Digest*, 38.
Tenny, R.I., Dakin, P.E. (1984). "History of the American Society of Brewing Chemists." *Journal of the American Society of Brewing Chemists: The Science of Beer*, 42(3).
Theodore Mack, Sr., Past President and Chairman of the Board of People's Brewing Co., Milwaukee, Wis., Accompanied by Ray Alexander, Member of the Board of Directors (June 1974). *Hearings Before the Subcommittee on Small Business of the Committee on Banking and Currency, House of Representatives, 1974.* U.S. Government Printing Office.
Thirteenth Census of the United States: Population Schedule, Sheet 19-B (1910). *Department of Commerce—Bureau of the Census.* Government Printing Office.
Thirteenth Census of the United States Taken in the Year 1910, Statistic for Wisconsin (1918). *Department of Commerce, Bureau of the Census.* Government Printing Office.
3 Milwaukee Brewers Are Accused of Payoffs (April 10, 1976). *The Milwaukee Journal*, 7.
Tolnay, S.E. (2003). "The African American 'Great Migration' and Beyond." *Annual Review of Sociology*, 29, 209–232.
Town 'N' Country Liquors Advertisement (January 21, 1972). *Kenosha News*, 8–9.
Town 'N' Country Liquors Advertisement (June 1, 1973). *Kenosha News*, 4–5.
Tremblay, V.J., Tremblay, C.H. (2005). *The U.S. Brewing Industry: Data Analysis and Economic Analysis.* The MIT Press.
Trotter, J.W. (2007). *Black Milwaukee: The Making of an Industrial Proletariat, 1915–1945.* University of Illinois Press.
Twelfth Census of the United States: Population Schedule, Sheet 17–18 (1900). *Department of Commerce—Bureau of the Census.* Government Accounting Office.
25 Business Leaders to Advise Governor (January 19, 1971). *Appleton Post Crescent*, 4A.
UBE Will Fight Tehan Decision (July 26, 1969). *The Greater Milwaukee Star*, 12.
United Black Enterprises: All Media Release (July 9, 1969) *United Black Enterprises.* Crosby Papers, University of Wisconsin–Milwaukee.
The U.S. Beer Industry 2021 (N.D.) *National Beer Wholesalers Association.* Retrieved from https://www.nbwa.org/resources/industry-fast-facts.
U.S. Census of Population: 1960. Vol. I, Characteristics of Population. Part 51, Wisconsin, U.S. (1963). *Department of Commerce, Bureau of the Census.* Government Printing Office.
United States of America, *Plaintiff vs. Jos. Schlitz Brewing Company and General Brewing Company*, Defendants: Final Judgement and Decree (March 28, 1966). *The United States District Court for the Northern District of California Southern Division.*
United States of America v. Albert Fuentes, Jr., and Edward J. Montez (October 5, 1970). *U.S. Court of Appeals for the Fifth Circuit.* Retrieved from https://law.justia.com/cases/federal/appellate-courts/F2/432/405/17901/.
United States v. Pabst Brewing Co., 384 U.S. 546 (1966). Retrieved from https://www.loc.gov/item/usrep384546/.
Visitors Flock to Oshkosh Home of People's Beer (October 11, 1970). *The Milwaukee Courier*, 3.
Wagner, R. (2019). "Post Prohibition Brewing in Reading, PA." *Museum of Beer and Brewing*, 40.
Wakesfeld, W.E. (1997). *Playing to Win: Sports and the American Military 1898–1945.* State University of New York Press.
Walker, J.E.K. (2009). *The History of Black Business in America: Capitalism, Race, Entrepreneurship.* The University of North Carolina Press.
Wallace Called Advocate of Evil (March 25, 1964). *The New York Times*, 25.
Wallace in Wisconsin (March 31, 1964). *The Afro-American*, 4.
Warner, A.G. (2010). "The Evolution of the American Brewing Industry." *Journal of Business Case Studies*, 6(6), 31–46.
What Kind of Man Is Your New York Life Agent? (October, 1965). *Ebony*, 8.
Wigs Worth $700 Stolen at Hotel (October 12, 1970). *Daily Northwestern*, 4.
Wilson, E. R. (2022). "'It Could Never Be Just About Beer': Race, Gender, and Marked

Professional Identity in the U.S. Craft Beer Industry." *Journal of Professions and Organizations*, 1–17.

Winship, K. (April 29, 2012) "Malt Liquor: A History." *Faithful Readers*. Retrieved from https://faithfulreaders.com/2012/04/29/malt-liquor-a-history/.

Wrong Way to Go at It (March 5, 1964). *Racine Journal-Times*, 7.

Youth Council Swells United Fund (January, 28, 1971). *Daily Northwestern*, 2.

Index

Alexander, Ray 52, 59, 63, 65–69, 86, 132, 137, 142, 143
American Federation of Labor (AFL) 33, 47
Anchor Brewing Company 154
Andrews, Gordon F. 106
Anheuser-Busch Brewing Association 30, 31, 117–120, 122, 123, 130, 153, 156, 158
Anheuser-Busch InBev SA/NV (AB InBev) 155, 156
Associated Brewing Company 51, 54
August Krug Brewery 23
Autauga County, AL 7, 8
Autauga County Training School 13–15
Ayandele, Ayantayo 139

Barbee, Lloyd 39, 41, 42, 135, 151
Barrel & Flow Fest 160
Beer Kulture 160
Bell, Daniel 36
Bequai, August 119–122, 130
Berger, Victor 25
Best, Jacob 22
Black bagging 120, 121, 155
Black capitalism 62, 63, 99, 128, 148
Black Pride Beer 107–109, 111, 114
Black Thursday 76, 77
Blatz, Valentin 44
Bloom, Leo Israel 105, 106
Bolden, Darwin W. 137
Bonga, Jean 32
Booker T. Washington High School 15
Boone, Levi 81
Braun, Johann 44
BrewDog 160
Brewers Association 159
Brewers' Union No. 1 25
Brooklyn Brewery 21, 22
Brown vs Board of Education 39
Budweiser Malt Liquor 110

Canadian Ace Brewing Company 122
Carling Brewery 130
Champale 110

Chicago Lager Beer Riots 81
City Brewery 44
Clayton Act 45, 120, 153
Clix Malt Liquor 109
Coggs, Isaac 34
Colony House Brewing Company 104, 105
Colt .45 110
Commandos 42
Congress of Industrial Organizations (CIO) 47
Congress of Racial Equality (CORE) 34, 37, 40, 41, 111
Coors Brewing Company 153, 156
Country Club Malt Liquor 109, 110
Crosby, Henry S. 52, 59, 60, 63, 65, 66, 68, 69, 82, 83, 86, 111, 123, 124, 132, 134, 143, 144
Crown & Hops 160
Crusaders Civic and Social League 37

Duquesne Brewing Company 51

Falstaff Brewing Corporation 119
Federal Alcohol Administration Act 122
Federal Trade Commission (FTC) 120, 122, 153
Fitger's Brewery 131, 132
Founder's Brewing Company 157, 158

Gambrinus Brewery 21, 22
Gary, Indiana 96–98, 112, 113
Giese, Heiner 135
Glatz, John 21, 23
Glatz, William 21, 23, 24, 26, 28
Gluek Brewing Company 109
Goetz Brewing Company 109
Goodbout, Edward 125–129
Gordon, Myron 144
Grain Belt Brewing Company 51, 54, 119, 122
Gray, Fred D. 136
Gray, Reuben 53
Great Migration 32
Gregory, Dick 151
Groppi, James 42, 56, 151

Index

Grupo Modelo 156
Guiles, Roger 76, 77

Hall, Gaines 13
Harpole, Reuben, Jr. 150
Hatcher, Richard 96
Hayes, Woody 17, 161
Heilman Brewing Company 51, 54, 56
Hemings, Peter 104
Horn, August 21, 23
House Resolution 13, 37, 155
Howe, David 125, 128

Inner Core 19, 37, 42, 43, 56, 68, 95, 99, 151
Intact Busing 39, 42, 52
Iroquois Brewing Company 131

Jackson, Grady 53
Jackson, Hal 52
Jackson, Harold B. 52–59, 69, 83
Jackson-Beckham, J. Nikol 159
Jefferson, Thomas 104

Kargus, William 26
King, Martin Luther, Jr. 37, 99
Klein Industrial Corporation 145
Koerber, Clarence "Click" 109
Korean War 15, 16, 62
Kreuger Beer Company 30
Kriz, Harold 94, 95
Ku Klux Klan 72, 73
Kuenzl, Lorenz 21, 23

Laiken, Michael B. 59
Levin, Edward S. 134, 135
Long Hot Summer 43, 56
Lucey, Patrick 101
lynching 13

Mack, Thomas 17, 18
Madison, James 104
Maier Brewing Company 131, 132
malt liquor 109, 157
March on Washington for Jobs and Freedom 37, 41
Marquette University 18, 43
Marshall & Ilsley Bank 61, 64, 141
Maytag, Fritz 154
McAuliffe, Jack 154, 155
McClellan, Edward J. 107–110
Mendocino Brewing 155
Miller Brewing Company 22, 23, 30, 115, 119, 122, 130, 153, 158
Milwaukee Council on Human Rights 34
Milwaukee County 19
Milwaukee Labor Reform Association 25
Milwaukee United School Integration Committee (MUSIC) 40
Molson Coors Beverage Company 155

Murken, Byron 84, 86, 143
Murray, Richard D. 143, 148

NAACP Youth Council 42, 151
National Association for the Advancement of Colored People (NAACP) 33, 40, 41, 107
National Union of United Brewery Workmen 25, 47
National Urban League 33, 47
Nelson, Gaylord 125, 126
New Albion Brewing Company 154
New York Life Insurance 48
Nigerian Breweries 138
Nigl, Joseph 21, 24, 26, 27, 28, 65

Oak Park Brewing Company 150
Office of Minority Business Enterprise (OMBE) 63, 128
Ogbomosho, Nigeria 138
Ogbomosho Investment Club 139
Ohio State University 16
Old English 600 Malt Liquor 109, 157
Oshkosh Brewing Company: 21, 23–29, 31, 93–95
Oyewumi, Oladunni 138

P. Ballantine and Sons Brewing Company 31, 131, 132
Pabst, Frederick 23
Pabst Brewing Company 22, 23, 30, 31, 45, 46, 48–50, 56, 64, 65, 115, 117, 119, 120
Pan African Business Information Center (PanAf) 137
Paradise Distributing Company 53
Peeple, Robert 52, 68
Peoples Brewing Company: advertising 116, 118; auction 145, 146; boycott 78, 79, 89; closure 133; demolition 149; expansion 92, 93; first year's loss 102; founding 27, 28; lawsuit 134, 135; post-prohibition 29, 31; purchase 58, 67, 68; purchase of OBC 95
Peoples Brewery of Nigeria 139
Phillips, Vel 151
Potosi Brewing Company 131
price fixing 119, 120
Prohibition 28

Rahr Brewing Company 23, 31
Reconstruction Finance Corporation 62
redlining 19, 39
Reinheitsgebot 22
Reusse, Henry 148
Reynolds, John W., Jr. 34, 41, 73

SAB Miller 156
St. Ide's 157
Saint Matthew's Christian Methodist Episcopal Church 40
Schaefer Brewing Company 31
Schenley Industries 45, 50

Index

Schlitz Brewing Company 22, 23, 30, 31, 64, 94, 115, 117, 119, 121–123, 130, 153
Schlitz Malt Liquor 110
school segregation 39, 42
Scott, Alexander 106
Section 8(a) Business Development Program 63, 123–128, 147
Securities and Exchange Commission (SEC) 119, 122, 123, 130
Seidel, Emil 25
service football 16
set-aside loans 63, 124, 125
Sherard, Calvin 36, 41, 151
Siebel Institute of Technology 88, 114
Sierra Nevada 155
sharecropping 8–11, 61
Small Business Administration (SBA) 61–63, 123–125, 129, 131, 133, 134, 141, 143, 144, 146, 158
Smith, John Randolph 104, 105
Southern Christian Leadership Conference (SCLC) 37
Sparkling Stite Malt Liquor 109
Starr, A. Bart 105, 106, 147
Stroh Brewing Company 51, 54
Sunshine Brewing Company 105, 106, 147

Teamsters 98
Tehan, Robert E. 46, 49–51, 53–57
Thom, Reinhold E. 26

Uihlein, David 94
Union Brewery 21, 22
United Black Enterprises (UBE) 51–59, 64, 68, 77, 78, 82, 83, 143, 147, 152
United Milwaukee Committee for the March on Washington 38
United People's Brewery Ltd. 64, 68
University of Alabama 15, 39
University of Wisconsin-Oshkosh (WSU-O) 74–77

Valentin Blatz Brewing Company 44, 49–51, 53–56, 58, 59, 115, 117, 120, 147, 152

Wallace, George 73, 74, 112
Wartime Prohibition Act 28
Watson, Everett 53
Weigel, Stanely 153, 154
Windham, James 46, 101
Workmen's Compensation Act 25

Ziegenhagen, Harold 58, 59, 91